CROCODILES AND ICE

"I totally buy Jon Turk's argument that we have lost our connection with the wild, and that 'environmentalism' must proceed via ecstasy and rapturous immersion in nature, not an agenda of fear-driven ideas. A spiritual connection with nature is the only thing that will save us because it will hook us and engage us in ways that mere rational arguments can't."

-Marni Jackson, author of Don't I Know You? and Pain: The Fifth Vital Sign.

CROCODILES AND ICE

A JOURNEY INTO DEEP WILD

BY

JON TURK

OOLICHAN BOOKS
FERNIE, BRITISH COLUMBIA, CANADA
2016

Library and Archives Canada Cataloguing in Publication

We gratefully acknowledge the financial support of the Canada Council for the Arts, the British Columbia Arts Council through the BC Ministry of Tourism, Culture, and the Arts, and the Government of Canada through the Canada Book Fund, for our publishing activities.

Published by
Oolichan Books
P.O. Box 2278
Fernie, British Columbia
Canada V0B 1M0

www.oolichan.com

Printed in Canada

To Amos and Pearl, who lived a
long time but didn't quite hang in there
long enough to read this book.

TABLE OF CONTENTS

PROLOGUE

The iceberg drifted lazily in the current, surrounded by a phalanx of smaller floes and basketball-sized bergy bits, compressed into a daiquiri-thick slurry. Then, as if the Himalayan Mountains were rising from the sea, the iceberg slammed into the cliff, stalled, shuttered, cracked with a loud groan, and smeared vertically against solid rock.

Boomer and I were trapped.

Below us, our yellow and orange kayaks were lying on the beach, flimsy shards of day-glo plastic. If we slipped into the cockpits—right now—and paddled bravely out into the current, the ice would crush us within seconds, as it flowed inexorably southward, propelled by the heat of the sun and the spin of the earth, planetary forces, powerful beyond comprehension.

We were low on food, the season was progressing toward Arctic winter and we had 600 nautical miles of Arctic wilderness to traverse before we returned to civilization: houses, people, food, warmth. There must be a way through this mayhem. There has to be a way.

I had persevered before, on so many adventures, through a mysterious cornucopia of patience, boldness, skill (perhaps) and luck. Yes, you can't discount the times I had exhausted all the tools in my bag of tricks and then been pulled out of trouble by blind, old-fashioned luck. I'll take it—without apologies—if it brings me home alive.

The ice would relax for us, and we would make a mad dash through the gauntlet. Or maybe it wouldn't. I looked across at Boomer, the young, blond, alarmingly blue-eyed Scandinavian powerhouse that he was, and I thanked the fates that at least I had him beside me. Just wait, and make your move when the time is right. That strategy had worked before, to emerge from that prison in Jordan, and to escape from the jaws of the crocodile.

CHAPTER 1

FROM A PRISON IN JORDAN
TO THE JAWS OF A CROCODILE

HOTEL ROOM
SOLOMON ISLANDS

OCTOBER, 2009

I woke from a deep afternoon nap. You know the kind. When you open your eyes, you think: "Where am I?" "What day is it?" "Whose bed am I sleeping in?"

Then I focused on the ceiling fan, revolving slowly—whompata, whompata, whompata—swaying on a frayed wire beneath the cracked and peeling ceiling paint, as if it were about to fly off its moorings and crash down on my nose.

"Right. I'm in a run-down hotel in Honiara, capital of the Solomon Islands, in the tropical South Pacific. I'm naked. Slimy with sweat. Stuck to the sheets in dried blood.

"Okay, let's see; I need to focus here. It's Tuesday. My return flight to Montana leaves on Friday. Three days. Seventy-two hours. How am I going to pass the time?" Then, after a moment of contemplation: "I have to pee."

To accomplish this, I had to peel myself off the bed, ripping off the newly dried scabs, like yanking a hundred Band-Aids off at once. The slow, millimeter by millimeter approach wasn't going to work. I lay there for some time, building up my courage, and then in one swift smooth motion, rolled off the bed and landed on the floor, kerplunk, on all fours. The pain wasn't totally debilitating, but enough so that I stopped for a moment to catch my breath.

While I was down there on the floor, I looked around, swaying my head back and forth, to shake off the pain.

"Wait. Something is wrong with this picture. I'm sure of it. Absolutely positive."

I looked again to be certain I hadn't missed anything. But no; my initial assessment was correct. Before I went to bed, I'd raced around the room, smashing cockroaches with my flip-flop. And then, in a rare act of domesticity, I'd swept all the dead carcasses under the bed. Now, they weren't there. Gone. Every last one of them.

I pondered this mystery for a while, but, really, I had to pee. So, using the bed as a support, I slowly lifted my worn, injured, 63-year-old body until I was more or less vertical and trundled off to the bathroom…where the mystery was solved.

There, oblivious to my presence, a long column of ants was carrying the last of the dead cockroaches down that suspicious yellow-brown hole next to the toilet. Every time I had used the bathroom, I was afraid that the toilet and I would fall down into this hole—an inglorious ending for me, after surviving the crocodile attack, monster waves, and all that. But now I understood that the mystery hole had a purpose; this was where the ant clean-up crew lived.

As the insects made their exit, I took care of my business and, with nothing better to do, went back to bed.

Brains are handy things sometimes, such as when you have to take a driver's license exam or do your taxes. But brains can be a down-right pain in the neck when you're trying to fall asleep, for the second time, on a hot afternoon, in a run-down hotel in Honiara. My mind fired off, doing what evolution has trained it to do— think—even though thinking was neither necessary nor desirable at this particular moment. So, my pesky, know-it-all-think-tank started ranting on and on, and the thoughts drifted up into the blades of that creaky old fan, where they got chopped to pieces and got spun around, with a definite and annoying "woe is me" overtone.

What are you doing here, Jon, all banged up—again—in pretty sorry digs, alone and exhausted, in this rank and dirty hotel room? You're an old man. You don't see very well. You're half deaf. You pee too much. Shouldn't you be in some fancy resort sharing a Mai Tai with your charming and beautiful wife?

I tried to argue that I had lived a wondrous life of high adventure. I could close my eyes at any time and see lonely oceans, colorful kayaks, sparkling mountains of untracked powder, spindrift cascading from limestone cliffs in a soft veil, the snow bouncing off the rock and falling upward in the storm. Just over the past weeks, my sea kayak adventures had taken me on long, exposed, open ocean crossings—gloriously alone—an infinitesimal, improbable speck on the tropical ocean. I had camped in mysterious jungle villages, slept in grass huts, gotten stoned on kava with elders and Rastafarian hippies, camped on uninhabited white coral sand beaches and survived a potentially lethal crocodile attack. Occasional injuries and frequent suffering aside, what more could a man want out of life? I was exactly where I wanted to be. But my think-too-much-know-it-all brain was having a bad day—we've all been there. So, it decided that it was high time to tally up my ego's résumé—you know, that worthless list of accomplishments, possessions, and failures:

One PhD; four pairs of skis; co-author of twenty-seven environmental textbooks; four wives; two cheery daughters; a son who barely talks to me; four adventure travel books; a small house in the Montana forest with a productive garden and broken plumbing; and a workshop that is always a mess. That sort of list.

I knew I was on dangerous ground, one to be avoided at all costs. Any stand-up guru worth her website would patiently explain that the real ME was separate from all that bullshit. But I wasn't in a philosophical mood, so I tried to escape by closing my eyes and going back to sleep. Unfortunately, my brain was too clever and persistent for that rusty old trick and began running through my past, complete with tallies, questions, and endless accusations that spun in slow tired circles with every turn of the rickety, squeaking, ceiling fan, revolving on tired bearings.

Okay, okay, brain. Enough already. Will you leave me alone if I simplify things and at least give a good answer to part of your question? Why am I here? You can say that I'm here because that crocodile didn't eat me.

CROCODILE ATTACK

I had just finished paddling, solo, along the Solomon Island chain, northwest from Honiara to the island of Choiseul, where I was within sight of the next nation, Papua New Guinea, although there is no geological, meteorological, oceanographic, or ethnographic reason for one country to end there and another to begin. I made the journey on a sit-on-top kayak, which all experts will agree is a toy, a recreational craft, suitable for crossing to the other side of a protected bay at that resort I didn't go to, and certainly not the craft of choice for an oceanic expedition. I had my reasons, as I always do whenever I make a big mistake. A sit-on-top is the most minimalist of crafts, little more than a surf-board with a seat, rising only a few centimeters above the water, with no deck or covering. It is slow, inefficient, and awash in the sea—a speck in the infinite. I wanted to navigate the rolling, mature waves of the South Pacific trade winds in such a craft, to be afloat on the broad ocean and out of sight of land—intentionally seeking vulnerability.

Since the Solomons are an island chain, my route followed coastlines interrupted by numerous island-to-island, open water crossings. The first crossing, on the second day of the expedition, was a fifteen-mile[1] strait called Iron Bottom Sound, named for

---

1 I generally use metric units throughout this book. But when I am at sea, I navigate using nautical miles and knots, because these units are precisely tied to latitude. Therefore, miles in this book refer to nautical miles, which are just slightly larger than a statute mile. 1 nautical mile = 1.8 kilometers.

that bloody day of human madness in 1942 when Japanese and American forces blasted away at each other, sending ships, aircraft, and human bodies to the bottom in a battle for an airstrip on Guadalcanal. Since my previous kayak expeditions have taken me around Cape Horn and across the North Pacific, I reasoned that a fifteen-mile crossing in an equatorial ocean should be trivial.

But once again, for the umpteenth millionth time, I underestimated the sea. Palm trees, coconuts, trade winds, and all those posters in the airport featuring old men, like me, strolling on coral sand beaches in the sunset with much younger, bikini-clad women had fooled me into thinking that this would be an easy trip—easy enough that I could intentionally make it more difficult and dangerous, just for the fun of it.

I set out in the early morning, hugging the lee of a narrow peninsula that provided a temporary harbor of nearly calm water. Leaving this finger of land, I paddled into the wind, which had been lazily forming waves across this vast and primordial ocean. When you watch a three-meter wave approaching a kayak, it seems that the wave should bury the boat, but then magically, it doesn't. A physicist will tell you that the water isn't actually advancing; it is just rolling in place, transmitting energy, not matter. If you feel your kayak while watching the sea, the physics of this becomes tactile, as the boat tilts, rises to the crest, hangs momentarily motionless in space, and then settles into the next trough, surrounded again by blue-green canyon walls of water.

An hour into the passage I felt the tug of a tidal current running through the channel. A quick GPS reading informed me that the current was carrying me off course, so I adjusted my compass bearing. Then, in the distance, I saw a line of white, rising incongruously at an odd angle to the wind. After all these years at sea, I should have known. The tidal current running through the strait was undercutting the trade-wind swell, like a line-backer grabbing the ankles of a running back, so the swell steepened, fell forward, and broke, creating surf-like conditions in deep water.

I had to maintain my course, or I would wash out to sea, so I crossed the deep-water eddy-line into the breaking waves. Immediately, I reached out with my paddle, feeling the break, as I had felt breaking waves so many times before in a lifetime of kayaking. Foaming white hissed toward me, raced over my paddle, and slapped me hard in the face, transmitting fear and joy, the two emotions entwined like lovers in a tango. As I leaned against my paddle, I rotated my hips instinctively, to set the edge of my kayak into the wave, as a skier sets edges while racing down a mountain. But to properly set an edge, I needed a real kayak, so I could press my thighs against the underside of the deck and use my lower torso for balance and stability. Instead I was perched on top of this stupid toy boat, flopping around like a rag doll. I briefly considered turning and riding down the breaking waves, like a surfer, but that course would take me straight down the channel, where I would wash out into the broad Pacific. So my only choice was to hold course, and paddle at right angles to the white, foamy, treacherous seas. I managed to make landfall by bracing aggressively with my paddle and maintaining my balance with my butt. The only problem was that this newly learned butt-control technique generated sores, which eventually lead to the bloody mess that I became by the time I returned to Honiara at the end of the expedition.

My second major crossing, from Hanesavo Island to Santa Isabel was 19 miles, just a little longer than the first. There was a small village of friendly people and grass huts at my launching point so I stopped early in the afternoon to rest and visit. A young man with an engaging smile offered me dinner and a place to sleep on his porch. With the Iron Bottom Sound incident fresh in memory, I reasoned that since I would be battling a cross-current the following day, my speed would be substantially reduced, leading to the danger that I would make landfall on an unknown coastline in the dark, with the ocean swell breaking against unfamiliar reefs. To avoid this eventuality, I might need more than the 12 hours of tropical daylight, so I decided to play it safe and leave at 3:00 AM, in total darkness. While this strategy would allow me to make landfall on the distant island in daylight, I would have to paddle out to sea, through a narrow channel in the reef, in early-morning darkness.

That evening, after dinner, I stood on the beach, watching the sea, to memorize the structure of the reef and the angle of the dangerous breaking waves. In this liquid landscape, changing continuously with the tides, what indicators would I have, without much vision, to guide me through that chaos for a safe passage? I slid into my boat and paddled into the lagoon. At my back, a tall coconut palm tilted out to sea, pointing like an unmistakable road sign toward my route. I felt certain that I would see its shadow illuminated in starlight. Following the palm, I memorized the feel of the waves when I was on course, toward the smooth green tongue of the narrow, safe channel. Then, I purposely paddled off-course, to feel the turbulent swash behind the reef. Yes, even with my eyes closed, I could tell the difference. I told myself, confidently, "I can do this in the dark."

I woke early the next morning, as planned, and my friendly host, along with a friend, helped me carry my boat and belongings down to the beach. Then I loaded up, waved goodbye, took a bearing off the palm tree, and ventured seaward. I inched closer, feeling the sea, listening to the woomph as the breaking waves expelled air from their curl, like the sound of a fat man who was punched in the belly. Yes, this is exactly where I wanted to be, in a reciprocal relationship with nature, feeling its moods, reacting to its voices, and putting my own physical body directly within this line of communication. I tacked back and forth, feeling the sea here, then there, comparing and listening. Then, confident that I was in the channel, I paddled blindly but resolutely toward deep water. Within a few moments, I could see, hear, and feel breaking waves both to my left and right, surrounding me, embracing my passage with their chaos.

I passed safely through the channel, reached the rhythmic swell of deep water, and paddled for fifteen minutes to clear the island, watch the stars, and enjoy the sea. Then, I reached for my GPS to calculate the current and my rate of drift. But when I picked up the waterproof bag that housed my GPS, I had a sickening feeling; it was too light. I opened it up, and sure enough, the instrument was gone. How could this be?

When I am camping around people, I always sleep with my GPS, money, passport, and ticket home tucked under my pillow inside my sleeping bag, so no one can steal them during the night. That morning, I'd packed all my critical possessions in the boat. I was certain of this. So what had happened? I reviewed every detail carefully. Yes, yes. In the pre-dawn blackness, my new-found friends had helped me carry my loaded kayak down to the beach. But then, before I set off, I fixed my starting position on the GPS, replaced it in its waterproof bag, secured it on the boat, and slipped off into the jungle to pee. In those few moments, my host must have opened my bag and stolen that life-saving, yellow bundle of electronic wizardry.

Now, out at sea, I decided to get angry at the thieves, and then at me for being careless. But I was alone, in the dark, now out of sight of land, and the trade winds at my back were so strong that I couldn't return to the village. Anger and recrimination were useless emotions out here. No, I was going to have to navigate as the Polynesian and Melanesian sailors had navigated before me, estimating current speed and direction by the shape of the waves, and plotting a course accordingly. I was afraid, as anyone would be afraid if he was at risk of drifting off into the boundless oceanic blackness in a kayak, but for the second time that morning, I felt euphoric as well.

Starlight danced off the tiny wavelets that rode on the backs of the larger waves, giving me a field of vision of a few meters. Thus, I could see a wave only moments before I could feel it, but I didn't need vision now. The angle of the wave-face tilted the boat, bypassing my eyes and transmitting information directly to my pelvis—the center of my balance, my ability to reproduce, and myself. Automatically, I knew where the wave would be, knew how steep it was, and—most importantly—how strong the current beneath it was. I understood now, why long-distance Pacific Island navigators placed their scrotums against the bow-stem of a boat, because that is the level of communication you need to steer a boat across the vastness, from Tahiti to Hawaii. I wasn't going nearly that far, but by emulating, in some small way, these great bygone navigators, I calculated the current and plotted a near perfect course. By sunrise I was within hazy sight of the distant island, lined up to make safe landfall.

A few weeks later, as I prepared for my third major crossing, I took stock of my situation. Even though the loss of my GPS had added a risk that I might get washed out to sea, I was managing well enough with old fashioned map and compass. Time on the water had taught me to calm down and treat the ocean with the respect I should have shown it from the onset. The last point of land, before this crossing, was an uninhabited tropical island, with palm trees and a white coral sand beach. I decided to stop, camp, and rest for a day—alone in paradise. I would snorkel along the coral, but more importantly, watch the currents and tides and carefully plan the timing of my next passage, in order to cross the deepest part of the channel at slack tide, when the current would be minimal. I was looking forward to the solitude and the opportunity to do nothing but watch the ocean, to study its moods, and then once again, to venture out into this fluid world on a tiny plastic platform, paddle in hand.

As I approached the beach, in this relaxed, peaceful state of mind, I saw, or thought I saw, a flash of motion on the periphery of my vision. Did I imagine it? I was travelling alone, numbed by the tropical heat and the repetition of paddling, as if I were wandering through a dream world. I couldn't ask my partner, because I had no partner, and when I scanned the sea and the shore, I saw no movement other than the waves and the swaying palms. Slightly on edge, I pulled my boat onto the beach and walked along the shore. And that's when I found the pie-sized tracks of a man-eating crocodile. As I stared down, the tracks closest to the ocean filled slowly with water, indicating the footprints were formed only minutes ago. Thus, the beast was close by.

I have this propensity, when facing imminent danger, to respond with initial curiosity and wonder rather than terror. I don't know where this reaction comes from; it has frequently alarmed my expedition partners, and maybe it will eventually lead to my demise. But, I can't help myself. Even when I was somersaulting down a mountain, in the maw of a horrendous avalanche and my skeleton was being torn apart, I took a second or a millisecond out of time and reminded myself to absorb the experience into my innermost being, in a positive way, because "You will never be here again."

Maybe this brief millisecond to stop and focus is foolishness, or worse yet, suicidal madness, but sometimes I think it is the thread that has kept me alive because focus, not fear, is my greatest ally in dangerous times. In this instance, my first reaction was: "Man-eating crocodile—probably longer than my kayak. Cool. I've never seen one of these before."

I walked back to my boat, got out my camera, and photographed the tracks, careful to frame the shadow of a coconut palm in the viewfinder, to give the image depth and perspective. Then realization set in.

"Man-eating crocodile. I am a man."

More alert and adrenalized now, I slowly followed the tracks toward the high-tide line, where the blazing hot coral sand met the damp, decaying jungle vegetation. In the subdued shadows of the jungle, trees, shrubs, and vines were twisted together as if everything grew out of one common trunk. Shade, steaming heat, and ubiquitous moisture had combined to create a deep, soft floor of decaying vegetation. And yes, there it was. Two mysterious yellow-green eyes, with brown splotches set into the background, like camouflage, and with an oval, blue pupil, oriented vertically. Reptilian eyes. And below those eyes, there was a barely discernable outline of a torso, with a few dragon scales lying in a field of brown leaves. Like a still-life. No motion. Looking into those unblinking eyes, then backing up and re-examining the tracks, I understood the story.

The reptile had been basking on the sand, facing the sea. When it saw me, it slithered on its belly into the water, swam down the shoreline for a hundred meters, and then turned back onto the beach. When it traversed inland, across the sand, toward the jungle, its belly was raised off the ground and its footprints were spaced farther apart, indicating that it was running, with its tail whipping back and forth, like a snake. Once in the foliage, it had turned again, and buried itself in the duff, with only its eyes peeking above the brown, fallen leaves. Now it was inching very slowly, almost imperceptibly, toward me.

Most of the time, when we see wild animals, they are running away, fearful of that upright, meat-eating, strange-smelling creature in its environment. Very occasionally, a wild animal stops to look at you. Over the decades, I have been fortunate enough to stare at close range—eyeball to eyeball—with a few potentially dangerous carnivores—wolves, polar bears, walrus, and killer whales. Big eyes, smaller ones, mammalian eyes. And now a crocodile. What was each of these animals thinking, as it looked at me? That's impossible to ascertain and prone to anthropomorphisms. But it was my definite impression that this particular crocodile wanted to eat me.

I stared into those unblinking eyes above the nearly motionless body. Crocodiles have an ancient lineage, appearing in the fossil record at the end of the Triassic Period about 30 million years after the first dinosaurs evolved. Sixty-six million years ago, a giant asteroid crashed into planet Earth, ejecting a dust cloud into the atmosphere that blocked out the sun and cooled our planet. Plants withered, and one by one, individual by individual, species by species, order by order, the great dinosaurs settled into the Cretaceous ooze and perished. But the crocs hung on. I guess that they don't experience much in the way of human-like emotions, like joy, anticipation, jealousy, or sadness, but they have a very long record at being excellent, efficient, and remorseless killers. And historically, I surmise, they haven't been particularly choosy about their prey. They like flesh, any sort of flesh.

I backed away, toward my boat, focusing on the jungle, prepared to sprint should the croc lunge. Soon I lost sight of those yellow eyes, and only the memory remained. Then, very carefully, I pushed out to sea, and paddled a hundred meters offshore. Scanning the seascape, I saw a second large crocodile floating, log-like, in the channel. I turned, calculated a quick compass bearing, and without bothering to worry about the currents in the channel, paddled away from this place, toward the next island.

As luck would have it, I began my crossing just at the worst part of the tide cycle, so I reached deep water when the cross current was at its strongest. I had a rough crossing, as all other crossings had been. But as I reminded my brain later, at the end of the expedition, in the urban filth and safety of that Honiara hotel room, at least I wasn't in the belly of a crocodile.

CROCODILE ANCESTORS

After my reptilian adventure, I spent more time seeking the security of human company and fewer nights camping alone in the rain-forest. Even now, at the beginning of the 21st century, villages in the outlying Solomon Islands mostly consist of grass and stick huts. There are some places where mining and logging companies have introduced western-style wood frame houses (along with bribery, social and economic hierarchies, slums, wife-beating, and other evidence of imported western civilization). But I tried to avoid those places.

When I travel, I bring gifts for people who offer me food

and shelter. On my first expedition to the South Pacific, a few years earlier, I brought Vise-grips to give away. A Vise-grip is an ingenious, beautiful, and handy tool—if you have rusted bolts to pry free or machinery to fix. But because my host lived in a pre-industrial home of wood and grass, the Vise-grip had no function in his society. He thanked me profusely and set the tool on a shelf above the hearth, as a piece of art, perhaps a status symbol, useless, but as a fond memory of a visitor from far away.

That experience helped me understand South Pacific village societies. Every person in the islands carries a machete, wherever they go. It can be scary, at first, to encounter a couple of muscular young men emerging from the jungle wielding sword-like knives; or to glimpse a four-year-old running across the village square with a jagged, rusted blade, broken off at the end. Or to meet a toothless, shirtless grandmother, with flat sagging breasts, also armed and seemingly dangerous. But after a while you get used to it. A machete, after all, is a wonderfully versatile tool, useful for planting, harvesting, clearing forest, opening coconuts, butchering chickens, preparing food, building houses, and making kava (the mildly hallucinogenic drug of the islands). To complement the machete, every family also owns a shovel and an axe, as well as cooking pots, fish hooks, and a few other utensils. But often, those are the only metal items they own, even today.

Solomon Island village houses are, by western standards, primitive affairs, with a frame constructed of posts set in or on the ground, roof of one kind of thatch, and walls of sticks, bamboo, or another type of thatch. Primitive, yes, but supremely comfortable. Sea breezes waft through the walls and rain cools the interior by evaporating off the roofs. And, not incidentally, the houses are free and easily replaceable after they are destroyed by a typhoon or an insect invasion. Neighbors cooperate to build a new home for a family; and then there are no 40-year mortgages leering from behind the sofa, forcing the owners to punch the time clock, and shadowing them into their graves.

In the soft, first light of early morning, when I lay on my sleeping pad on the rough plank or dirt floor in one of these houses, before the sun had filtered through the foliage, I gaze at each stick, each bundle of grass, twisted, bent, out of level or plumb, certainly not neat and orderly, but rather perfectly messy, like the forest itself—deep-order, a perfection of inhomogeneity, relaxing to the soul.

In my humble opinion, our propensity in Western Civilization to create neat and tidy living environments, with planar surfaces and sharp right angles, is way overrated. I know that it's supposed to be our patriotic duty to march down to the mall and purchase all the stuff we need to create an interior space that will boost the GDP and lower unemployment. Well, nature isn't orderly, love isn't orderly; our futures aren't orderly, why can't we flow through life embracing a little cheery chaos in our homes? A lot of people will accuse me of inventing a lame philosophical excuse for not fixing the plumbing at home, but that's how I feel.

Chickens and children, both noisy and random in their trajectories, add to the jolly chaos in the villages. Chickens are loose descendants of the dinosaurs, which puts them up there with the crocodiles as dogged survivors of asteroid impacts, human development, and other planetary catastrophes. These two dissimilar creatures just utilize different evolutionary strategies, that's all. The strategy of allowing yourself to be domesticated, and thus readily available to be eaten, wouldn't necessarily seem like such a good idea, but it has worked well enough as a method of passing on the DNA. Children, on the other hand, have a different genetic strategy, which is to convince grown-ups to dote on them because they are cute. But in other respects, they behave pretty much like chickens. They run around totally unsupervised, scratch in the dirt, dart in and out of houses, and chase bugs. Solomon Island children, unlike chickens, spend a lot of time playing soccer, but unlike their western counterparts, they play without coaches, level playing fields, or strict rules, and certainly without parents driving them to practice and then standing around, while cheering halfheartedly and talking on their cell phones.

Everything that the villagers do is less efficient than the performance of a similar task in Western Society. I cut firewood more quickly with a chainsaw than a Solomon Islander can with a machete or an axe. It takes five minutes to put a load of dirty clothes into the washing machine versus a few hours to wash them by hand in the stream. Yet, paradoxically and intriguingly, people in this inefficient society appear to have more free time than their opulent counterparts in the west. Walk through a primitive village at any time of day, and chances are that women will be sitting by the well chatting and gossiping, while men will be lounging in the shade of their gathering place, goofing off.

As I spent time in the island villages, I reasoned that these folks had survived for millennia among the crocs, so I asked the elders, the chiefs, the young Rasta hipsters, the dudes wearing "Ammo is the Currency of the New Generation" T-shirts, and above all, the fishermen and divers: "How do you manage the crocodile menace?"

The answer was universally consistent. People reminded me that I live in the Rocky Mountains of North America where mountain lions and grizzly bears are the dominant large-animal predators. A mountain lion will kill you nearly instantly by ripping out your jugular vein and a grizzly bear will crush your skull with one quick blow of its powerful paw, but a crocodile is much easier to defend yourself against. Crocs grab you in their ferocious jaws, drag you into the water, and then sink to the bottom. Because they can slow down their reptilian metabolism and need to surface less frequently than humans, they just hang out down there until you drown. Then they bury you in the mud, let the bacteria do the advance work of digestion, and return when you are soft, like a nice ripe brie, for dinner.

But there is a strategy for avoiding this fate. Drowning takes at least a minute, so you have time to calm yourself and react.

Everyone told me that the trick to surviving a crocodile attack is to determine whether you are right-side-up or up-side-down in the croc's jaws. Then you wait, focus, and in one swift motion, rotate around and: Poke him in the eyes. Everyone I spoke to assured me that it works every time; the croc will let you go and swim away. And if I didn't believe this story, in every village there was at least one survivor, who could bear witness with terrible scars from this Paleolithic hand-to-eye combat between man and beast.

Every time someone told me this story I repeated my mantra. "OK, got it. Calm yourself, orient your body position, focus, and poke him in the eyes." Not something I could use back home in Montana, but presumably handy in this place.

So one day, I was paddling alone in a calm sea, in the late afternoon, when I met a slightly corpulent gentleman with a benevolent smile, about 50 or so, traveling along the island coastline in a dugout canoe. I pulled over to within speaking range:

"Hi? Wanem nao nem belon' iu?" (Hi. Wanto know name belong you?) I asked in Solomon Island Pijin.

"Hi. Nem blo' mi Basil. (The name that belongs to me is Basil) Mi olraet nomoa! (Me alright; normal.)," he replied.

There are hundreds of distinct languages throughout Melanesia. In the 1800s Europeans kidnapped islanders to work in the sugarcane fields both in Queensland and on the neighboring islands of Fiji and New Caledonia. In order to communicate with each other and with their captors, the diverse Melanesians developed a bastardized language, called Pijin that combines bits and pieces of English with local logic and a uniquely structured grammar. Today, while some people spoke to me in pure Pijin, most spoke some unique, personal hybrid of Pijin and conventional English.

Basil invited me to join him and visit some friends for the evening. I accepted and we continued paddling, talking about the weather, the sea, the declining fishery, Indonesian logging companies, the latest antics of Paris Hilton, and other topics of local interest. We came to a small delta around dusk and he turned up-river toward his friends' village. That's when my pre-expedition research kicked in.

Before I embarked on this expedition, I'd read the *Lonely Planet Guide to the Solomon Islands*. And one of the tips I remembered, very clearly, was: "Crocodiles feed mainly in river mouths at dusk." Now, I had been mentally practicing my eye-poking croc-battle-plan, but had no real desire to test it out. So, as casually as I could, I mentioned this to my new companion.

"You know, it's really nice to paddle along with you, and this is sure a nice river mouth with a hint of an early moon rising above the forest greenery. I'm enjoying your company, and looking forward to meeting your friends, but, you see, I read this book, back home, in America, and it says, 'Crocodiles feed mainly in river mouths at dusk.' So I'm just kind of wondering if we might happen to be at the wrong place at the wrong time."

Basil smiled and patiently explained to me that while crocodiles do feed mainly in river mouths at dusk that generalization applies to crocodiles in general. If we were in another river, we would indeed be in grave danger right now. But this was his home river and the crocodiles in this river were not real crocodiles at all, but Grandfather Crocodiles, reincarnations of his ancestors. He concluded by assuring me that, "As long as you are with me, under my protection, you are safe."

Then he instructed me to wash my face in the river water, which would introduce me to the local crocodiles and assure my safety.

I could have bolted for the relative security of the open sea, but, wherever you draw the line between truth and myth, it was an undeniable fact that Basil had somehow managed to survive in this crocodile infested environment for half a century. As a result, I figured that the probability was in my favor that we would make it through one evening, together, without being eaten. I calmed down, changed the subject, and asked him how far it was to his friends' village. He replied, "Two to three minutes or an hour or something like that."

The jungle was deep and primeval. Shafts of evening light filtered through the foliage, highlighting vines and epiphytes. Birds sang overhead and flitted in and out of the light and shadow, revealing flashes of bright colors. Between the shafts of light, the impenetrable jungle was nearly jet black. My butt was sore and I felt more tired than I thought I should be. Old age, setting in. Just when I was beginning to become even more concerned at the prospect of paddling in crocodile infested waters in the dark, we rounded a bend to see a huge, incongruous, and incomprehensible open space, harsh and barren, where the jungle had been soft and verdant. Here, people had hacked the rainforest with machetes and axes, leaving a death-like landscape covered by a single agricultural crop. On the edges of the giant clearing, brush fires glowed red in the twilight and smoke rose in curling columns, giving me the feeling that I had come across a recent battlefield.

"What is this?" I asked incredulously.

"Rice," answered Basil. "My friends are planting rice."

All the Island agriculture that I had seen up until now consisted of a variety of crops, planted together: various tubers mixed with banana and papaya trees, an occasional pineapple plant and a variety of other foods, some of which were familiar to me and some of which were not. When you eat dinner in most villages, you are likely to eat lap-lap, which is a starchy pudding made from tubers, mixed with a variety of other fruits and vegetables and maybe even a little morsel of fish or chicken. I had never seen monoculture in the Islands before. I wrote in my journal that the rice field seemed like drawings in those children's books showing scenes where you were supposed to point out "what's wrong with this picture." And then you see a snake playing the piano.

The living dwellings were hastily thrown together, without any of the art of stick and thatch dwellings in normal villages. There was no village square, no chickens, no children playing soccer, and no flowered walkways, all of which were common in normal villages—there were only the symmetrical rows of rice, pinched together by perspective at the edge of the clearing and the beginning of the forest. Next to the crude dwellings stood a rusty rice-mill, spinning away noisily, shaking and vibrating on worn bearings, milling wholesome brown rice into bland pure white carbohydrate, with no redeeming nutritional value.

A curly-haired woman, named Mary, in her mid-50s, welcomed me. Her hair was almost blonde, indicating some European DNA in her system, perhaps from the slavery days in the sugarcane fields. She held her machete easily, swinging it casually, as if she never knew that it was possible to stop working. We chatted for a while and I asked her if the farm was successful. She shook her head mournfully, "Insects are eating the crop." I asked her if insects also ate her traditional home garden and she replied "Yes, but never like this." The woman had left her native village, her husband, and her children to "get ahead" on this rice farm. Now, along with her partners, she was in debt and impoverished, unable to return home, like the feudal peasantry that I thought we had freed from bondage at the end of the Middle Ages. For dinner, we had a big pile of white rice and nothing else. I felt hungry and weak, so I shared a few crackers that I had in my boat, but they were devoid of nutrition as well.

After dinner, Mary poured some hot water through a sorry-looking strainer of old, well-used, soggy, moldy tea leaves. Then Mary, Basil, and I sat quietly on a log. Mary asked, almost in a whisper, "Jon, is life hard in America?" I thought about my happy friends who are itinerant ski bums, and then about the unemployed street people, or those festering in prison for petty drug charges, or those who were stressed out, seeking psychotherapy, despite living in penthouse opulence—and I didn't know how to answer her question. So I asked in return, "Mary, is life hard in the Solomon Islands?"

"When people want too many things, then life becomes hard. When I was young, living in a village, we had very few things. But life was easier. Now we owe money to the man who gave us the rice seed, and I don't know how I will ever return home."

Night fell, the conversation broke up, and people drifted off to their evening tasks. Under the glow of my headlamp, I walked down to the river bank and shined the light across the muddy waters, looking for crocodile eyes. All I saw was the orange reflection of my light bouncing off gently flowing water. Then I turned my beam onto Basil's canoe. He had hollowed it out of a single log, and from the look of the tool marks, he had used a sharp adze, not a chain saw.

I splashed some water on my face, to remind the crocodiles that even though I was a white man, I was part of the family.

MOOLYNAUT

Back in my present situation, in the third-world civilization of that grubby hotel room, the sun was dipping and the stifling afternoon heat had been broken by shadow and sea breezes. I was hungry, so I rose out of bed again, dressed, and hobbled into town to my favorite Chinese restaurant. As soon as I opened the door, the young, stunningly beautiful Chinese-Melanesian waitress scurried over to greet me.

"Good evening, grandfather." She touched me lightly on the shoulder. "Just a moment; I will bring your chair." Then she raced into the back room, where her thin, wrinkled father was half shrouded in steam, as if in the haze of an opium den, as he stirred vegetables in a wok, moving his arms with a graceful flourish, conducting a symphony.

Being called "grandfather" has its advantages, despite the not-so-gentle reminder of looming mortality. And one of the perks, in that Chinese restaurant in Honiara, was a fine chair, with throne-like arms, and a soft cushion for my half-mangled butt.

"One beer, again, tonight? You could have more," she teased with a mischievous grin and another gentle touch.

"Let's start with one."

It was a cool Pilsner, brewed in the islands, with a faint essence of jungle. That's exactly what I needed at that moment, a little buzz to take the edge off of pain and boredom.

So where were we now? Yes. Washing my face in the river. By this time in my life, Grandfather Crocodiles no longer surprised me. Nine years earlier, while I was on another expedition, kayaking along the east coast of Siberia, from Japan to Alaska, I had met Moolynaut, an old Koryak shaman. She was 96 at the time, one of the last of the old time healers who was born into a near Stone Age existence, on the Siberian tundra, at the extreme eastern edge of Czar Nicholas II's vast empire. We met briefly in 2000, and she asked me and my Russian partner, Misha to: "Come back. Because it will be good if you do." Misha and I returned the following spring. During that second visit, while traveling on the tundra, with our friends, Oleg and Sergei, I slipped on an icy rock and reinjured my pelvis, which had been dislocated a few years before in a horrendous avalanche in British Columbia. While I was wracked with pain, Oleg calmly told me not to worry, because he would take me back to the village where Moolynaut would heal me. At that moment, lying helplessly in the snow, unable to stand, I would have preferred to call a helicopter to transport me to a modern hospital, with its tubes, machines, and taciturn surgeons. But that option was not available.

Two days later we returned to the village. I was a little better by that time, and Moolynaut asked me to stand naked, balanced on one leg, with one hand stretched out in front of me and the other tucked behind my back, in the shamanic pose of flight. She closed her eyes and transported herself into the Other World, where she implored Kutcha the Raven to fly to The Old Woman Who Lives on Top of the Highest Mountain and to ask her to fix my damaged body.

Moolynaut rocked slowly back and forth for some time, then straightened, looked at me, and asked me whether I believed in this journey.

She was a tiny woman, barely as tall as my chest. Yet, on that day, as I stood naked before her, she looked deeply into my eyes, penetrating the reality that I had been born into; the reality that I had so laboriously defended, and then challenged, minute by minute, layer by layer, all my life. She leaned over slowly, emphatically spit on my pubic hair, and then told me that I had to believe in the journey we were about to take. If I didn't believe, it would be very bad: Bad for Her. Bad for Kutcha the Raven. And especially Bad for Me. I was terrified. Her eyes, often soft, had become fierce. How much did she know? How deeply into my mind could she see? The only thing I knew for certain was that, for her sake, for Kutcha's sake, and for my sake, I couldn't lie. Yet, throughout my life, I had essentially zero experience embarking on spiritual journeys, of any kind, through any religion or medium.

I started slowly, not knowing what I was about to say, until, thankfully, the only possible answer arose. I told her that I was a white man. I hadn't been raised to believe in Kutcha. My mother never taught me to seek healing from The Old Woman Who Lives on Top of the Highest Mountain. And then some overpowering emotion welled up inside. A certainty that I was about to embark on a wondrous new journey. A transformation, if you care to call it that. I told Moolynaut that I would try. I would try to fly with the Spirit Raven and the mysterious ancient wisdoms that rode on those jet black wings. I promised her that.

Moolynaut nodded and started chanting again. I lost track of time. Minutes passed, I guess. Then, from the other side of a dream-state, I heard her tell me that I could put my foot down now, and stand on two legs. That confused me, because I somehow forgot that I was naked, standing on one leg. "Oh, yes, of course."

So I stood on both legs and I was better. Healed. I could ski again.

On my next visit to Siberia in November, Moolynaut had me eat the amanita to help me journey to the Other World through the drug-power of a red hallucinogenic mushroom with little, threatening (or promising) white dots on the top. But I became frightened and couldn't complete the journey. After retreating from the dream journey, I felt that I had failed her and myself.

The next morning, at breakfast, Oleg announced, "Pack your things, we're going fishing."

So Oleg, Sergei, Misha and I traveled upriver in Oleg's speed-boat. Over the course of three days, we filled the boat with fish, as the first blasts of winter formed a thin film of ice across the river. When it was time to return to the village, Oleg adroitly steered the speedboat around sand bars and snags that were invisible to me. The ice made a sing-song tinkling sound as the aluminum hull blasted its way through, in the late afternoon autumn light of this remote Siberian landscape. Oleg was smiling contentedly because we had been successful enough to feed his family, with excess to give away to those too old or sick to fend for themselves.

Suddenly he cut the engine and the silence of the tundra engulfed us again. The boat drifted aimlessly, spinning slowly in the current, and bumping gently into the ice. I looked up, expecting that there was a mechanical malfunction, but I hadn't heard anything amiss.

He held my gaze. "Jon…" I looked into his broad weather-beaten face, short cropped moustache and four-day stubble beard, half indigenous Koryak and half Russian Cossack; two of the toughest races on Earth. His eyes were hidden behind dark goggles that bulged outward like fish-bowls, and his head was covered by a dog-fur beaded hat, with protruding lobes that resembled the ears of a friendly, inquisitive wolf.

Oleg continued, "Do you know why you failed to complete your journey to the Other World?"

"What?" In all the time I had known him, through all our adventures together, Oleg had never talked about spiritual matters; it was always about motors, route-finding, ice and snow, hunting and fishing.

I looked up at his calm, almost beneficent smile. "Nyet. No, I don't know why I failed to follow Moolynaut on a journey she had trod so many times."

"Jon. You are a lousy traveler into the Other World. You are a hunter like me. You are an excellent traveler in the Real World. You must make your spirit journeys on real oceans and tundra, where you will be cold and hungry. Tired, frostbitten, and strung out. Because the Spirit World and the Real World are the same. Maybe you will die out there." He shrugged and smiled his warmest bear-smile, pulled the starter cord on his outboard motor, and spun the boat into the current, because there was nothing more to say.

A week later, I returned to North America with all its wondrously seductive technology and wrote a book about my experiences with Moolynaut and Oleg, called, *The Raven's Gift.* And now, coming full circle, I was back into the Spirit World of our ancestors. So, the question at hand: "Did I really believe that by traveling with Basil and washing my face in the river, I would conjure up a magic spell that would give me safe passage through a cauldron of Mesozoic-minded, meat-eating crocodiles?"

Sorry, but I refuse to answer the question. It's that pesky think-too-much-know-it-all brain getting in the way, again. It's not a matter of believing this or that and I'm certainly not in a mood to try to convince anyone (myself included) into believing anything. Here in the jungle, far from home, alone, in a world ruled by dangerous reptilian predators and predatory landlords who were enslaving the people with debt and horrendously inappropriate agricultural practices, I was once again, balanced between disparate worlds—magical and logical—aboriginal and modern. And I washed my face in the river because regardless of where The Real World ends and The Dream World (or The Delusional World) begins, Moolynaut and Basil have become gentle, reassuring, and guiding presences in my life.

By the third beer, I reminisced even further back in time, on a rambling wayward journey beyond the shadow of the real or spirit crocodiles floating in the muddy current of that lazy river, before Moolynaut even, because as important as she was in my life, my encounter with her was not the beginning of my journey. The beginning was that nothing speck of time, two hours at most, when I was nineteen years old, traveling across the steppe of Asia Minor with the Gypsies.

HITCHHIKING ACROSS
THE MIDDLE EAST
SUMMER, 1964

I was born in December 1945, four months and a day after Japan surrendered to the allied powers, thus ending World War II, that era where the most powerful and supposedly civilized nations of the world incinerated, vaporized, cremated, machine gunned, bombed, tortured, and starved 50 to 85 million people: soldiers and civilians—men, women, and children—infants and centenarians. At that time, physicists had invented the atomic bomb, but there wasn't a single fully operational electronic computer in the world, and no television stations. (In my grandfather's time, Reuters News Service used passenger pigeons to transmit stock price changes from city to city.)

Just to keep things in perspective, I was also born approximately 3,600 years after the extinction of the wooly mammoth, 280 years after the last dodo bird expired, 9 years after Tasmanian Tigers (Thylacines) perished, and 2 years after the last known Ivory Billed Woodpecker pecked on a dead spar. And by the way, I was born as one of the 4% of the people on the globe who just luckily bumbled into unimaginable opportunity and opulence, so that I can safely say that I have lived in the age of shaped skis and before all the snow turned to rain.

Now, I'm an old man.

In college, I did my physics homework on a slide rule, and I wrote several of my early textbooks with a fountain pen. Just to remind myself of my age and frailty, I gingerly shifted my weight in my fancy chair here in this restaurant in Honiara. Actually, my wounds, for all the commotion they caused, were only superficial—nothing more than infected butt sores, from sitting in my kayak too long, or really, from sitting in the wrong kayak. Because, once again I had followed some self-defined romantic image rather than logic or common sense. You'd think I would know better by now.

I grew up in a traditional, loving family, with an older sister and a younger brother, in a house on a small New England lake, nestled in a forest that had overgrown old cow pastures on land that the pilgrims stole from the Mashantucket Pequot and Mohegan tribes. My parents, teachers, and clergy never talked about the Mashantucket Pequot or the Mohegan and incredibly, I had to Google, "Connecticut First Nations People" to write this, because I never knew the tribal affiliations of those who had lived, hunted, farmed, had babies, and died here before us. Oh, of course, around Thanksgiving, we all talked about "Indians" as a generic catch-all term for all the varied, independent, pre-contact nations of the Western Hemisphere. But, most of the time when we talked about people from a bygone era, we focused on the Middle East, where, I learned over and over, Abraham had destroyed the multiple gods of the savage heathen and established the monotheism that anchors refined civilization.

After a happy childhood and a year at Danbury High School, I left home at the age of 14, not in anger or rebellion, but to attend Phillips Academy, Andover, where young boys from working class families, like me, played stickball next to George W. Bush and his compatriots, who even at that young age, knew that they were destined to rule. When I think about my classmates, I can't shake an old Kurt Vonnegut quote from my head, "True terror is to wake up one morning and discover that your high school class is running the country."

In any case, my grades were good enough for admission into the Ivy League, at Brown University. In those days, I had a neat and tidy outline for the rest of my life. I would study chemistry, like my father, earn a Ph.D., and eventually partner with him as an air pollution control consultant. We would become financially solvent enough so I could afford a private airplane and fly up to Vermont on weekends to go camping and hiking, which I loved to do above all else. I would marry what my mother always referred to—generically—as "aniceJewishgirl" (always spoken as one word), have kids, and so on.

That's what I told myself, because that's what I was expected to tell myself, but that's not what I dreamed about. During my freshman year at Brown, my roommate, Dave Robinson, and I hatched a plan. As soon as school got out, we would take off, a mandated five dollars in our pocket, not a penny more or a penny less. Traveling fast and light, and hungry perhaps, we would hitch-hike to Ohio and immediately get jobs as roughnecks on an oil drilling platform. We would work there for a few weeks or until the first of July, when we would have enough money to buy fast motorcycles. Then we would zoom off to California, with wind in our hair and smoke blowing out our exhausts, and drive up and down Highway 1 partying and getting laid in and around Big Sur. By the end of July, we figured we would be out of cash again, so with enough money left for one last tank of gas, we would zoom up to the deep forests of Northern California, where we would get jobs in a logging camp. We would work there long enough to earn the money needed to drive home, back to our classrooms for the fall semester.

After my last final exam, I tossed all my pens and pencils onto the campus green in a ritual purging of academia, because they were symbols of a world I was now joyfully abandoning, if only for three months. I went home briefly, scrambled together the five dollars, and grabbed a few pieces of fruit and a couple of sandwiches from my mother's kitchen. Obtaining free food, by whatever means possible, was within the rules we had established for ourselves. Then I hitchhiked up to Melrose, Massachusetts to pick up Dave. When I got there, he told me that he had neglected to tell his parents about our planned adventure. We broached the subject to his mother, and she absolutely F-R-E-A-K-E-D-O-U-T.

This wasn't good. I looked into David's eyes for some sign of rebellion, but it wasn't there. After a heart-to-heart talk with Mom, while sitting on stiff-backed flowered chairs in their meticulously ordered Victorian living room, we made a deal. Dave and I would paint the Robinson's house, and they would pay us. Then, only a week behind schedule, we could head west with a greater financial cushion in our pockets. Painting your partner's mother's house in suburban Melrose isn't nearly as romantic as the mud and blood of an oil drilling platform, but there seemed to be no choice. So we worked long hours to finish the job in as short a time as possible, drew our paychecks, and then announced that we would leave the next morning.

As soon as we started packing, Dave's mother ran into the bathroom, crying. Dave looked at me with a forlorn, "I'm sorry" expression, and again no indication of rebellion. So I walked out the driveway by myself. I found a phone booth and called my parents. My mother's first reaction was, "Well, if Dave's mother won't let him go…" But she knew me well enough to know that I was on the verge of taking off, permission or no permission, and that to hang onto a thin thread of control, she needed to come up with an alternative—fast. I would go to Israel and work on a kibbutz.

Israel was far away and a foreign country, and these two factors lent an air of mystery that seemed almost as good as the old plan, so, under pressure, I agreed. After a flurry of activity, obtaining tickets, shots, and passports, I boarded an airplane to Tel Aviv.

Somewhere along the line, I became attached to a romantic

image that native-born Israelis, called *sabras*, were so tough that they put stones in their mouths while working in the desert heat to stimulate the flow of saliva and trick the body into thinking that its thirst had been quenched. But, all the romanticism and mythology aside, a kibbutz is a farm, and regardless of its underlying philosophical, political, or economic theory, farming is hard, often monotonous work. Because I was young and strong, the kibbutz leaders assigned me to a crew that woke in pre-dawn semi-darkness and loaded heavy straw bales onto a wagon in the hot desert sunshine. The crew consisted of several kibbutz members and two foreigners, an Argentine guy and myself. After working for about a week, two women appeared on the scene, one from Great Britain and the other from Holland. Naturally, the Argentinean guy and I wooed them and after a few days the women mentioned that they were feeling vulnerable, traveling alone in a potentially hostile world. I suggested, as casually as I could, that perhaps it would be safer to travel together, as a foursome—and to my surprise, they agreed.

We rode buses across the stark, barren Negev and snorkeled in the blue waters of the Gulf of Aqaba. Then we hitchhiked north to kibbutz Ein Gedi, adjacent to the biblical King David's Falls, where a massive spring of fresh groundwater rises out of the coolness of the earth to tumble over a rock cliff into the Dead Sea. We arranged for short-term work at the kibbutz, and then hiked across the tan, baked desert to the fabled springs. Short bursts of gun-fire split the still air, whether from target practice or hostilities, no one would ever tell us. We were alone at the springs, with exotic vegetation and rainbows rising in the mist, so we stripped off our clothes to soak, Jacuzzi style, in the frigid bubbles from the waterfall. Then we sprawled out on hot rocks, naked, to bake in the sun.

We paired up as couples that day, almost randomly, because, really, we were friends as a foursome. During the following week, the Argentinean guy and I helped a kibbutz crew pour concrete for an irrigation system and our partners staked tomato plants.

The woman I had partnered with (sorry, I simply can't remember her name) asked me if I would like to go to Greece with her. I told her that my money from painting Dave's mother's house was running low, but she assured me that she would pick up the tab for a few weeks in Greece together before she returned home to resume her job.

My flight back to New York at the end of the summer was from Tel Aviv, and I didn't have the money to return to Israel after we parted, but that kind of logic didn't register in my 19-year-old male brain. So we boarded a ferry for Athens, but even before the boat touched shore two days later, my girlfriend decided that I wasn't as cool as she had thought, and she ditched me.

So I ended up in Greece, alone, with very little money. Of course, I could have gone to the American Embassy, acted contrite, and asked them to place a collect phone call to my mother. If I told Mom that I was stuck here, she assuredly would have chastised me, but equally assuredly, she would have wired me enough money to return to Israel where I could repent and finish the remainder of the summer on the baling crew.

But, instead, I decided to hitchhike across Greece, Turkey, Syria, Lebanon, and Jordan, and return across the border to Israel. In those days, 1964, Jerusalem was a divided city, with East Jerusalem being part of Jordan and West Jerusalem belonging to Israel. A famous border crossing called the Mandelbaum Gate, formed the checkpoint between the two countries. Even though Jordan and Israel didn't get along that well, they were still civilized enough to allow tourists to transit back and forth. One of the guys at the youth hostel warned that I might get in trouble if immigration officials in Syria or Jordan saw the stamp of the Israeli visa in my passport. So I went down to the Red Cross, sold a pint of blood for $10, and spent the blood money on a new passport.

My first ride was with a Frenchman who thought my story was hysterical and drove his sports car very fast.

I stole food from farmers' fields as I waited for rides. There is no meal quite like an illicit, juicy watermelon, warmed by the sun until it almost tastes like hot, sweet soup—a sensation Eve must have felt when she ate the apple.

A Greek farmer drove by on a horse-drawn cart and asked me if I knew anything about fixing machinery. I shrugged and said I could always try, not knowing if the problem was a loose spark-plug wire or a blown piston. He took me to his village, handed me a screwdriver and a pair of pliers, and led me to the small irrigation pump that was the lifeline for all the farms in the entire region. It turned out to be a simple Briggs and Stratton, almost identical to the lawn mower engines I had worked on routinely back home, with a loose throttle cable. With my farmer friend looking on expectantly, I pulled the cable taught, tightened the set screw, and fired the machine to life. Back in town, the news spread rapidly, and someone quickly ushered me into a house where his wife prepared a feast. After dinner, the village men left their wives at home to do the dishes and we retired to the bar to dance together and get very drunk on ouzo.

I left the village with my pack stuffed full of food, which lasted a few days until some German tourists picked me up and spread a wonderful smorgasbord of breads, cheeses, and meats out on a blanket for an afternoon picnic.

In Istanbul I spent a little of my precious money to buy green figs and yogurt in an open air café, as James Bond had done in one of the Ian Fleming novels. In this youth hostel, young travelers were smoking hash and having casual sex. I didn't get in on the action, probably because I was too awkward and bewildered.

Traveling across the Turkish highlands, I quickly learned to introduce myself as Jon Turk, not simply, Jon. Invariably, people would ask, "How did you get that last name?"

My meal ticket was to lie, "My grandfather was Turkish and I am coming home."

A large truck dropped me off in front of a roadside restaurant just before a catastrophic locust plague descended in Biblical ferocity. We watched as the grasshoppers ate the entire wheat crop in a half an hour. Then a car pulled up with American tourists. The owner of the restaurant quickly told me in French, our shared language, that the Americans would be pleased, and he could inflate the prices, if I would quickly become a waiter. When I showed up in my Turkish waiter uniform speaking flawless English, the Americans were pleasantly surprised, ordered a big meal, paid the bill, and left me a generous tip. The restaurant owners paid me with food, a shower, and a place to sleep.

A few days later, as I walked along on a particularly desolate stretch of road in central Turkey, Gypsies picked me up in a brightly painted wagon pulled by a dusty old mule. I climbed onto a splintery board bouncing on rusty springs, and sat next to a mustached man in his thirties and a teenage mother who was nursing an infant. We didn't go far, long, or fast—maybe an hour or two, and we had no language. The couple didn't talk much to each other, so the only sounds were the plodding hooves, the squeaking wheel bearings, and a gentle clucking as the driver guided the faithful, patient mule. Nothing happened. No action, no narrative. I remember smells of strange spices from inside the wagon and a sweaty mule outside. Wheat fields stretching across the horizon. An occasional car or truck whizzing past.

The incident could have faded into mental oblivion. But it didn't. In that brief time, with no overt excitement, I silently journeyed into a reality that reached into the past and stretched across the globe. A reality that, with minor changes in costume, culture, or draft animal, was universal, but so completely alien from anything I had ever experienced back home. It jolted me. It was a call. But I didn't know all that at the time.

Shortly after my sojourn with the Gypsies, I crossed over into Syria. On my first night, I was sleeping in a field, when a young man woke me and pantomimed that he wanted to have sex with me. I said no, emphatically, and he left peacefully. I should have packed up and moved on, but I was young, tired, and naïve, so I dozed back to sleep. Then, I heard the muffled sound of shoes in soft earth. When I opened my eyes, the man was standing above me—with a long knife. I had talked my way out of the first encounter, but that approach wasn't going to work this time. So with both feet still in the bag, I reared up and kicked him in the balls, my feet rising under the knife. He dropped in surprise and pain, giving me time to scurry free and kick him in the face, before I understood what I was doing. He collapsed, bleeding, and I escaped into the night, stumbling, alone and vulnerable, over irrigated fields, terrified at the intensity of my own violence, smelling moist earth and fear. I walked all night, paralleling the road, but avoiding all human contact.

In the morning, I was close to Damascus, which seemed like an exotic place to be, so I caught a ride to town. I don't know what I expected, maybe another youth hostel full of happy-go-lucky travelers, like the one in Istanbul. I found someone who spoke English, but when I tried to get directions to this hostel that existed only in my imagination, the man asked, "Who are you? Where are you from? Do you hate the Israelis as much as we do?"

It turned out to be a harsh day. In retrospect, I never got a fair chance to see Syria inside and out. I never sat down to dinner with the philosophers and artists of Damascus. If my memory serves me correctly, I never spoke to a woman, or to children. I hung out in bazaars and truck-stops, alone, without language. Given those circumstances, and recognizing that I only experienced a small part of the total culture, the Syria I witnessed, personally, was a hotbed of intense animosity and anger. Every conversation, with anyone, descended almost instantly into virulent hatred, punctuated, almost invariably, with loud, accentuated spitting onto the sidewalk. I'm not exaggerating. And that was fifty years ago, before the current civil war that has destroyed the nation and its societies, before ISIS institutionalized rape and random beheadings as a policy initiative. I got freaked out at the innate violence, and high-tailed it into Jordan.

Finally, I arrived in East Jerusalem. I had a little bit of money left, so I checked into a hostel and visited the holy mosque that rises over an exposed chunk of bedrock that had been the site of the Second Jewish Temple during biblical times. This is the place where Abraham prepared to sacrifice his son Isaac, according to God's command. Much later, Jesus tossed the money lenders out of the Second Temple, an act of defiance that quickly led to his crucifixion. The Prophet Muhammad ascended to Heaven from this rock, accompanied by the angel Gabriel.

An inscription in a mosaic frieze on the walls of the mosque, reads, "So peace is upon me the day I was born, and the day I die, and the day I shall be raised alive!"

These words reverberate against thousands of years of warfare on the most contested piece of real estate on Earth. They echo with the silent screams of dying soldiers and civilians during the Roman Siege of Jerusalem in 70 CE, of clashing metal as crusaders and Arabs cut each other to bloody ribbons by the tens of thousands, and the unmistakable staccato bursts of modern submachine guns.

A group of Irish Christian pilgrims were gathered around an Arab guide in the massive courtyard. I stopped on the fringes of the group out of loneliness? Curiosity? The tour guide gave a brief history of the long, complex Christian and Arab presence in the city, but made no mention of the Jews. I could have walked away and shrugged, and today I certainly would not bring attention to myself in such a volatile environment—after all, I have no desire to be beheaded. But back then, I was young and stupid. So from the back of this group that I had no association with, I commented, as casually as I could "And what about the Jews? Didn't they have a historical presence in this city?"

The guide looked at me and asked sharply, "Why do you say

this?" He squinted at me hard for a few seconds, and then asked, "Are you Jewish?"

Sensing trouble, I backed away without answering, and tried to disappear in the crowd of international tourists, but it was too late. The guide whistled sharply and yelled something in Arabic. Immediately, two guards, who were positioned nearby and armed with AK-47s, moved in quickly from the sidelines.

All summer, I had been casual and cavalier, following my whims, changing plans for any reason at all, assuming that I could be a little bit outrageous and somehow get away with it. It had been so much fun, the dreamed-about, and unrealized, motorcycle journey up the California coast, the desert romance, the stolen watermelons, the party mode in Istanbul that was exciting even from the sidelines, the Gypsies, and the locust plague. All of that, even the glint of the knife in the moonlight, had been child's play. I guess that in some way, deep down inside, despite all evidence to the contrary, I didn't understand how much anger, hatred, violence, and hostility infused this holy land.

For just an instant, I thought that I should run, ducking and weaving through the milling crowds of tourists. But I was in a medieval walled city, surrounded by ancient stones, with only a few narrow, arched gates, and armed guards at every gate. A dramatic, over-the-wall dash was definitely a bad idea. So I stood there placidly until the guards reached me. I can't explain why I felt the way I did, but I remember a deep calmness, which has since become familiar, as I have faced danger repeatedly throughout my life. It wasn't something I thought about or decided to do; it arose out of that mysterious electrochemical interaction among DNA, nerves, and brain that I had no control of. I would save my energy for when I needed it.

One of the men jabbed the barrel of his weapon into my kidney and the other poked me in the stomach with his submachine gun and pantomimed that I should put my hands on my head. Then the guards—young, grim-faced and tight-lipped—herded me through the marketplace, where shopkeepers in open stalls sold religious trinkets and exotic fruits. As we passed, men spit at me. Most of the time they missed, but every once in a while, a glob of phlegm landed on my shirt, and one hit me square in the cheek. Keep your hands on your head, I told myself. Don't wipe it off; you've been stupid enough already. Suck it up; let some time pass for all of this to calm down; make your move when the time is right.

The guards walked me into a building. Funny, I have no recollection of the exterior of that building. Was it new? Built of wood or masonry? Or was it made of old stones erected under the orders of King Solomon? King Richard II? Saladin? King Henry III? Ayyubid Sultan Al-Kamil? I can't remember.

We walked through a hallway. The guards opened a door and ushered me into a windowless, pale room, empty except for a worn and cracked desk with a bare surface, a stiff, wooden highback chair for an interrogating officer, and a three-legged stool for me. They motioned for me to sit on the stool, demanded my wallet and passport, and then backed out, guns still pointing, until the door slammed shut. Alone, I finally had the opportunity to wipe the spit off my face, but it was dry by now.

Some time passed. 15 minutes? An hour? I think less than an hour. Certainly enough time for my brain to slide into absolute silent nothingness. There were no images of home overlooking the quiet lake with geese and the occasional muskrat creating V-shaped wakes, of nubile naked bodies splashing in the Ein Gedi spring, no girlfriends, no motorcycles, no chemistry lessons, just raw emptiness, which might have been beautiful if I could reimagine it from a different perspective. But under the circumstance, I felt no cathartic beauty.

Eventually, the door opened and an officer strolled in, followed by an enlisted man who locked the door behind him and put the key in his pocket with a flare of showmanship, daring me with his eyes to respond. The men were unarmed. They didn't need to be. I was deep in the labyrinth. The officer sat down in his chair. He placed my passport and a thin file on the desk, and moved them absently about, as if they were chess pieces. Even after all these years, I remember his words almost verbatim.

"Nobody knows you are here," he began slowly and evenly in accented but grammatically perfect English. "Your mother doesn't know where you are; your embassy doesn't know where you are. The Israeli army doesn't know that you are here. You are in this room." He slapped the desk hard with an open palm. "I own you. You are mine. I can do anything I want with you, and nobody will ever know."

He folded his hands and looked across the desk at me.

I experienced a terror beyond thought or description.

Torture is a very heavy word, implying almost unimaginable insensitivity on one side and inconceivable pain on the other. The enlisted man didn't torture me. That is too harsh a concept. He roughed me up, slapped me around, punched me in the belly, pushed me down, pulled me up, and slapped me around some more. I had played lacrosse in college and could handle a little contact. But this was not the same as a hard cross-body block on an Ivy League playing field, with rules, a sense of fair play, and a referee to monitor against unnecessary roughness. The contact was familiar, but the terror was new. Terror because he owned me. Possibly forever. If he decided to escalate, he could do whatever he wanted to destroy my mind and my body.

At a word in Arabic from the officer, the enlisted man released me, and stepped quietly into the space behind the desk. The officer spoke again:

"I own you and I hate you. Do you know how much I hate you?"

I didn't think that the question warranted an answer, so I said nothing.

"I hate you enough that I want to inflict great suffering on you." He was silent for a moment, letting the words sink in. "But, I'm not sure how to do it." He slid my passport absentmindedly back and forth with one lazy finger, and then continued pensively, "Maybe I will just own you. Maybe I will keep you here for 20 years. No, maybe 40 years." He opened my passport. "Yes, you are now 19 years old. I will release you when you are 59. That is a good age to release you—when your life has passed and when you are old and broken. Maybe toothless. Yes, toothless. And then you can go back to your people and tell them how much I hate."

He stared at me silently for a moment, scooped up the papers, rose abruptly, and left the room, with his henchman behind him. The door slammed and the sound of the clicking lock echoed in the bare room and seemed to hang in the still air. Then I was alone again, longer this time. Most of the afternoon. I hadn't had any water for a while. I had to pee. I tried to imagine if, in fact, my brief life was already over. Could I really just disappear? I day-dreamed, as if in a haze, about David Robinson's mother's Victorian living room, which I had previously thought to be mildly ridiculous, with its plush but uncomfortable chairs, all straight-backed, so you had to sit bolt upright, as if true relaxation were a crime. I imagined the printed roses against an ivory background on the upholstery and the strategically placed cut-glass bowl of candies on a well-polished wooden coffee table. If I could just reach out, open the wrapper, and slip one sweet candy into my mouth, I might magically time travel back to New England.

The door opened and the officer returned, this time with three men. I didn't like the idea of three men; one was bad enough. The officer sat down behind the desk, again laying out my passport and the file folder. Moments passed in silence. Then he stood, pushing his chair back, so it screeched across the bare wood.

"Yes, I own you; and I hate you. But for certain reasons, I will let you go. These men will take you to the Mandelbaum Gate and will release you to Israel." He handed my passport to one of the men. "But don't ever, not ever, return to any Arab country. Do you understand me? If you return we will not be so lenient next time."

The officer strode abruptly out of the room without looking back. After the door closed and silence settled around us, the man with my passport motioned for me to follow him. Together, the four of us walked from the dark hallway into the desert sunlight, so bright that we all had to stop and blink. An armored car was idling by the front door, clad in heavy, brown, desert-camouflaged, steel plate, with a light machine gun poking out of the top. I climbed into the back seat and one man sat on either side of me. The third man slammed the back doors shut and joined the driver in the front seat. No Ak-47s this time. With the exception of the vehicle we were riding in, it was all very civilized and almost cordial. We drove through the city, and then stopped in front of a small building at the border crossing. Tourists were waiting in a long line to get their passport stamped. Everybody looked up when they saw the armored car stop, and their silent questioning faces watched me step out. No one objected as we moved to the head of the line. My captors spoke briefly to the immigration officer in Arabic, and he stamped my passport without a word.

I remember a bridge, like a drawbridge, made of steel. There were towers on the Israeli side, voices, and men in the towers, peering from behind armored steel plate, with heavy machine guns. I started to walk across the bridge, leaving the terror behind and slowly journeying toward that lake in Connecticut. But I wasn't home yet. Perhaps they might shoot me in the back as I walked away. What would it feel like as the first bullet penetrated? I wanted to run, but with all those guns on either side, I walked with a calculated casualness, as if nothing had happened, as if I were like any other tourist, crossing the border between friendly nations, thinking about a quiet cup of coffee on the other side.

No one shot me. When I was three quarters of the way across, gaining certainty that I was going to emerge unscathed, my body started to relax, a blissful relaxation with a bottomless depth as bottomless as my fear had been. Then, unexpectedly, the adrenaline rose with a very clear thought:

"You Fuckers. You dirty grimy filthy Fucking Fuckers." Imagining the interrogator before me, speaking directly into his face, I announced, "You asshole. You just fucked with the wrong guy, Mister. I'm going to join the Israeli Army and wrap my trigger finger around superior weaponry. And then I will shoot to kill."

The anger flowed through me, so thoroughly that it seemed to liberate me, washing away fear, helplessness, and adrenaline.

I continued the last few steps across the bridge. A door opened on the other side and I stepped into a clear, bright, friendly room where an Israeli colonel greeted me.

"Who are you? What the hell is going on?" he asked.

REVENGE

When I returned home, my mind was incapable of processing what had happened, so robot-like, I followed the path of least resistance, and returned to school. Back at the university cafeteria, I wolfed down food, as my fellow students picked at their plates while loudly complaining that their mothers were better cooks. Classmates thought I was weird. It was the start of a socially challenging year.

At Brown, students "rush" fraternities at the end of their freshman year, and if they get the nod, move in with their "brothers" after summer vacation. Most of my friends got into fraternities, but I did not. I don't know why; I tried. My old buddy Dave Robinson came back from summer vacation to move into one of the most socially prominent fraternities. I saw him around campus a few times that fall and we were friendly enough. "Hi, How'z it goin?" But he was involved in his new world of secret Grecian handshakes and I was not a "brother." That fact, coupled, I suppose, with all the baggage surrounding our failed adventure, established an unspoken barrier between us. We never sat down over a glass of beer and talked about that prison in Jordan. I must have told someone, but I don't remember any conversation of that nature. My fellow students laughed at me when I tried to explain hunger through a mouthful of overcooked, institutional, canned string beans. If they couldn't understand hunger, how could they comprehend primordial hatred and abject terror? I was alone and isolated with my memories.

To exacerbate this isolation, the Dean of Students assigned me to sensory-deprivation housing. All the fraternities were located in two giant squares on campus, in extended buildings that surrounded central courtyards. Each fraternity was separated from its neighbor by a steel barrier which could be moved one way or the other to add or subtract dormitory rooms if the membership of one brotherhood increased or decreased.

That year, membership was down, just slightly, in two adjacent frats, leaving three rooms unoccupied. The Dean of Housing moved people around so these three unoccupied rooms were stacked vertically, one room to a floor, three floors. Then he assigned six non-fraternity people, including me, to live here, our perimeter separated from the two boisterous fraternities by those heavy, impenetrable, gray, steel barriers.

Today, I'm sure it would be illegal because there were no fire exits, and should a conflagration occur, I was perched inside the top of a virtual chimney. My room felt like a prison, enclosed like that interrogation room in Jordan, on a third-floor tower, with a roommate that I didn't relate to, and no social life. I had this recurring dream that during the night the steel barriers would slowly close in on us, enlarging a room where the frat boys were drinking and laughing, while shrinking my living space, crunching the furniture, like one of those crushers that flattens cars, eventually squeezing me until my eyeballs popped out. My roommate went crazy, turned latently violent, and dropped out of school. I went to classes, studied, didn't have any friends, and don't remember any joyful moments, whatsoever, during that fall.

When I returned home for Christmas break, the Rabbi at our local synagogue held a symposium with the promising college youth. The topic was some theme along the lines of: "What did I do on my summer vacation?" I sat up there on the stage in an uncomfortable folding chair, with my childhood friends on either side of me, my parents and their friends sitting in the audience, proud of their youth, and the Rabbi, moderating. He was a large man who could have been strong if he wasn't old, decrepit, and woefully out of shape, with a deep sonorous voice and a dignified, bushy mustache. One by one, my compatriots told stories of their summer vacations, contorting the narrative through all sorts of permutations and combinations to arrive at the same conclusion, which was to explain, to loud applause and enthusiastic affirmation, how their life experience had increased their dedication to being Jewish. That was the point of this exercise, was it not?

Then it was my turn. I was and felt Jewish, don't get me wrong, and I knew they wanted stories about baling straw on the kibbutz, while singing Zionist songs, and increasing my commitment to the faith. But that's not what happened.

At that moment, I didn't feel rebellious. I was alone; sad; socially isolated. I had told my parents the skeleton of the story, and they met me at the airport when I was worn, tanned, hungry, scared, and emaciated, so at some level, everyone knew about my journey and the afternoon in the Jordanian prison. But I hadn't exorcised the fear or reached any equilibrium about the experience. Now all these good people were here to listen. We could talk about what happened—on an emotional level—couldn't we? We could discuss the anger, the hatred, and the warfare, the poison of seeking revenge that had been festering inside me, cursing cancerously and randomly through my think-too-much-know-it-all brain as I studied differential equations and quantum physics. How would my Cub Scout den mother react to my promise that I was planning to become an efficient and remorseless killer? It was time for the understanding and the healing to begin.

I started my story about baling straw, followed by sex, drugs, selling blood, German tourists, and locust plagues. And then I flashed into an image of the Gypsies—the endless steppe, the plodding mule—freedom in its purest form. Hold on everybody. Give me a second—or a decade—so a thought, an image, an action can germinate. Hold on. It's so simple that the words are falling apart in front of me and I can't grasp them.

I must have rambled. Assuredly, I was too long-winded. But I didn't even get to the good part before the Rabbi cut me off. He didn't want to hear it.

As a clergyman, as a person who was supposedly dedicated to the emotional and spiritual well-being of his flock, didn't the Rabbi understand that I needed to speak to someone—to anyone? Wasn't there a course in the rabbinical college that taught basic psychology—fundamental human compassion? Right now, I needed my childhood tribe to listen and to hug me. To tell me to put down the gun I hadn't picked up yet. Instead, I looked around the room at all those smiling faces—my peers, my elders, and my Rabbi—all wrapping me up in some ridiculous Halloween costume, which was their image of me, of what had happened to me, which bore no resemblance to the truth, or not the truth as I remembered it.

I had just hitchhiked across Asia Minor and the Middle East, across steppe and desert, perpetually hungry. I had survived a potentially lethal knife fight and been roughed up in a Jordanian prison. Suddenly, I saw the Rabbi, not as an inspiring spiritual or physical leader, but as an overweight, feeble, irrelevant old man. Insensitive, uncaring. During my entire life, he had demanded physical, and intellectual obedience, without reciprocal compassion. When I was eight or nine, he had smashed my head against a steel post—much as the Jordanian soldier had beat me—because I was insubordinate, that is, running around, laughing, yelling, and chasing my friends, acting like a normal healthy, happy, rambunctious young boy. And as a result, he had left an emotional wound that was deeper and more infected than I imagined. For a brief instant, I considered sprinting out of my chair, like the first quick move after the opening whistle at a lacrosse game, and hitting him with a bone-crunching, cross-body check that would send him flying off the stage to land in a crumpled heap below.

But of course I didn't do that. That flash impulse flooded my brain like a roiling river bursting through the levee, and then with equal speed, the emotional wave washed all the anger away, to dissipate peacefully across some broad and featureless delta. To this day, over fifty years later, I remember that moment of catharsis—a heavy veil lifting. The Rabbi continued to drone on and on, and the elders of the congregation sat in rapt attention.

The evening was a smashing success. After completing the symposium, we sipped wine and snacked on bagels and lox. The Rabbi shook my hand warmly and thanked me for participating. I smiled graciously when people trooped by to tell me how nice it was that I had stacked straw bales on a kibbutz.

These people were my family, my tribe. They had loved me since I was an infant; they still loved me, and I loved them. June Goodman taught our Cub Scout troop to make candles like the pioneers. Pat Goldman effused goo-goo and ga-ga when I built a clunky, overweight, aesthetically displeasing stone barbecue for her. Sylvan Saul, who was the local athletic guru because he had played junior high school basketball, took time off from his busy life running a retail textile store to teach me how to ski, even though he had never skied, and refused to put skis on during our lesson. (His signature advice was, "Bend your knees." So I bent my knees and ran head-on into the first tree.) Yes, I had felt anger at the Rabbi, but I kept it inside and didn't denounce my faith or otherwise say or do anything stupid—or rude. Perfect.

But internally, I had changed. In those moments, I understood, so clearly, that I didn't need to fight and win (or fight and lose) because instead, I could step back, look at the world from a new perspective, and make choices that I hadn't even known were possible. Functionally, the first step in this new resolve was to stop practicing Judaism—or any organized religion for that matter. From that moment onward, I couldn't go there.

This decision had nothing to do with an argument for or against the existence of spirituality or some entity we call God. Furthermore, I'm aware that a great many people find rapture and/or tribal unity in organized religion. I understand that there are countless religious-sponsored charities that help the poor and downtrodden. But, from that day to the present, I simply could not, and cannot, ignore the fact that I, personally, had not experienced one single nano-second of spiritual awakening in a synagogue. Not only that, but within my childhood tribe, the people in my synagogue, including the Rabbi, never—not for an instant—discussed deep rapture or ecstasy as an inherent emotion, difficult to achieve, but out there and fundamentally accessible. Instead, my religious education was all about rules to follow and history to remember. And then of course, leering from beneath the floorboards, how could I honestly ignore the abysmal record, since the beginning of recorded history, of religious fervor being successfully hijacked by unscrupulous leaders to justify killing, burning, bombing, beheading, raping, slashing, and maiming. Thus, despite all the accumulated weight of my upbringing, and the continued beliefs and lifestyles of my family, whom I loved dearly; despite all the sophisticated philosophical denials that violence wasn't an inherent component of organized religion, just an unfortunate and perhaps occasional byproduct, I believed that as soon as we define ourselves as members of a group—any group—with an US and a THEM—we opened the doors to tribal, religious, or nationalistic warfare. So I quit. It's a personal decision—a feeling—not an argument about what others should or should not do.

Today, it has become a cliché to say, "I am spiritual, but not religious." But it wasn't then, in 1964, or if it was, I didn't know about it. In fact, when I rejected religion on that day, I didn't have the slightest conscious clue that I needed to discard the dogma before I could open the door to what is supposed to lie beneath all those prayers and regulations. That was over half a century ago, so I can't be trusted to recall accurately the thoughts that meandered through my marvelously complex and poorly understood brain. Or perhaps, even more importantly, I can't be trusted to understand what was determined by circumstance and what was pre-determined by genetic disposition. But the fact is that I discarded organized religion. And then gradually, over the decades, almost as if I had no free will regarding the matter, I began to perceive, or acknowledge, or peek into the window of a consciousness shift—some transcendence, some at-one-ness that I now know is out there, attainable. And even if, most probably, I never attain it, even thinking about this transcendence has become a wondrous and ecstatic journey.

A single event can't redefine a life or create a new personality. If I had gone to California with Dave Robinson and gotten stoned on a beach in Big Sur, or stayed home and mowed lawns in Danbury, Connecticut, or done a zillion other things that I could have done that summer...If no one had ever poked me in the kidney with the barrel of a tommy-gun in a holy city, or if the Rabbi had never convened that silly symposium, or if he had been compassionate...I would have still ended up as a partial drop-out from society, living in the deep forest, an adventurer, a long-distance expedition sea kayaker and a back-country skier. Given the DNA I was born with, the end result was inevitable, because this wasn't a simple, petulant, adolescent rejection of Middle Eastern warfare, or religion, or the Rabbi. There was something inside of me that was seeking something that was so far out of the norm of my loving, generous, financially comfortable family and society that I didn't even know it was there. I did know it, but I didn't know that I knew it. So I had to make a lot of mistakes and take a lot of goofy turns along the way.

Although privately I dropped out of religion that evening, there was too much inertia in my upbringing to make immediate and radical changes in my life. When vacation was over, I returned to school. Chemistry is intellectually challenging, but emotionally inert. Both molecules and people "react" to situations, but molecular reactions are predictable and reproducible (if you are clever enough), without ego, anger, hatred, malice, love, duplicity, or anything messy like that.

The following summer, I started a small landscaping company and worked in the open air with rocks, flowering plants, and the rich smell of soil. At the start of my junior year at Brown, the administration stuck me back in another social-torture, sensory-deprivation, prison-cell-buffer-dorm room, squeezed between locked steel barriers. I walked into my room, sat down on the bed, and reminisced again about the broad plain of Asia Minor, with an infinite sky above, stretching from the Mediterranean across the Asian Steppe, bridging between Aristotle and Genghis Khan, plodding along at the speed of a weary but faithful mule who was in no hurry to get anywhere, because here and there were all about the same. Suddenly, the price of admission into society was too high. I was expected to go to school and get good grades and marry and have kids and become a respected professional. Fine, I would do my best. But not if they imprisoned me while I was playing the game according to their rules.

School policy allowed transfer into an off-campus apartment in your senior year, but not before. At the beginning of my junior year, I marched down to the Dean of Housing and told him that I needed to move off campus immediately—or I would quit school. There must have been a resolve and urgency in my voice or body language that convinced the Dean that this was not a bluff, so he relented. Given my freedom, I moved in with a rock'n'roll band and became their road manager. Despite my previous failure to fit into the Brown University fraternity scene, I made friends easily in this new social environment. I bought a fast motorcycle, spent an inordinate amount of time hanging out in a local guitar shop, and socialized mainly with the artists at RISD (Rhode Island School of Design). For the first time in my college career, I had a girlfriend. I rode around Providence with a dear friend who drove a shiny black Mercedes with the license plate W-8. At the end of the semester, I reeled in two F's, a D, and a C-.

That was 1966. JFK had been shot in 1963 and a year later Lyndon Johnson lied to the American public about the Tonkin Gulf incident to stir up patriotic-racist hatred and convince a bunch of young men to run around in the jungle and blow away men, women, and children with slanted eyes. While my band was playing the mellow folk-rock of The Lovin' Spoonful and the traditional rock'n'roll of The Young Rascals, out on the coast, The Grateful Dead were jamming at Ken Kesey's Electric Cool-Aid Acid Tests. One of my friends jumped on his Harley and headed to California to "Join the Hell's Angels, or maybe follow The Dead." He never sent us a postcard.

After my grades came out, the Dean of Housing called me into his office. He explained sternly that he had made an exception to the rules specifically for me. Now my malfeasance was a personal embarrassment, a blot on his résumé. He sent me to the school psychiatrist, a pompous dandy who was all duded up in a somber gray suit and a white pressed shirt, sitting behind an ostentatious oaken desk, like the Rabbi's desk, like the desk of all the hierarchal command systems in the world. Then he put on his most fatherly voice and asked me to trust him.

No. I didn't trust him; not one tiny, little bit.

I didn't trust him because I felt, rightly or wrongly, that he was hired by the school with a mandate to guide me away from being a bad boy (poor grades) toward being a good boy (straight A's). I didn't need that form of guidance right now. To get him off my back, and end this charade as quickly as possible, so I could go down the street and meet my buddies at the pool hall, I feigned contriteness and told him that my poor grades were just temporary adolescent confusion. I would do better next semester.

Did he actually believe me? Or was he playing this silly, superficial game as well, smiling with his faux Cheshire Cat grin, while secretly watching the clock till quitting time, so he could go down the street and shoot some pool, or go home and mow his lawn, or do whatever he did for peace and relaxation after work? Didn't he know that there was no confusion about smoking pot and dancing all night with my girlfriend, or lying flat on the gas tank of a stripped down, sooped up crotch-rocket, legs spread out behind like the tail feathers of a hawk, throttle full bore, watching the roadway blur by at 100 mph, until the pavement lost its identity as a horizontal structure of pebbles and tar, while spring pollen and urban air pollution packed into my nostrils like a ram-jet—until the cosmos became an emotion.

As our hour dragged on, we descended into a pathetic exchange of useless vapid platitudes, until the man behind the words seemed to disappear. I couldn't shake Alice's comments about the Cheshire Cat—that she had often seen a cat without a grin but never before a grin without a cat.

But I still wasn't ready to jump on my motorcycle and follow The Dead. It was just too scary, to reject everything I had been born into, and run towards...what? A street scene in San Francisco? No, that wasn't what I was seeking. Until I had some conscious inkling of what my honest alternatives were, I rebelled against my own rebellion, heeded the psychologist, and listened to my mother. Perhaps I became intellectually challenged by my studies. Perhaps I wanted to show the world, or myself, that I wasn't a failure. Whatever the reason, or reasons, in my senior year, I got straight A's, excelling in organic synthesis, thermodynamics, and chemical kinetics. At graduation, in June of 1967, all the folding chairs were aligned on the lawn and flowers bloomed beside the stage, as the Six-Day War raged in the Middle

East, with bloody battles between Israel and her neighbors in the Golan Heights, West Bank, and Sinai. Sitting in the sunshine, in my black graduation gown, next to my proud parents, I shook my head in disbelief at the notion that I had once resolved to be part of that battle. It wasn't going to help anyone if I grabbed a gun and ran around the desert shooting people.

On the other side of that warfare, there was Jerry Garcia. All graduation speeches can be summed up in four Garcia and Hunter lines:

> There is a road, no simple highway,
> Between the dawn and the dark of night,
> And if you go no one may follow,
> That path is for your steps alone.

I thought I saw a middle road between the AK-47 and hits of purple blotter acid. Maybe I could step back onto the well-manicured pathway that had been there all along. Once again, I resolved to follow in my father's steps, and specialize in air pollution research.

I gained admission into graduate school at the University of Colorado, in Boulder, where I worked on a mass spectrometer, firing electrons at molecules in a high vacuum, blasting the molecules apart, and accelerating the fragments through powerful magnetic fields, probing mysterious forces called chemical bonds that hold all matter together.

In those days, every mass spectrometer in the world was located in a basement, bolted to bedrock, in a room that was held precisely at 70 ° F and 40% relative humidity. I had instrument time from 10:00 PM till dawn, giving me time to catch a nap and grab a quick cup of coffee before my 8:00 AM class. The research was fascinating. I loved the intensity and challenge of discussion with my colleagues, but eventually the mass spec lab began to feel like any confined, subterranean, airless dungeon. I had escaped from the sealed dormitory room at Brown, and here I was again, in a room lined with concrete block, steel doors, and humorless loneliness. I missed the easy camaraderie of the guitar shop.

In September 1969, two years into my graduate studies and five years after my Middle Eastern caper, I attended a lecture by Dr. Timothy Leary. He walked onto the stage in a white guru-suit, entering from left to right, and sat cross-legged on a red cushion. In a slow, calm, measured voice, Leary explained that the press had simplified and distorted his message: "Tune In. Turn On. Drop Out." Yes, drugs were part of his life and awakening, but his real message was:

Tune In to discover your inner self.
Turn On to this inner self.
Drop Out of any path that interferes with
this journey—whatever the cost.

The message is so simple, obvious, and seemingly innocuous that today it could be hidden inside a fortune cookie—an aphorism that we chuckle at as we reach for a credit card to pay for our chicken chow mein. It's hard to imagine, or remember, in this day and age when self-awareness has, in many ways, become commercially mainstream, what a huge backlash Leary provoked. Yet it happened. And Richard Nixon, who was busy bombing cities, napalming babies, and defoliating Vietnam, called Leary "the most dangerous man in America." Leary was considered such a threat because he wrapped his message around LSD, which opens the synapses to a spiritual journey and slams the doors shut to corporate advertising, political warmongering, and parental expectations.

If you had asked me, five minutes before I walked into Leary's lecture, "Are you happy?" I would have looked at you like it was a dumb question and replied, "Of course I'm happy. Why do you ask?"

If you had followed up with, "What are you seeking in your life?" I would have been confused because no one had ever asked me that question, in that manner, and I would have answered as if the question had been posed by my mother asking, "What do you want *to be* when you grow up?" With the verb "to be" implying a physical state. So I would have answered, "I'm planning *to be* a chemist and get a job, preferably as a professor in some major research institution, but if not, I'll take an industrial position, making adhesives or searching for oil, or something like that."

On October 1, 1969, just a few weeks after the Leary lecture, John Lennon, also in a white coat, walked across the iconic album cover of *Abbey Road* on a mysterious journey "to the other side." I was in the computer room, entering data on a punch-card machine, when a friend burst in waving his newly purchased stereo 8-track tape of the album.

"Drop that shit. We're going to San Francisco."

"Huh?"

"We're going to the aquarium, to visit the Octopus's Garden."

We put *Abbey Road* in the recorder, on automatic replay, so it ran continuously for the next twenty hours. I was driving as dawn rose over the desert, highlighting the granite peaks of the Basin and Range with a soft red glow.

> I'd like to be under the sea
> In an octopus' garden in the shade

I was driving again as the city loomed before us, towering concrete and glass reflecting sunlight in the late afternoon rush, and we swung onto the Bay Bridge:

> We would be so happy you and me
> No one there to tell us what to do
> I'd like to be under the sea
> In an octopus' garden with you.

We went to the aquarium and the octopus crawled out from under his paisley, iridescent purple, yellow, and red glowing, pulsating, shape-changing cave. He winked one bulging eye at me, as a private conversation between the two of us, and jauntily waved a tentacle. I swear it's true.

On the drive back across the desert, I decided that I simply couldn't spend my life indoors, in what had become a series of prisons, lined up, one after another, endlessly streaming toward the distant horizon of old age. I was old enough now, close enough to graduation, to see a career in proper society as too full of "deadlines and commitments," painful, harried decisions about "what to leave in; what to leave out.[1]" Sure, there was a hedonistic component to my decision. It was more fun to hang out in the octopus' garden than in the mass spec lab. But woopie-ding hedonism didn't explain the whole story. Somewhere along the line, although I didn't express it explicitly back then, I was beginning to see something on the horizon, still vague, unfocused, and undefined, mysteriously interwoven with the coolness of King David's spring, the Gypsies, the quiet music in the guitar shop, the ecstasy of a high speed run on a motorcycle, the paisley octopus, and a desert dawn.

External events moved quickly. In January, 1970, just a few months after *Abbey Road* appeared, "they"—whoever "they" is, sentenced Tim Leary to ten years in prison for two marijuana roaches, which he claimed were planted in his car by a Federal agent. While he was at it, the judge added an additional ten years for an earlier bust where Leary was caught with possession of 0.01 grams of pot. Twenty years. The same sort of sentence violent criminals draw for manslaughter or rape or some horrendous atrocity toward another human being. The government also ordered Leary to undergo psychiatric treatment, to seek—what? The same state of being that the school psychologist was steering me toward? Normalcy?

Much later, Joanna Harcourt-Smith, Tim Leary's lover for a

brief period, wrote, "Psychedelic research, from its inception to its prohibition...has always been inexorably bound up with spiritual quest." And the government was deathly afraid of that raw quest, aided by drugs and bypassing organized religions, which are modeled after 12,000-year-old agricultural monarchies that shattered the multiple Earth Gods of the hunter gatherers. Joanna continues: "Normalcy was defined to include the endless war that seamlessly moved from the Cold War to the War on Terror. The sixties was recast as sex, drugs, and rock'n'roll *only*. No politics, no consciousness revolution, no explosion of creativity.[2]"

That spring, Leary was a political prisoner, and his jailors, perhaps aware of the irony and perhaps not, administered him the Leary Interpersonal Behavior Test, which he had designed years before when he was a psychology professor at Harvard. Meanwhile, one Saturday afternoon, I sat on a hilltop, high in the Colorado Rockies, watching a bug crawl across the rounded crystals of spring corn snow, marveling that I had never before in my life sat on a stone and watched a bug. I giggled as I hadn't giggled since childhood. People laugh all the time when someone tells a joke with a clever play on words, but the bug made me giggle. Or more precisely, I giggled because it was so revolutionary and life-changing to watch that bug; to marvel at how it would find food in that frozen landscape; and how it kept warm with those skinny legs and no woolen socks or long underwear.

When the snow melted, I joined my dog digging holes in an alpine meadow, and shoving my nose into the holes to smell the earth. And then, when greenery began exploding across the land, I wrapped my arms around the smooth, cool, gray bark of an aspen tree and held my ear against the trunk to listen to the living gurgles as sap rose out of the earth toward the tiny buds that were blossoming into leaves. This wasn't a youthful, temporary, or petulant rebellion *against* anything. So many times, I had started to rebel, or question, or mold my own life according to my inner voices, and so many times I had retreated back into convention and expectations. Now, denial had become unacceptable, impossible. I had no choice but to discard my twenty-five years of trying to adapt to twelve thousand years of human progress toward ever increasing separation from the life-giving spring sap rising skyward inside that budding, silvery, aspen tree.

By the time I walked out of my final oral exam, in June 1971, and people could legitimately call me Doctor, I tucked my Ph.D. diploma in the glove box of a 1964 Ford Fairlane, lashed a canoe on top, and drove north to paddle a lazy river that flowed through the Canadian Arctic. When I returned to Colorado late that summer, I took a job as a carpenter in Longmont, framing tract houses. I lived in the woods and went skiing. Eventually, I developed a lucrative gig writing environmental and earth science textbooks, which supplied me with money and free time.

I wandered for the next thirteen years: Colorado, Connecticut, California, Montana, Wyoming, California, Maine, Colorado, Washington, Colorado, Montana, and Alaska, living in a teepee, a sailboat, a renovated chicken coop, a dirt floor cabin, a broken down trailer, an old miner's cabin in a ghost town, a wall tent, and a crude log structure on the edge of the great swamp beneath Mt. Denali. My personal life was chaotic, with failed marriages, children bouncing back and forth between single parents, and trouble with divorce courts. I had successfully broken the bonds that tied me to religion and a career, the two foundations of "normalcy" as defined by my upbringing. But once I started running away, with wind in my hair and imagined demons chasing me, I didn't stop long enough to make any sense of where I was going, how I would get there, or who I might hurt along the way.

In September 1984, my elder daughter, Reeva, who was then 14, and I drove up from our current, temporary home on the southern Kenai Peninsula to meet my girlfriend, Chris Seashore, in Anchorage. I had worked on a commercial salmon fishing boat that summer and stashed $15,000 in hundred dollar bills in a brown paper bag that was tucked in the springs behind the driver's seat of my trusty, white, GMC pick-up truck. The three of us drove down the Alaska Highway to Montana, where Chris and I got married and bought a small house, some call it a cabin, deep in the forest, on the flanks of the highest peak in the Bitterroot Mountain Range. That was over thirty years ago. Tragically, Chris died in an avalanche in 2005. The following year, I married her best friend, Nina. Today, Nina grows a cold-weather northern garden that provides us with abundant fresh vegetables while I hunt deer and elk on the mountainsides. We migrate north every winter, toward the deep snows of Fernie, British Columbia, to ski among Devonian limestone cliffs that were tilted, fractured, folded, and thrust skyward during continental collisions.

Now an older woman, Joanna Harcourt-Smith recalls that Leary was "Harvard professor and trickster, genius and crackpot, spiritual leader and imposter, adventurer and iconic manipulator, devil and angel, guru and scientist." It is never simple, is it? She continues, almost forlornly, "I attempt the truth for Timothy's sake, for my sake, and for the sake of the generation brought to its knees in those Nixon years."

I don't know what "the truth" is, and my almost-adult grand-children didn't play any role in the Counterculture '60s, because they weren't born yet. All I know for certain is that my convoluted journey eventually led me into the misty, crocodile and butterfly-infested jungle, where one man would teach me to wash my face in a slow, muddy river, so both the real and the spirit crocodiles wouldn't eat me.

I splashed another handful of river water on my face that eve-ning to inhale the smells of pollen, rot, bacteria, and crocodile poop. The French call it *terroir*, the taste of climate, soil, and the land. But, for those of you who still squirm uneasily and can't quite accept Grandfather Crocodiles, let's start with comfortable, unassailable, irrefutable facts. Facts that we can all believe in and agree on: A historical journey starting with a stone axe.

A STONE AXE

One day, just before I made one of my riskier kayak crossings in the Solomon Islands, a young man approached me with grave solemnity and offered what at first appeared to be a smooth stone. But when I looked at it closely, I realized that it was a polished piece of basalt carefully shaped into an axe head.

Following my gaze, he explained, "This is my grandfather's axe. My grandfather was a warrior. You are a warrior who is crossing the sea in the old way. You must carry this ancient weapon with you on your dangerous journey."

I protested that this was a family heirloom, but the man insisted.

I took it. The axe head fit comfortably into the palm of my hand and now, several years later, I sometimes pick it up to feel its texture, imagine its journeys as a tool and as a weapon, evoking images of painted warriors clashing at dawn in shadowed rainforest, scenes of victory, defeat, bloody death, and cannibalism. An axe.

I live in the Montana forest and heat my house with wood. As a result, I am familiar and comfortable with steel axes, hand saws, and the noise, acrid burnt-oil smell, and efficiency of a chain saw. One day, after I had returned home from my expedition, just to dramatize what I already knew, I took my Solomon Island stone axe out to the wood-pile and whacked at a pine log. The surface of the wood mushed in a little. I whacked again. The indent became imperceptibly deeper. And then I gave up. It would take me a week to cut a single piece of firewood in this manner.

Yet, only a few generations ago, young navigators and shipbuilders walked into the forest with stone tools like this one. With the additional use of fire, bone, coral, and possibly with other materials and techniques lost in antiquity, they cut down huge tropical hardwood trees, removed the bark, hollowed out the logs, and fashioned ocean-going canoes. And then they sailed across two thousand miles of open sea from Polynesia to Hawaii. And back. (At the same time, European sailors, building ships with the use of steel tools, were sticking mainly close to shore.) Although no one knows how the Polynesians discovered Hawaii the first time, once the initial settlement was made, sailors plied to and from their old homeland to the new one.

The modern double-hulled voyaging canoe, the *Hōkūleʻa*, is a full-scale, working replica of a *waʻa kaulua*, an ancient Polynesian double-hulled voyaging canoe. It is a catamaran, built on parallel hulls, 19 meters (61.5 feet) long with graceful, arcing upturns of the twin bows. When loaded for sea, the *Hōkūleʻa* carries 16 people and 450 kg (1,000 pounds) of food, water, and supplies. She is rigged with two triangular "crab-claw" sails, with booms that rise steeply off the deck, so the boom and the mast, together, look like outstretched arms of the triumphant. European explorers, from Magellan to Cook, noted that the *waʻa kauluas* were faster, more seaworthy, and more maneuverable than the bulky, square rigged European ships of discovery.

I tried to imagine entering the damp, verdant semidarkness of a mature tropical rainforest, like the one I was standing in right now, to find a massive old-growth tree with a trunk wide and tall enough to fashion into a hull as long as a six-story building is tall. With buoyancy in my brain, with thoughts of open sky, blue water, and Arcturus the "star of gladness," (a guiding zenith for Hawaiian navigators) I imagined taking a deep breath, winding up, swinging, and bracing for the impact of rock against the tree's thick bark. The start of any worthwhile journey—physical, intellectual, or artistic—is like that first swing against a giant tree, a step so puny that you dare not imagine the travail and danger ahead.

No one alive in the world today could do that. The feat aligns almost unfathomable complexity, patience, strength, engineering skill, bravery, and endurance. This is not shamanic magic that you might choose to believe in or not. This is history. Yet, it is on the edge of magic—to me anyway—that a human being could be so synchronistically connected to the natural rhythms of the forest, the ocean, and the orbit of the Earth to accomplish this feat.

The central theme of this book is that no modern human could build an ocean going canoe with stone tools, and sail across oceans to distant islands, because our thought and behavior patterns are too rooted in technology and too distant from the subtle, intangible, and inexplicable secrets of nature. There are two important consequences to this loss of skills and connectivity. First, as we have turned our back on nature, we have turned our back on ourselves and are trudging along with lots of fancy stuff, but a reduction of our fundamental, aboriginal, glorious humanity. Second, as we learn to believe that technology is sufficient, we have altered the planet in perhaps catastrophic and irreversible ways, and at the same time, we have created huge and perhaps unsurmountable consciousness barriers to overcoming the real, factual, serious problems that our complex society faces today. For those of you who argue that 21st century technology will solve our problems, I simply disagree.

But before we proceed, let's make one point clear:

CANNIBALS IN THE FOREST

I thought back to an expedition in 1994, when I paddled with my now-deceased wife Chris, in the Vanuatu Chain, also in the tropical South Pacific. The trip was inspired by a breakfast conversation one morning when Chris asked, with a quiet smile: "Why do we always have to go to cold places, Jon? Why can't we kayak in a warm ocean some day?" Several weeks into our island hopping across the deep blue waters of the equatorial Pacific, we stopped in a small village, on the island of Uripiv, where a young man named Wigley asked us if we would like to hear a story. When I nodded, he explained that this story could only be told in the forest, so we followed him as he tread barefoot, along a curvy, well-trodden trail. After fifteen minutes, we reached a clearing beneath a huge banyan tree. Wigley sat without speaking, picked up two sticks that had obviously been left there by a past visitor, and beat a jungle rhythm on a hollow log.

The drumming echoed through the forest, ricocheting through trees, softening in the brush, chasing ancient mysteries, while high above, the tropical trade winds wafted through the foliage.

Old stone platforms and fire rings, some of which were now partly overgrown, told me that people had congregated here through the ages. The banyan tree that loomed above us was not so much a tree as a complete ecosystem, dominated and supported by a single living plant. A banyan tree starts its life as an epiphyte, a vine that sprouts in the branches of a host tree, where it is already high in the canopy, so it can capture sunlight. After the young banyan spreads its leaves and thus gains a toehold on life, it sends a long shoot downward, to find earth, sprout roots, and form an initial trunk. As the trunk grows in girth and sucks life-giving water and nutrients from the soil, the banyan's branches spread, and then these branches, in turn, send more shoots downward to create more trunks. Eventually, the banyan smothers its original host and continues to spread, building its structure from above and below simultaneously.

As the tree matures, it consists of many smaller trunks supporting a single organism. At ground level, the multitudes of interconnected trunks create walkways and caves that allow you to stroll within the bowels of this damp, shaded mini-forest, consisting of a single tree, and smelling of rot and rebirth. Its total girth makes even the largest redwood tree seem spindly by comparison, while above, the foliage spreads across the landscape, providing homes to myriads of other epiphytes like the original incipient banyan. Birds nest in the branches, and lizards crawl, while ants and bees form their own, mysterious colonies; life thrives. Hindu scripture teaches that the leaf of the banyan tree is the resting place for the god Krishna. Buddha is believed to have achieved enlightenment while meditating under a banyan tree. Robinson Crusoe made his home in the elevated safety of this sprawling giant. Powerful landscapes are universal; they draw people to them, to seek enlightenment, secure shelter, or practice cannibalism.

Wigley softened the drum-beat until it was barely audible, but still emphatic, and started his story:

"Not long ago, in my grandfather's time, the men from this village paddled their dugout canoes to Pinaloum Point where they ambushed and killed a man from the neighboring tribe. They brought him back to this tree and built a large stone oven to cook him along with a local food called lap-lap. The warriors used mangrove sticks to build the fire because there are many mangrove bushes on our island. But one of the mangrove sticks got full of the man's spirit and flew back to his people. And when his people saw the burned mangrove flying into their village, they knew that it was the spirit of the man who was in the oven. But Uri Island, just to the northwest of here, also has many mangroves, so the men from Pinaloum Point thought the invaders came from Uri Island. So they went over there and killed a man from that tribe and ate him. And then, even though they were fooled into murdering a man from the wrong village, they felt satisfied that they had achieved revenge."

I retell this story because in following the journey of the stone axe, from history into magic, it is essential that we do not over-romanticize our past. I revere the practical skill of Polynesian sailors. But no sane person would choose to live in a cannibalistic Stone Age tribal society or, for that matter, would choose to ignore modern medical attention, motorized vehicles, and electronic advances. Anyone who advocates "turning the clock back" and reversing course back to "the way it was" belongs on the dismissible delusional fringe.

This book is not about an impossible and undesirable

re-creation of hunter gatherer societies. It is about honoring the intimate, life-supporting, reciprocal synergy that existed between our aboriginal ancestors and the natural world and assimilating that synergy into a sane and sustainable 21st century society.

The problem is that in honoring the wisdom of our ancestors, we smash headlong into modern opulence, which is so seductive that it is easy to forget about the magic of nature. No. Stop right there. I'm too old to grin at you sheepishly and offer a limp handshake, accompanied by a few wishy-washy platitudes. Can I please back up and rephrase that?

In our urban industrial society, corporations and politicians have launched a conscious and carefully strategized effort to dupe us into thinking that we can and should forget about the magic of nature. As a result, on a day-to-day, minute-by-minute basis, without even questioning the magnitude and consequences of our infidelity, most of us communicate with machines, shopping malls, and electronic devices, not storms, crocodiles, baby tomato plants, or crisp, yellow, falling leaves. This shift in our consciousness snuck up on us while we were taking an afternoon nap, so that we woke up groggily, forgetting what day it was, and just took the path of least resistance, accepting this pasted-on, sugar-coated, diabetes-inducing myth that 21st century urbanization is "normal." And "acceptable." But this is not normal, and it is not acceptable. No. Not at all, given any long-term perspective of how *Homo sapiens* have related to our environment and ourselves for 99.99% of our tenure on Earth. No. Not at all, given any long-term scientific perspective on how delicately balanced and interconnected Earth's systems behave.

It is so easy to lose perspective and assume that what is happening *now* is normal. But, from the dawn of humanity, a few million years ago, until a couple of generations ago, at the most, the vast majority of the world's people lived in a feedback loop where survival was so tactilely and immediately connected with the ebb and flow of nature's cycles that they couldn't ignore it. Go to sea on a whale hunt during a storm and you drown. Plant your crop too early, or too late, and you starve.

To understand the speed of what has happened to humanity, let's not forget that the entire computer revolution, from its infancy to the iPhone, fits into one lifetime, 70 years, which just happens to be my lifetime. Also during my lifetime: the human population has almost tripled from 2½ billion to over 7 billion. As our sheer numbers and technological sophistication have grown, there has been an astronomical and unprecedented migration of billions of people from farms and woodlands into concrete cities. Global petroleum consumption has increased 17-fold since I was born; tropical rainforests, which once covered 14% of our planet, have been chain-sawed and bulldozed until they now cover only 6%; and the carbon dioxide concentration of the atmosphere has increased from 300 ppm to over 400 ppm.

Over the 4.6-billion year history of our planet, there have been times when Earth's systems have been relatively constant for tens of millions of years and also times of rapid atmospheric, geological, hydrological, and biological change. Our planet has alternately been covered with humid swamps and then glaciers that spread from the poles to the equator. It has been teeming with life and almost devoid of life. The Earth is now caught up in such rapid change that most geologists agree that we have entered a new geological epoch, called the Anthropocene, the time when the earth became dominated by two-legged, hairless, big-brained animals with arms that can throw a spear and fingers that can thread a needle.

During the 250 years since the invention of the steam engine, or 12,000 years since the invention of agriculture, wherever you want to draw the starting line, humanity has created glorious opulence for the lucky ones—including me and probably you. There have been doomsday and apocalypse predictors since biblical times: But if the global human population were to triple every 70 years, then in about 500 years there would be 46 trillion people, three-quarters-of-a-million humans living on every square mile of land, including Antarctica and the Arctic tundra. Or, if global petroleum consumption were to increase as fast as it has during my lifetime, then in about 6½ lifetimes, people would be burning as much petroleum every year as there is water in all the Earth's oceans. Way before this impossible exponential increase in fuel consumption occurred, a runaway greenhouse effect would heat our planet until the oceans and atmosphere boiled off into space and Earth became like Venus, hot enough to melt tin on the surface, with toxic clouds raining steaming sulfuric acid onto the lifeless surface.

You can argue that these apocalyptic scenarios represent journalistic gamesmanship: long-term and impossible mathematical extrapolations of existing trends. That's fair. But the short term, realistic, well-documented projections are dire enough. The global temperature has already risen by 0.85°C, leading to the melting of almost half of the permanent arctic icecap, dramatic increase in the frequency of violent storms, death of millions of acres of forests, and on and on. Many prominent scientists argue that for civilization to maintain itself in an orderly fashion, we need to keep global temperatures from rising no more than 2 ° C because, according to World Bank scientists, "it is not clear that adaptation to a 4 ° C world is possible."

And you know, we all get caught up in the crisis of the decade syndrome. Remember, during the height of the Cold War, when we all worried about "Nuclear Winter?" Well, that's been out of the news for a while. But, let's not forget that today nine nations, collectively, own about 16,000 thermonuclear warheads, primed and ready to blow civilization to smithereens. They tell us that these things are monitored by carefully engineered technical safe-guards, but in reality, those safeguards are ultimately controlled by individuals—Vladimir Putin, Nawaz Sharif, and Kim Jong-un, to name a few. And you know, in my opinion, people don't have that great a long-term record of keeping violence, evil, and mayhem under wraps. Evil happens. Mistakes happen. You don't think that a nuclear holocaust is a possibility? Ah shucks. As U.S. presidential candidate Jeb Bush famously said, "Look, stuff happens. There's always a crisis."

So…

How do we, as individuals and as a society, respond to the complex problems that we face?

I worked first as a scientific researcher, and later as an environmental educator. Those activities are absolutely essential. But, over the past 20, or 50, or 100 years, science and education have simply not solved our problems. In fact, you could argue that our problems are becoming even more acute. The changes required in our society are so drastic that—beneath the science, education, economics, and politics—each individual needs, as an unshakable foundation, a deep commitment to compassion for our fellow humans and for our planet, which cannot be adequately generated through science and technology alone. And one possible starting point toward a visceral, unshakable environmental ethic and human compassion is through a personal, euphoric, and—yes—magical relationship with nature. Without some sort of a collective consciousness change, we run the real risk of being seduced by imagined opulence.

I got an email the other day, as part of a rejection of this manuscript: "I don't think a spiritual response to the matter [impending global catastrophes] is going to help very much; what is really needed is intelligence and forceful action."

We can argue this back and forth forever. Political activism is very nice. Science, education, "intelligence and forceful action" are all very nice. But a great many people, including me, argue that they are not sufficient. "Forceful action" mentioned in this email implies striving within the current political-economic paradigm. But the current political-economic paradigm is just nuts, because it relies on continued exponential growth. As Dr. Paul Ehrlich, professor of Population Studies at Stanford University and the author of the 1968 blockbuster, *The Population Bomb,* famously wrote: "Anyone who believes that exponential growth can go on forever in a finite world is either a madman or an economist."

Or as Einstein said: "The significant problems we face cannot be solved at the same level of thinking we were at when we created them." What does he mean by "the same level of thinking"? George Schaller, one of the preeminent wildlife biologists alive today, wrote, "Unless we can convince people of the spiritual value of wilderness, the cause is lost." In other words, science got us here, but science—alone—is not going to get us out of this mess. An elder woman in Siberia named Marina told me, "If you lose the magic in your life, you lose your power." In school they taught me that Reading, 'Riting and 'Rithmetic gives you power, and that magic is somehow frivolous—not real. Not real? Marina's definition of magic launched the Polynesian canoes from Tahiti to Hawaii; it carried humanity through the Ice Ages and out of Africa, across woodland and steppe, into every habitable environment on earth.

Steven Koonin, a prominent energy scientist in the United States, with roots in industry, government, and education, wrote in *The New York Times* in the fall of 2015, "Even as the world struggles to reduce (carbon) emissions, human influences on the climate will not be decreasing for many decades. Thus adaptation measures…become very important."[2]

Which leads to the question: "How do we adapt?"

In a private conversation, over coffee in Telluride, Colorado, Dr. Ehrlich told me that he thought that the sustainable human population was about 2 to 3 billion, less than half of what it is now. When I asked how we could achieve this goal in any humane and realistic manner, he answered that humanity was in dire need of a "Spiritual Revolution" before we could move into the 21st century with a reasonable hope of creating a peaceful, healthy, and equitable world.

There it is, that word "spiritual" again. A holy journey to fast for 40 days in the desert and return with the Ten Commandments. Elves and fairies. A slippery concept. I'm going to disagree with the use of this word for the purposes of this book, even by a scholar as eminent as Paul Ehrlich. Let's replace "Spiritual" with "Consciousness" and rephrase the statement above to, "Humanity is in dire need of a 'Consciousness Revolution' before we can move into the 21st century with a reasonable hope of creating a peaceful, healthy, and equitable world." I think it's simpler, less controversial, and more inclusive. A "Consciousness Revolution" is any change in our paradigm that may include the intervention of "spirits" but also includes the simple, mundane, every day, home and garden, electrochemical workings of our marvelously intricate and still largely poorly understood brains. Along these lines, I'm particularly fond of the quote, "The biggest challenge we face is shifting human consciousness, not saving the planet. Because the planet doesn't need saving—we do…" coined by Xiuhtezcatl Martinez of Boulder, Colorado, when he was only 14 years old.

I recall an evening watching TV with my granddaughter, Avalon, who was then five years old. After a cartoon, a screen appeared with a fancy logo—the Green-Channel. Fade to a beach with gentle surf and piles of unsightly litter in the sand. A group of young children—multiracial of course—jauntily skipped and hopped into the camera view. They stopped abruptly and looked in horror at the litter. Miraculously, recycling bins appeared and immediately the children began to clean up. Whenever an offending pop can flew into the bin, all the children jumped up and down, waving their arms in unadulterated joy. After a few seconds, pink cartoon mermaids floated into the scene, landing on the children's ears, and cheering them onward. Green-Channel logos joined the mermaids in the digital cosmos, and, in case we hadn't gotten the point yet, idyllic banana trees appeared and bumped into the mermaids like soap bubbles.

Fundamentally, the Green Channel entertains children so they will stay glued to the boob-tube and watch ads, to convince them, to convince their parents, to buy stuff. The Channel never presented an argument that consumption itself is the root of the problem—that drinking sugary, nutritionally-vapid, diabetes-producing soda pop is a bad idea—with or without recycling. In fact, quite the contrary; immediately after this environmental lesson, we were subjected to a long string of ads. Thus, the TV was teaching our impressionable children that everything will turn out rosy if we continue business as usual, and amend our ways only very slightly by putting our pop cans in the recycling bin. I am not against recycling, but the changes we need are way more basic and complex than was offered that evening by some wealthy media executives running a children's TV program for profit. Or to put it in the understated, laconic words of Garrison Keiller, host of the NPR radio show, "Prairie Home Companion," if stuff like the Green Channel is what society considers "normal," then "maybe we should think about the advantages of being weird."

This book, told through the lens of my experiences, the voices I have heard, and the landscapes I have visited, is a chronicle of my attempt at "being weird" through my journey into Deep Wild. I believe that a similar sort of personal journey, with an infinite number of possible variations, permutations, and combinations—on the Antarctic Ice Cap, or in your own living room, or back-yard—is an essential starting point toward building a sustainable society. Call me a romantic Pollyanna that we can save the world by skipping into La-La land, singing "The Sound of Music." But every time I read some book or magazine article proposing that we can save the world by relying on logical, concrete, political, legal, and economic strategies, I get this hopeless feeling that these "solutions" have an element of Pollyannism as well. Because it's not that simple; it hasn't proven to be that simple over the last 5, 50, 250 or 10,000 years. When scientists come up with an observation or a technological solution, the world hasn't just said, "Oh! Woopie Ding! That's a good idea. Let's make the necessary changes." Even though it is a self-evident cliché, people sometimes forget how horrendously complex our problems are. For one, as Kurt Vonnegut famously summarized, humanity is diverse.

> *Oh, a lion hunter in the jungle dark,*
> *And a sleeping drunkard up in Central Park,*
> *And a Chinese dentist and a British queen*
> *All fit together in the same machine.*
> *Nice, nice, such very different people in the same device!*

And because the people of Toronto think and behave differently and have different problems than the people of Ashgabat, Turkmenistan, or Kigali, Rwanda, concrete solutions, as simple and logical as they may seem from the onset, usually turn out to become horrendously complicated. And then, pasted on top of global cultural differences, humanity is complex and diverse within each culture, country, city, or village, torn between the contradictory, primordial survival techniques of cooperation versus warfare, submission versus power. I read in the newspaper today that certain politicians in the US were "for" torture and "against" nutritious school lunches. You can't make any sense out of that.

Given the madness out there, I find it mildly presumptuous and slightly terrifying to jump into the fray with some kind of a formula or a grand plan. But we have to start somewhere. So how about this? Every time a single person—maybe you or me—seeks some sort of ecstatic state as a primary life-journey, then we, the people of the world, will be $1/7,125,000,000^{th}$ of the way closer to a really cool place to live.

That's my contribution. That's the best I can do.

I tell this story frequently from the cockpit of my kayak. It's no mistake that after all the rebellion and confusion, after "dropping out" of my religion, my scientific career, and a couple of marriages, when I finally stopped running away, caught my breath, and calmed down long enough to discard the chaff and follow my own inner voices, I went to sea in a diminutive, one-person boat, uncomfortable and vulnerable, with no responsibilities other than to myself. I wouldn't make it as captain of an aircraft carrier with the mandate to carpet-bomb small nations until the soils glow orange, or at the helm of a cruise ship to create opulence for those who can afford the price of admission. A kayak suits me just fine, thank you, where every wave washes over the deck, where I am battered by tumultuous surf and sudden storms, and where I am captain and crew, first mate and chief dishwasher. Scrotums on the bow-stem, ladies and gentlemen, because our GPS doesn't really tell us where we are or how to reach the distant shore. Technology has the potential to create a sustainable world, but, in practice, it hasn't brought about equanimity, peace, equality, and sustainability. Science does not necessarily generate compassion and a widespread human communication with our planet.

CHAPTER 2

TRIAL BY ICE:
CIRCUMNAVIGATION OF ELLESMERE ISLAND

2011

THE BIRTH OF AN IDEA

When *The Raven's Gift* was released in January 2010, I piled a bunch of books in the back of my blue Ford pick-up and hit the road, giving readings at any place where people would listen to me, couch-surfing when possible, and sleeping in roadside bivouacs or in the cab of the truck, if no one offered me a place to sleep. I was in Boston one day, when a thin, frail-looking, white-haired woman asked me how I could preach the spiritual value of nature while I was living in the concrete jungle, driving on freeways, grabbing coffee at Starbucks, and sustaining myself on wraps, sandwiches, and pizza when kindly bookstore owners felt benevolent.

I smiled. How else could I respond? "Thank you for that. I guess that this book tour is part of the journey," I told her. "But you're right, only part." Then I smiled and the woman smiled back—the silent muse in the amorphous crowd.

That evening, after I shook my last hand and signed my last book, Moolynaut's chants and Oleg's directive hung in the air.

The Koryak people had taught me that if you spend enough time in nature, Tundra will initiate your spiritual journey because, in its silence and fury, it will somehow, eventually, irrevocably, guaranteed, seep into your think-too-much-know-it-all brain and soak up those extraneous, chaotic thoughts that distract you from living in the moment and becoming that glorious, perhaps unattainable, bundle of pure awareness and action.

Of course there are other ways to do it, but in my experience, the journey we seek is a walking meditation, not a sitting one. Hunter, moving through the tundra, aware of muscles, bones, and body position, often tired, frostbitten, hungry, strung out. Hunter, not necessarily in the final thrust of a spear or crack of a rifle, but as the athlete, whose consciousness is based on an intimate synergy between body and spirit.

Once Tundra and Hunter have cleared the decks, there's Shaman, the woman with the drum or the man in an eagle headdress. Wonder. Ecstasy. Journeys to the Other World, if it is your inclination and within your ability to go there. Magic, if you want to use that word. But we don't need the Other World to need Shaman. He or she is also the dancer, the artist, the musician, the person who leads the rest of us on a path into ecstasy, because without ecstasy, we can never realize our full potential as whole, complete human beings.

I was 64 years old. Social security was about to kick in and I had a comfortable nest egg from decades of textbook writing. But the journey all the way from my childhood, the whole enchilada, complete with all the adventures and disasters—physical and emotional—had been too wondrous, and still incomplete, jam packed with mysterious twists and turns, doors opening and dead ends, soft snowfall and horrendous avalanches, moments of anger and insights of clarity, threatening polar bears, spirit crocodiles, and a raven that came to comfort me as I was carrying Chris' ashes through a summer thunderstorm to the summit of her favorite mountain. Now, I needed to return to the Far North to be cold, tired, frostbitten, and hungry again.

When I say that "I needed to return to the Far North," it wasn't a "need" of desperation. No dramatic narrative here. It was a deep inner "need" to continue to grow, to journey back into the ice for all it had taught me in the past, and as a recognition that however many times I returned, I could never resolve (or even define) the mystery. I wouldn't want to. There would always be more to "learn" or to "feel" or to "absorb." The journey wasn't over, nor would it ever be over, nor did I want it to be over. Wildness has lifted me out of a life that wasn't suited for me, into a life that fit perfectly—it has given me passion, joy, a community of dear friends, and as much inner peace as I am capable of right now. Tundra, Hunter, and Shaman. And when I am so old that I can no longer sleep in a tent, or walk into the woods, I can only hope that I will be able to roll out of the old folks' home in my electric, motorized wheelchair, into the garden, and be content watching spring blossom into summer, listening to the birds, or turning my face upwind to feel the first cold blasts of a snowy winter, as I have felt such winds from so many mountain ridge-tops.

In 1988, four years after we were married, Chris, and I kayaked up the east coast of Ellesmere Island in the Canadian Arctic and across to Greenland, following a journey undertaken in 1853 by an Inuit named Qitdlaq, who was an *angakkuq* (a shaman) as well as a charismatic leader, madman, outcast, and murderer. The east coast of Ellesmere remains one of the most remote landscapes on earth, complete with towering glaciers, treacherous sea ice, abundant walrus, polar bears, and magical narwhal, and above all, isolation from civilization. Because currents in the channel run north to south, originating essentially at the North Pole, there is essentially zero trash or detritus from Western Civilization—none of the ubiquitous plastic cups or bits of fishing gear that litter coastlines in most of the world. Chris and I were alone, together, without books or media, adrift in a world of infinite simplicity, yet infinite complexity, a world of wind, currents, and moving ice. We were hungry and hurting from the raw pain of hard travel, making life and death decisions together, every day, quietly, without drama. And as a result of all that, we deepened our love of each other at the same time that we slid ever more intimately into our shared love of the landscape we were traveling in.

We traveled 600 nautical miles in 60 days, or 10 miles a day, over pack ice and through tempestuous seas, and felt exhausted at the end. But when we were on the flight home, I began to think about a complete circumnavigation of Ellesmere, which would be 2½ times as long, 1,500 nautical miles. I ran the numbers through my head, researched the difficulties and obstacles involved, and decided that the expedition was physically impossible.

Ellesmere, the tenth largest island in the world, lies in the extreme northeastern corner of the Canadian Arctic archipelago, separated from Greenland by a thin strip of ocean, only 12 nautical miles wide at its narrowest point. The southernmost extremity, King Edward Point, lies a smidge above 76° North latitude, about 10° or 600 nautical miles (1100 kilometers) north of the Arctic Circle. The northernmost extension, Ward Hunt Island, is 83° N, only 7 degrees of latitude from the North Pole. Ellesmere was the last piece of solid land for the earliest attempts at crossing the frozen Polar Ocean to reach the North Pole, by Frederick Cook who claimed to be the first to reach the Pole in 1908 and by Robert Peary, who disputed Cook's expedition and claimed to have been the first in 1909 (a claim that has also been disputed).

A great many people have skied to the Pole since the days of Cook and Peary, a journey that Arctic historian Jerry Kobalenko dubbed "The Horizontal Everest." Yet no one had even attempted the circumnavigation of Ellesmere. According to *The New York Times*, Ellesmere has "the highest misery-per-visitor ratio in the world." Kobalenko posted a challenge on his website, calling the Ellesmere circumnavigation "one of the last great unfinished passages of Arctic exploration."

I decided to set that as my goal, for numerous reasons. First and foremost, I wanted to return to a landscape that had so much poignancy for me. At the same time, I also felt that this would be the proper place to say one more final goodbye to Chris. One more final goodbye to youth. But perhaps more than anything, the journey would be one more affirmation of Moolynaut's worldview. Tundra, Hunter, and Shaman. It would be a physical outreach of my promise "to believe" in the journeys and powers of my distant Paleolithic ancestors who had accomplished so much with so little. But why couldn't I have chosen a less ambitious route, a fun jaunt, rather than a desperate push? You ask me (and I asked myself) why I thought I could ski, walk, and paddle 1,500 nautical miles across one of the harshest environments on Earth when I was 65 years old, after thinking the journey impossible at 43?

When Misha and I paddled into Moolynaut's home village of Vyvenka, in Eastern Siberia, for the first time in 2000, it was part of a two-year expedition to kayak across the North Pacific Rim, from Japan to Alaska. Sitting around the dinner table during our first evening, people asked us why we were expending so much energy and money, and placing ourselves in so much danger, to make this journey. I explained—as if this were actually an explanation—that we were following in the wake of aboriginal maritime migrants who first colonized the Western Hemisphere. After discussing this Paleolithic aboriginal migration for a while, one of our Koryak friends Sergei, always the joker, commented, "You know, you and Misha are white men and therefore you're not very tough. But you're paddling to Alaska. If you could do it, tough guys—like our ancestors—could paddle to Alaska with no problem. And they probably wouldn't have made such a big fuss about it."

Sergei was being friendly and mischievous, with no insult intended or taken. Yet, I knew, in my heart, that throughout all previous expeditions, I had never, in my life, truly gone all out. Now, I decided that I wanted to push my body to the utmost limit, within one of the deepest, most remote and hostile environments on Earth. At the time, I had no idea how close I would come to tickling that "utmost limit."

Does this personal experiment on my own body have any importance to anyone but me? I think the answer is yes. Exploration and journeying is an integral part of our DNA. After all, for better or worse, it was humans and our hominid ancestors who crossed deserts and oceans and walked out of Africa, while chimpanzees and bonobos, to say nothing about wildebeest and hippopotamuses stayed put. I believe that our ancestors, with their primitive technology and aboriginal wisdoms, have something important to teach modern humanity about our current journey into the future. We've already discussed Paleolithic cannibalism and intertribal warfare. But those injustices don't negate the mystery of Moolynaut's healing, the flight of Kutcha the Messenger Raven, or the real and quantifiable journey of the Polynesian navigators. The story of aboriginal people is about the power of connection: Connection to nature and our own bodies. Many people, over many centuries, have told this story—it is not new. But at the same time, many people, over many centuries, have not listened. So I decided to retell it, in my own way, first by experiencing this connection, by skiing and paddling, (and although I didn't know it at the time, crawling) across this beautiful, remote, Arctic environment.

Now I just needed to find partners and organize logistics.

I have a friend in Montana, who is five years older than me, named Bill Bradt. Bill has a son named Tyler. When Tyler was a little boy, Bill decided to teach him how to kayak. At that time, Tyler looked so tiny in an adult's cockpit, arms raised almost above his head so he could reach his paddle into the water. We were all afraid that he would have a bad experience, and reject water sports forever, so someone came up with the bright idea that we would camouflage this inherently adult activity by announcing that we were "looking for frogs." Over the years, Tyler grew into a teenager and soon surpassed all of us in his skills. Then he became a young man and continued to get better and better and better. Before we knew what was happening, while Bill and I and the rest of our geezer tribe were progressively getting older and slower, Tyler was dropping radical runs all over the globe, including breaking a world record by launching himself over Palouse Falls, a waterfall that is 57 meters, or about the height of an 18-story building.

Shortly after I started dreaming about Ellesmere, and was trying to find a competent partner, an email popped up from Tyler out of the ether. "Hey, maybe we should do an expedition together?" I was totally surprised, and honored. The old man and the youngster—

passing the torch from one generation to another. So we teamed up and started organizing logistics.

Using two food drops, we planned to pack provisions for 100 days, meaning that we needed to average 15 miles—half a marathon—every day for over three months. Experienced polar explorers warned us that rough ice on the North Coast would slow our passage to a mile a day, or a few hundred meters, or zero. And once the ice broke up in late summer, we would be paddling overloaded boats through open water ravaged by Arctic storms. Over coffee in Duluth, Lonnie Dupre, the accomplished polar explorer who had circumnavigated Greenland, advised me that our bodies would simply not withstand the torture of a hundred continuous days and that we needed to rest along the way. But we didn't have enough food or time for rest days. And somehow, for no rational reason, I still had faith that Moolynaut's power and legacy would give me the strength to complete this circumnavigation.

One day, while studying maps and ice conditions, Tyler announced that we needed more firepower and suggested we enlist a friend of his, an extreme kayaker named Boomer. I didn't say anything, but my first thought was, "Oh, Boy. What kind of guy would attach a *nom de guerre* like "Boomer" to himself?" It turned out that Boomer was off kayaking the Stikine Canyon, one of the most difficult and committing whitewater runs in the world, but he was due to return to Hood River, Oregon, soon. Nina and I hung out with Tyler for a day or so until we got word that Boomer was on his way, driving straight through the night from west central British Columbia to connect up with us.

We went to a local coffee shop, caught up on emails, drank a latte, and waited. Soon enough, a beat up, rusted, generic white car pulled up. The first thing I noticed, aside from the fender that was about to fall off, was that the back seat was packed with everything imaginable, a clear sign that this was not only a means of transportation, it was also home, dining room, and toy shed. Most kayakers have a rack on the roof of their car to transport their boats. Boomer had saved a few dollars and sidestepped that purchase by pounding a huge divot into the roof with a heavy hammer, to create an indent that fit the shape of his boat. Then he simply nestled the boat into the depression and tied it off securely by running ropes through the windows.

A strong, burly, youthful man of medium height stepped out, walked across the street with the easy athletic grace of the world-class wrestler and kayaker that he was, blinking in the sunlight, ragged after driving all night. He had a thick mop of Scandinavian blond hair, the kind that changes color easily with sun and wind, and disarmingly blue eyes. If, in another lifetime, he charged to shore from a Viking longboat, splashing through the surf with a horned helmet, chain mail, and a razor-sharp, double-bladed battle-axe, I would turn like a jackrabbit and run for the hills.

He greeted Tyler then offered his hand to me with a warm, understated, boyish smile, "Erik Boomer, pleased to meet you."

"Oh, my gosh," I thought. "Boomer is his real name, the name he was born with, not some contrived nickname. I've already underestimated this guy."

We shook hands, went inside, and ordered another round of coffee. Tyler outlined our project and I carefully watched Boomer's tired but smiling face. When Tyler was finished, Boomer nodded casually as if we were discussing a trade run of a local river, "Sure, I'm in."

So, now as a threesome, we began firming up logistics. Eddie Bauer-First Ascent generously became our major sponsor and we won a Polartec Grant. Wilderness Systems provided boats and Adventure Technology donated paddles. By February of 2011, we were in full swing, buying and shipping food, acquiring boats, deciding on tents, and so on. Tyler visited our winter home in Fernie, British Columbia to field test some gear, and then charged off when he heard that river levels in Oregon were prime for launching off waterfalls in a kayak. Then:

Tyler was the force that would hold Boomer and me together—the apex of our human triangle. Now, Boomer and I were two strangers, a generation apart, preparing to travel together in total isolation, for over three months, with the assurance that we would face life-and-death decisions—daily. Was it madness to continue?

For some weird, inexplicable reason, I didn't think so. Another apex existed, stronger even than Tyler, with his magnetic personality and booming laugh. Boomer had experimented with possessions and jobs, but he put all that aside to follow his passions. He had already tested his mettle, repeatedly, in extremely dangerous situations, and had briefly experienced that quiet chuckle and mischievous grin of the Arctic wilderness. These shared experiences would prove to be the unbreakable thread that would bond us.

Many people have insisted that I must have had reservations about traveling so far and so long with a stranger a generation younger than me. We had no music, no books, no playing cards, just eight rumpled, torn out pages of the *Tao Te Ching*. What would we talk about? How would we resolve unavoidable differences in the face of tense situations? We had lots of worries in the days before flying north, but I always trusted Boomer. I think you can trust a person by recognizing the madness that propels them.

In the past, I had been able to kayak 500 miles a month under expedition conditions in tempestuous oceans. So I figured that this journey would take about three months. The problem was that the ocean freezes solid in the winter and the ice doesn't melt until mid-July, plus or minus a few weeks. If we started on July 15, we would complete the expedition about mid-October. But by that time, winter would be setting in, with all its polar ferocity, and the ocean would be freezing again. At the beginning of freeze-up, the ice is too thick to paddle through and too thin to walk over. If we were still traveling this late in the season, we would die. Balancing all these factors, we decided to start in early May, by dragging our kayaks across the solid sea ice until the ocean would start to break up under the relentless heat of continuous 24-hour daylight. Then we planned to finish the journey by paddling over open water.

INTO NOTHINGNESS

If I can just stop taking myself too seriously, the Ellesmere circumnavigation was nothing more than a grand walkabout, one in a long series of walkabouts that started when I chased a pretty skirt to Athens and ended up hitchhiking across Turkey.

The word "walkabout" originates in Australia and refers to a journey where Aboriginal adolescents would travel, alone, often for months at a time, to trace the paths, or "songlines," that their ancestors took. The Aborigines did this as part of their culture, without, in Sergei's words, "making a big fuss about it." Much later, white, male travel writers came along and defined a walkabout as a spiritual journey. But let's be careful here and not wrap ourselves up in some flag or another.

I like the various definitions of "walkabout" in the online Urban Dictionary[4]:

"A spontaneous journey through the wilderness of one's choosing in an effort to satisfy one's itchy feet, a need to be elsewhere, the craving for the open road, that space over the horizon…yes…something like that…you can't quite touch it so you have to go find it because you just know it's there…"

"A trek usually around woop woop (roughly: happiness, excitement, joy) which has little or no goal other than admiring nature, and the personal satisfaction of walking around the middle of nowhere and making it home alive."

"Usually the recount of the trek is exaggerated to add extra excitement and thrill. The trek in actual fact is usually very dull."

"Walkabout's really have no logical reason or appeal other than to combat boredom with adventure. Many people who participate in walkabout's are usually told they're 'crazy' and 'are gonna get themselves killed one day'."

Boomer, who had never been on a camping trip for longer than a week prior to this, was also on a walkabout, seeking a new vision of adventure, expanded from his already formidable accomplishments as an athlete on a wrestling mat and in extreme, but comparatively short, passages in a kayak.

In early May, I met Boomer in Ottawa, and together we flew to Grise Fiord, the farthest north hamlet in Canada, and the only civilian settlement on the island. The temperature was about ten below Celsius (mid-teens Fahrenheit) when we landed. We had arranged to stay with a Dene man named Raymond, who had moved north from the Canadian forested taiga decades before because he never quite fit in with civilization—even though his childhood home was far from "civilization" by most people's standards. Over the next few days, we packed our 30 kilo boats with about 70 kilos of gear, including 25 days of food, enough, we hoped, to reach our first food drop at the Canadian weather station in Eureka. Everything was a compromise because every piece of gear, from kayaks to underwear, had to function in three radically different environments—winter on dry snow, break up and slush, and open water arctic paddling. Every handful of nuts, candy bar, or cup of quinoa was also a compromise, because extra food gave us cushion, in case we were slowed down by soft snow, rough ice, or bitter winds, but every ounce of food also added weight and slowed us down, even if conditions were favorable. The Wilderness Systems Tsunami 135 kayak, was advertised on the company website as "ideal for female and small-framed paddlers." As a result, it was clearly smaller than we would have liked, but it was the largest boat that fit into the airplane that flies to Grise.

On the morning of May 7, we finished our preparations in this tiny knot of humanity, the last place, for the next hundred days, where people lived, married, raised babies, loved, argued, worked, hunted, grew old, and died. We stood, looking out across the frozen ocean that extended to the horizon, and ultimately around the earth in a circumpolar girdle of glistening whiteness. When the ocean freezes in the autumn, currents and waves crumple the ice into a kaleidoscope of flat surfaces interspersed by jagged blocks that can rise into a clustered forest of small individual towers, two to three meters high, or into huge "pressure ridges" ten meters high and extending for many kilometers. This was our highway, and we had no idea how smooth or rough it would be.

Boomer took off like a rocket while I remained silent and stationary, needing just a few moments to mentally absorb the task ahead. We would encounter two small enclaves of civilization along our way, the weather/research station at Eureka (on the west edge of the island) and the Canadian military base at Alert (on the northeast coast). Otherwise we were planning to live in a world defined by sky, ice, ocean, rock, and space, along with polar bears, wolves, walrus, seals, ducks, and geese, but with none of the normal trappings of civilization, like people, roads, cars, houses, TV, newspapers, doctors, computers, and fences. No distractions, no enclosures, and not much of a safety net. It's tempting to say that this is Moolynaut's world, but that's not true.

Moolynaut was born into essentially a Stone Age existence that consisted critically of her tribe—community. Here, Boomer and I were a tribe of two, unsustainable in the long-term because there were no women and therefore no promise of another generation. So this journey was a contrived experiment—a walkabout—to communicate directly with nature at the portal of old age.

Bob Dylan summarized my feelings, not only about this trip, but about life in general, when he wrote: "And it dawned on me that I might have to change my inner thought patterns.... That I would have to start believing in possibilities that I wouldn't have allowed before, that I had been closing my creativity down to a very narrow, controllable scale...that things had become too familiar and I might have to disorient myself."[5]

Oleg's words resurfaced, "The tundra will be your teacher."

"Teaching me what?" I asked myself.

"To disorient yourself," Dylan answered.

Before I realized that time had passed, Boomer was down the hill and onto the sea ice. So, finally, I took my first step. I tripped over my skis—and fell down. My kayak slid on hard-packed snow and smashed into my ribs. I got up, took a second step, fell down. Repeat. Onlookers giggled politely, wanting to laugh but trying not to embarrass me. Was I actually that incompetent? Skiing has been a central component of my life. I feel more comfortable gliding down a gentle snow slope than I do walking. Had my whole world gone upside down, a portent of disaster to come? I stopped and collected myself.

These were the skis I got married in, when Chris and I were young, before she perished in that avalanche. I had spent many glorious powder days on these skis, in steep descents in the high alpine of the Wasatch Range, in Utah. I don't generally fall down on skis. And I've never, in my life, fallen down three times in three steps, all on a gentle slope, less steep than a beginners run at the local ski area. What was wrong? I shuffled these old friends beneath me to feel their reaction to snow. Oh, got it. Shit. I've screwed my climbing skins on backwards.[2] That was about the stupidest thing I could have done.

Life had been so hectic in the months and days before the expedition. Boomer and I still didn't know one another. Maybe we should have taken a trial run, tested our gear, like every other Polar expedition in the world has ever done, for all eternity. Should've, would've, could've has no place out here. Now, I should definitely stop, take an hour, and repair my gear before I took another step. Maybe even leave tomorrow. One day would make no difference. But Boomer was way out on the horizon already, a thin black dot amid chunks of broken pressure ridges frozen into the matrix of sea ice. I was revved up and didn't want to start the expedition with a "Wait for me; I'm a stupid old man" ploy. So I hobbled, jumped, skipped, slid backwards, and jerked forwards to catch up.

"It's going to be a long 900 miles," I thought, "before the sea ice melts and we start to paddle."

That night, in the safety of the tent, after Boomer borrowed my superior spoon so he wouldn't melt the Chinese piece-of-shit, one-time-use, coffee-stirring device that he took from the counter at McDonalds, I had time to assess. Now that reality was staring me in the face, like a mother polar bear with bad breath and two cubs behind her, I concluded that this circumnavigation was a really dumb idea. It's too far. We don't have enough food. We'll wear holes in the bottoms of our kayaks, dragging them as far as the distance from New York City to McCook, Nebraska—as if anybody ever wanted to go to McCook. Our kayaks are too small. Too loaded down. Too much weight on the deck. We don't have the foggiest idea what the ice will be like. My skins are screwed on

_____

2 Climbing skins are modern, synthetic substitutes for the seal skins that early explorers attached to the bottoms of their skis. The skins have a nap, or fiber, like fur, that is smooth if you slide it in one direction, and grip the snow if you slide it the other way. Set correctly, climbing skins enable the skier to slide easily along on flat or downhill terrain and at the same time to climb up hills. Set incorrectly, the skins catch the snow when you try to move forward.

backwards. Boomer's spoon is going to break. He's too young and inexperienced. I'm too old and feeble.

OK, I'm going to wake up in the morning and say, "Hey Boomer, buddy. Sorry about this. All the planning and anticipation and all. Don't mean to disappoint you, but I'm going home."

I slept fitfully, and in the morning, tried to hide the internal tension by bouncing out of my sleeping bag into the cold, to start the stove, priming it just right, with not too much or too little fuel. I slid into the familiar routine, repeated so often in my life on mountains and by tumultuous seas. I watched the oatmeal bubble and adjusted the flame carefully. Boomer was cheery, enthusiastic, and excited and I loved the guy, already, with his mix of boyish innocence and deadly focus. I didn't have the heart to tell him that I was ready to tuck my tail between my legs and surrender to anticipation of hardship before any hardship actualized. I didn't have the heart to tell myself that I was prepared to quit, before the expedition began. We broke camp in silence. Boomer adjusted his harness, stepped into his skis, and took off while I was still fiddling with my gear. I remembered something a good friend, Brian Bell, once told me. "You don't turn back until you can't take even one more step. Never give up when you anticipate that some 'next step' in some indefinable space 'down the road' might become difficult."

I was rested, with only one day of travel behind me. It was going to be easy to put my left foot in front of my right on flat sea ice and proceed sixty centimeters or so, even though it would be inefficient because my skins were screwed on backwards. And the sixty centimeters after that was a no-brainer as well, and the step after that.

After less than a hundred meters, as I was rushing to catch up, Boomer stopped to inspect fresh polar bear tracks. A monstrous animal had passed close to our tent, during the night, on broad, flat, snowshoe-paws that were made to carry a heavy body efficiently over soft surfaces.

In Faulkner's classic novella, *The Bear,* the boy asks the old man, "You mean he (the bear) already knows me, that I ain't never been to the big bottom before, ain't had time to find out yet whether I..." Then after a moment, the boy continued, "It was me he was watching. I don't reckon he did need to come but once."

With my eyes, I followed the bear tracks across the ice and suddenly every block of pressure ridge appeared as a white bear, or a bear with cubs, or a piece of ice with a bear behind it. "It was me he was watching."[6]

So why didn't the bear eat us? Why didn't it creep stealthily toward our tent in the wee hours of the morning, and then pounce, as it would pounce on a sleeping seal, destroying our flimsy nylon tent with one ferocious swipe, killing us both within milliseconds? Why have thousands of hunters and adventurers before us traveled over this land and, most of the time, not been eaten by bears? I didn't have an immediate answer, but without formulating the thoughts, or understanding the depths where they originated, like the boy in Faulkner's story, I knew: "So I will have to see him, [the boy] thought, without dread or even hope. *I will have to look at him.*" (The italics are Faulkner's, not mine.) Somewhere, out on this ice, or on the ocean after the ice melts, we will meet him.

In this case the pronoun, "Him" was the living, breathing bear with one mangled foot, because he had already been wounded by civilization's steel traps. But, more importantly, "Him" was the wilderness, also living and breathing, crippled but still powerful and primordial.

Ten years ago, I ate the amanita with Moolynaut and started on a hallucinogenic journey toward The Other World. I was trudging through the labyrinth but got scared and ran back, desperately groping for reality. So now, I was free of the dark, threatening, mysterious labyrinth, traveling in The Real World, just like Oleg had told me to, beneath the limitless frozen arctic sky. What would it mean if I got scared and ran back again now that I was in Oleg's world, my world, Hunter's world? What does "turn back" mean, anyway? Yeah, maybe if I were born differently, I would be wearing pink shoes and playing the blues harmonica in a noisy nightclub, or journeying through life as a 350-pound couch potato with a bag of chips and the TV remote. Maybe I would have gotten a real job somewhere along the line and had a fat pension by now so I could waltz through retirement with a wife with breast implants gazing at me adoringly. But I didn't do any of that. So I have to make my journey on the tundra. On the ice. With my skins screwed on backwards. There is no turning back, no starting over, at this point in my life.

Once I settled that issue in my mind, I looked at the polar bear tracks with a fresh perspective. This was my world now. In every aboriginal culture, from the Amazon to the Arctic, people believed in the unity and consciousness of all things, from bears, to rocks, to windblown snow. Knud Rasmussen, the famed Arctic explorer and anthropologist, recounts a fundamental and oft-repeated Inuit teaching: "In the very first times, both people and animals lived on earth, but there were no differences between them…A person could become an animal, and an animal could become a human being…There were wolves, bears, and foxes… they all spoke the same tongue, lived in the same kind of house, and spoke and hunted in the same way…That is the way they lived here on earth in the very earliest times, times that no one can understand now."[7]

Boomer and I were living on the ice. On any given night, a bear could charge in fast and resolute, rip through our tent, and kill us in our sleep. So what was the thread that kept us alive? Well, there was that shotgun always within easy reach—the Real World—efficient, metallic, and deadly. That was reassuring, but it definitely wasn't enough out here. Our survival also depended on learning to "speak the same tongue" as the bear. I can't tell you exactly what that means, but I am certain that this communication exists and is as real, tactile, and effective as a shotgun's blast or a lover's whisper.

To the Inuit, Bear was food, clothing, mortal danger, and Spirit, all wrapped up in one 500-kilo package, with cute rounded ears, penetrating black eyes, and sharp teeth and claws. If a hunter managed to go out with a shaped rock tied on the end of a long stick, and kill this powerful predator, that was fine, even though "In the first of times…an animal could become a human being." The hunter would pay respect to Nanook's soul by hanging the skin in an honored place in his igloo for several days. Then he would offer spirit tools to Bear Spirit. The Inuit believed that polar bears allowed themselves to be killed in order to obtain these spirit tools, which they would use for their journey into the hereafter.

A thick, dense fog rolled in, reducing our visibility to a few meters, embracing us in the same silence and loneliness that embraced the earliest travelers who hunted here, who left no visible trace on this ephemeral sea ice, which melted every year and turned to ocean waves, just as their lives have melted into the fog.

For the next few days, we traveled westward along the south coast of Ellesmere, and then swung north to circumnavigate the island in a clockwise direction. On May 13, the end of our first week, the temperature dropped to -20 ° C (about -5° F) and the wind blew hard out of the north. We pulled our hoods tight against frozen faces and trudged past polar bear tracks and herds of musk oxen grazing in a nearby tundra meadow. One day we disagreed on whether to take a short-cut overland, and on another day we argued about whether we should take a short-cut across the sea ice. But, very quickly, we learned to trust each other. It wasn't a verbalized emotion, but like the eight water-stained pages of the *Tao*, it *just was*. And anyway, neither of us knew the answers to the most pressing questions, like, "How far can we push our bodies today and still maintain enough reserves to travel every day for three months or more?" "How many miles can we maintain on will-power alone, and when do we tickle the dragon of basic metabolic limitations?" We had no idea, at the start, how perilously close we would come to answering those questions.

I put on every stitch of clothing I had, including my life vest, which provided an extra layer of insulation when worn under a windproof shell. Boomer took a photo of me, with moustache encased in ice, head down, skiing over tiny wavelets of wind hardened snow called sastrugi, dragging an orange kayak, with a paddle lashed incongruously on top, seeking open water, which seemed like an impossible cosmic joke. Equally incongruously, a lemming ran in front of me, perpendicular to my line of travel, almost crossing the tips of my skis. Every couple of seconds, it smashed into another line of sastrugi, bounced off it, legs spinning like a humming birds wings, even while it was in the air, half carried by the wind. And then it was gone, disappearing into the mist, a tiny bundle of protoplasm and DNA, powered by a mysterious concoction of synapses, directing its muscles to race away from land, toward oblivion, I am sure. Was that a mirror of Boomer and me walking through the storm for no obvious reason?

We had purchased most of our food from Costco and the bulk bins at the Good Food Store, in Missoula, Montana using two criteria: maximum calories and nutrition per gram and quick cooking time. Thus, our diet consisted of varied mixtures of humus, tabouli, dried beans, quinoa, nuts and coconut, mixed with olive oil or butter. We traded cooking duties with every camp. One person would cook a dinner and a breakfast and then rest for the next two meals. When I wasn't skiing, making or breaking camp, or cooking, I concentrated intensely on doing nothing. This wasn't some abstract passage into meditation. I needed every ounce of muscle power and endurance I had in me, so I permitted no wasted motions, thoughts, or random sightseeing. As a result, the spurious, annoying, useless, emotionally damaging, "stories in my head" began to simply vaporize into the limitless Arctic sky. Deep Wild is a living entity that reaches inside and cleans out unnecessary distracting thoughts, opening peacefulness and clarity.

Of course, Boomer and I talked during breaks and dinner,

mostly about the route ahead, but conversation was slow and limited. And then after dinner, we slept, the loaded shotgun lying between us—because there is no contradiction in my mind between staying alive through groovy cosmic oneness, and carrying a loaded 12-guage, just in case.

The modern residents of Grise Fiord had built a few hunting cabins, partly for themselves and partly for rich hunters who brought cash into the community so they could hang a polar bear hide in their living room, showing their macho-ness, which is, in my mind anyway, breaking the spirit-bond between bears and people.

On May 16, our tenth day on the expedition, we located a train of three structures mounted on skids, and pulled into position decades ago by a bulldozer. One structure was a tool shed, a second was for fuel storage, and a third was outfitted in 1950s décor as living quarters. The plywood cupboards were painted a sickly pinkish-orange, and the counter surfaces were Formica with gold swirlies, a little the worse for wear from many cycles of freeze and thaw. We spread our sleeping bags out on steel beds with wire springs, covered first with cardboard and then with foam pads that were soggy but not terribly soggy. The hunting guides, knowing that their clients are high-end-fancy dudes, stocked the shelves with a few delicacies, like canned escargot, but mostly the left-behind food consisted of Saltines, Lipton's cup-a-soups, instant coffee, and coffee creamer that had been soaked by condensation and then frozen like lava after a volcanic eruption. We found a huge assortment of sort-of-rusted to very-rusted Campbell's soup cans. Boomer called it the "apocalypse cabin."

I borrowed some tools and refastened my skins so they were finally pointing in the right direction. Now, I would be able to glide a little on my skis.

Despite the end-of-the-world feeling about the place, it felt like civilization compared to a mountain tent, so we celebrated by sleeping in and breaking camp around 9:00 AM the next day.

We had skied approximately 170 miles, with 1330 remaining. I remarked, "We have a long ways to go." And Boomer replied, characteristically: "We only have 15 miles to go today." That's the way we talked, in short sentences, friendly but short, because chit-chat had no meaning out here and nearly all our energy was directed towards forward motion, eating, and sleeping. My foreleg hurt and I developed a persistent sore on my right toe, while Boomer's Achilles tendon was sore. Fine, I adjusted my harness, stepped into my skis, and headed north.

By this time of the year, the sun was warm, but the air temperature was usually below freezing, as if we were in a giant, brightly-lighted refrigerator, with sparkling crystals reflecting sunlight. This seeming paradox of hot versus cold is caused because snow and ice reflect about 80 to 90% of the sun's heat back out into space. Later, in the short polar summer, when the snow and ice melt, the exposed dirt, rock, and ocean water are much less reflective and absorb up to 95% of solar radiation. The net result of this difference in reflectivity, or albedo, is that snow and ice cool the planet, which maintains the snow and ice. If the air heats up a little, by some outside factor, such as greenhouse warming, and some of the snow and ice melts, then the rock and ocean absorb heat and Earth's climate gets a lot warmer, very quickly. This phenomenon, where a little warming suddenly accelerates into a lot of warming, is called a "tipping point."

Boomer and I stopped for a snack of nuts, chocolate, and dried fruit. This place, right here, on the west coast of Ellesmere Island, and throughout the circumpolar Arctic, too far north for anyone to live, is one of the key systems that determine global climate. If the snow and ice here melts a few weeks sooner than it did last year, all those people in New York City and Bangladesh, people who never think about polar bears and sea ice, lavishly rich and desperately poor, will be more vulnerable to storms, floods, droughts, and food shortages. Which is, without a doubt, what is happening in the world today. Right now. Not in some imagined or hypothetical future.

I don't know how to get this message across. No one does. I have worked as a research scientist and an environmental science educator. Now I write trade books. Every once in a while, after I give a book reading or a keynote address, someone will raise their hand and ask, "But do you really expect us—society—to change our ways? This fossil fuel-driven opulence that we enjoy is too seductive, too accessible, and too addicting to shrug it off."

In a recent article in *The New York Times*, Jim Hanson, the climate scientist who originally raised the flag about greenhouse warming several decades ago, wrote, "It's useful to show that you can have a lifestyle which produces less carbon, but it doesn't solve the problem. Because if that's all that happens, even if you convince a thousand people or a million people or a billion people to reduce their emissions what it does is reduce the demand for the fuel, lowers its price and somebody else will burn it."[8]

I munched slowly on my nuts, careful to chew completely so my stomach could utilize all the available calories. Clearly, this book isn't going to stop the relentless drive of civilization across the world, in Cincinnati and Beijing, London and Port-au Prince. Finger-pointing can be dangerous and hypocritical because we all burn fossil fuels in one way or another. But human civilization does change. Despite indisputably terrible local wars such as in Syria right now, overall human violence, across the globe, is considerably less than the violence in aboriginal societies in Papua New Guinea, and other tribal societies. When I was a young man, black people in the southern United States rode on the back of the bus; now a black man is president. We can change. We have changed. So each person does what he or she can do. It is my contention that it is important to remind people, for the umpteenth time—to remind myself—that there is a circumpolar mantle of ice out there, and that this mantle is fragile. If we disrupt it, the whole world will be affected.

It is simpler than that, and more complicated. As humans, we take care of our loved ones—aging parents with terminal illnesses, sick children, perhaps with permanent disabilities, stricken spouses. We take care of these kin, without regard to cost, because we love them. But when someone asks us to care for the earth, the all-too-common questions are: "How much will it cost?" "How many jobs will be lost?" The journey into Deep Wild is a journey into love of landscapes. Because we care. As simple as that. And as complicated.

Boomer and I were feeling the sun, skiing across hard ice, or slush, two specks of humanity, maintaining our body heat with nuts, some oatmeal, and a little bowl of quinoa in the evening. The shoreline was barely above sea level, so sometimes we would be skiing along and see grasses and rock poking out of the snow. Then one of us would say, "Oh, we're on land," or alternately, we'd pass a pressure ridge ice block and say, "Oh, we're on the ocean."

The mountains along the coast were fragmented by desert-like erosion, with sharp gullies and cut-banks, mud flows, deltas, and other evidence of moving sediment in a land almost devoid of vegetation. But, most of the time, I didn't look at the vistas around me; I concentrated on making every step as efficient as possible. The sea ice was covered by snow, molded by wind and temperature changes into a near infinite variety of surfaces. If we were lucky, we traveled smoothly and efficiently over firm snow lying on flat ice, while at other times we had to drag our boats over sastrugi or tilted blocks of pressure ice. These surfaces changed very rapidly with sun angle and time of day, melting into slush at midday and then refreezing in the evening. My boat was always about two meters behind me. Now that my skins were affixed properly, when both my skis and my boat were simultaneously positioned on the crest of a tiny, sometimes almost imperceptible, downhill surface, I gave a little extra push and then slid a meter for free. One extra meter forward with 1,000 miles to go doesn't sound like much, but it multiplies if you do it enough times, maybe enough to make a difference of a mile a day, times 100 days, equals 100 miles, which could possibly be the difference between completing the journey before our bodies broke down, or before winter returned—or not completing the journey. Perhaps this extra push would be the difference between life and death. Despite the long, hard miles and the frightful consequences of failure, this concentration on the next step became a joyful affirmation of what I was doing. It was my remedy for boredom in a deep visceral manner, because living in the moment was not only some abstract Zen joy, it was also a tactile form of survival. Just as Oleg said, "Tundra will be your teacher."

We followed GPS coordinates to a tiny shack, that appeared on the low-lying plain, in a seemingly random place, as if some Greek God had been blindfolded at a party, spun around three times, tossed out a thunderbolt, and whack, created the northernmost civilian habitation in Canada, and perhaps in the world.

The cabin was three sheets of plywood wide by four sheets long, with a flat roof that leaked as the snow melted under the sun's heat. The last visitors had tacked sheets of plastic on the ceiling, carefully positioned to funnel the dripping water away from the bunks and onto the floor, where it froze into miniature stalagmites. We arrived mid-afternoon, and rested for half a day. Boomer rebuilt his boots from an assortment of boot-like material he had accumulated at various refuges, and I worked on my skins again. It was very domestic. Previous visitors had recorded their presence on the walls. Some hunter from Montana wanted the whole world to know that he had bagged a trophy bear. I half expected to find a message, "For good sex, call…"

As the afternoon waned into evening, Boomer broke a long peaceful silence, "I like this more than the apocalypse cabin. That place was too duded up. This feels real."

"I disagree. The apocalypse cabin had chairs, a table, and foam pads on the bunks."

"No, sorry. That place felt like an old meth lab. This is plywood,

Dude, how much more real can you get? Look, you can live in the apocalypse cabin. I'll live here and come down to visit you once a month, and you can serve me some rusty canned soup. And anytime you want to visit me, your bunk is waiting for you. There hasn't been anyone here since 2005, so the chances are pretty slim that someone will be sleeping in it."

On May 29th, our 23rd day, we swung east into Slidre Fiord to travel a few miles out of our direct path to the Eureka weather station, where we planned to pick up an air-drop of essential food. Boomer accelerated and I tried running to keep up, but even that wasn't sufficient. As he pulled ahead and slowly morphed from a person into a small black dot on the ice, I felt old, decrepit, and slow. By mid-day, I was so exhausted that I saw double, and had to feel when my skis were in the track, because my vision was too blurry to focus.

I argued and pleaded, "Please, brain, it's distracting to see double. Just focus for me; just for today. I've asked you to direct my tired leg muscles to perform, and you seem to be able to do that. Thank you. Now I'm asking to stop making me see double. As a favor between two old friends." But my brain would have none of it. "You're getting old, dude. Systems start breaking down. Get used to it."

The track veered abruptly, and I surmised that Boomer saw the weather station and was adjusting his course. I stopped and closed one eye to override the double vision, but saw nothing. Twenty minutes later I tried again, and saw several blue and white dots that stood out in a world of blue and white ice because they were rectangular and nature isn't.

We had just traveled about 400 miles in 23 days, or 17 miles a day, slightly faster than our mandated 15 mile per day average, and had completed a quarter of the total distance around Ellesmere. I was exhausted, seeing double, half limping on sore muscles, aching tendons, and bruised skin. This was the last airstrip with regular flights, where we could catch a ride home without a forty-or-fifty-thousand dollar charter flight for rescue. Once we left Eureka, we were committed to another 1,100 miles—and the most dangerous passages lay ahead. Any reasonable outside observer might ask, "A thousand-plus miles is one heck of a long ways. You had already tickled the ceiling of old age, so why didn't you just call it a good ski tour and go home, spend the summer riding mountain bikes with your wife and your dear community of friends?"

But I had already rejected that argument. The polar bear had walked by our camp on that first night to pay us a silent visit. Then, he or she had opened the door to let us enter and pass through the portal. "It was me he was watching." Us. Boomer and me. We were guests on this sea ice, given the opportunity and honor to live within the sphere of this great power. So I didn't call it quits here at Eureka, just as I hadn't called it quits the first day out, because I was exactly where my whole life had steered me toward, exactly where I wanted to be.

Boomer was waiting patiently close to land, where the solid, glistening white ice had partially melted into a broad zone of mud-brown wet slush. After some discussion, we elected to splash on through and get our feet wet, because we weren't going to sleep in a cold tent tonight. We left the boats on the shore and walked up the hill, dancing, as it were, to the throb of a diesel generator. There was not a single human in sight. All the people were inside the blue alumascape, recording the weather by staring into computer screens. We reached the main building with a sign, "Welcome to Eureka Weather Station," and opened the heavy door into a large windowless vestibule that was warm but enclosed, dark, silent, and lifeless. Boots were neatly ordered below a second sign, "Remove Your Outer Footwear," but there were no people who had worn those boots, as if all the people had stood here and had been beamed up, out of their shoes, by the aliens. We opened a second door and meandered through a dark, silent labyrinth until we burst through a portal into a gleaming stainless steel kitchen with glass lined refrigerators full of food. A kindly, grandmotherly cook looked into our frostbitten and weather worn faces and said, "You must be hungry."

Our food resupply was waiting for us in the storeroom, so for the next day and a half, we ate, rested, played pool, watched TV, caught up on our emails, and packed for the next leg of our expedition, toward a food cache on the north coast, 300 miles away. If we continued to average 15 miles a day, we could travel light, with twenty days of food. But we had no idea of ice conditions on the north coast. So far, we had traveled over relatively protected bays and inlets, where the ice was traditionally smooth. In contrast, the north coast was exposed to the full ferocity of the North Pole Ocean, where winds and currents could churn the sea ice into a mayhem of perhaps impenetrable pressure ridges. Several modern adventurers, who had trekked to the North Pole, had warned us that rough ice along this north coast might reduce travel to ten miles a day, or one mile, or next to nothing. I had a theory that these explorers, leaving for the Pole, with 500 miles of fractured ice in front of them, might forget that the ice was smooth for the first hundred meters, or fifty meters, or five meters after they left land. But that's all we needed, a tiny path, just a ribbon. Furthermore, I predicted that this narrow band of shore ice, neglected and forgotten in the Arctic literature, would be our yellow brick road, and we would cruise along the coast at our mandated 15 miles a day. Several people thought I was crazy, stupid, or suicidal. Boomer wasn't as confident in my logic as I was, but due to his indomitable spirit, and faith in his boundless strength if conditions did worsen, he was willing to travel into the Polar unknown on my hunch. In my secret, quiet moments, lying in my sleeping bag in the early morning, before waking to the cold air and a meagre breakfast, I wasn't all that convinced that I was right either. But I kept my fears and doubts to myself.

Way back, seemingly so long ago, at the beginning of the expedition, the dispatch man at Ken Borek Air, the bush-pilot company, had asked, "What's your fall-back plan if you get in trouble?" I looked at him in the eye and said, "We don't have a fall-back plan. We're going to make it." He returned my stare, measured, measuring: "Ok, here's the GPS coordinates of a few stretches of smooth glacial ice, inland, where we can land an aircraft. Guaranteed." I wrote them down, knowing that if our journey was halted by rough ice, and we were starving, or hurt, we could ski to shore, attempt a difficult and potentially hazardous travel over the mountains, find those lifesaving segments of smooth ice, and call for a rescue that we couldn't afford.

Enough theory. Now we needed an absolute number. How much food should we pack? Twenty days? Twenty five? Thirty? We decided to fill our boats with as much food as we could carry—fifty days—and let the details sort themselves out according to the whims of the Polar North. With heavy loads, perhaps unnecessarily heavy, Boomer and I left the warm, food-filled civilized opulence of Eureka and headed again onto the sea ice.

In Montana, I live near the boundary of the Frank Church/Selway-Bitterroot Wilderness, the largest wilderness area in the US outside of Alaska, a little larger than the state of Connecticut. I can walk out my front door, and without crossing a single road, not even my driveway, travel through uninhabited forest and mountains for more than a hundred miles due west, or fifty miles north or south. But that is puny and insignificant compared to the remoteness of the region we were traveling in now. Above this latitude, there are no civilian settlements anywhere in the world, although there are a few scattered military and research stations, either on land or on floating ice. If we walked east or west, at constant latitude, we could travel forever, around and around the earth, without encountering a single person. To the North, the closest point of familiar geography is The North Pole, an astronomical peculiarity, set on ephemeral, shifting sea ice. If, in our imaginations, there were no radios or rescue aircraft, as in the days of Peary, and if Boomer and I decided to return to civilization by walking due south along a constant line of longitude, we would finally reach the road system of Manitoba after a long, cold, hungry, weary, perhaps impossible 2,000 miles. In short, we were traveling in the great open space, defined by sea ice, the great mountain ranges of Ellesmere on the east and Axel Heiberg Island on the west, and the sky. With the exception of an occasional satellite phone call, we had zero exposure to the chatter of civilization. Of course, our survival depended on logistics, strategy, gear, strength, and so on, but those are only the mechanical components. Fundamentally, our survival depended on being empowered, not crushed, by nothingness.

One of our pages of the Tao summarized our situation:

> We put thirty spokes together and call it a wheel;
> But it is on the space where there is nothing that
> The usefulness of the wheel depends.
>
> ...
>
> Therefore just as we take advantage of what is, we
> Should recognize the usefulness of what is not.

A WOLF THAT LINGERED

On the evening after Boomer and I left Eureka, I wrote in my journal:

> *"I don't have any great thoughts today. Just plugging along into the Dream World. Right now the journey isn't particularly difficult. We will be on the northwest coast in a week and we'll see."*

We swung north, anticipating that we would cross 80° N latitude that evening. 80° N is a line on a White Man's map, determined by some more or less arbitrary decision by an ancient Greek mathematician, that circles and spheres should be divided into 360 equal segments. When Robert Peary mounted his expeditions to the North Pole in the early 1900s, his Inuit companions were perplexed with his sextant and fixation on these lines that existed on Peary's maps, but not on the land itself. The North Pole was the greatest mystery of all. What could possibly be at this place that was so valuable that these men launched repeated expeditions to reach it, enduring great expense, suffering, and even death? The Inuit reasoned that the North Pole must be made out of iron, the most valuable commodity in their world, and they called it The Great Nail.

Regardless of logic or absurdity, Boomer and I put considerable emotional importance on crossing 80° N, because we felt that it was the transition from the High Arctic to the Polar Zone, 10° latitude, or exactly 600 nautical miles, or 1111.2 km, or 690.468 statute miles from The Great Nail.

On the afternoon of June 1, I was trudging along in Boomer's tracks, so exhausted that I was seeing double again, and trying to focus well enough to travel efficiently over a kaleidoscope of smooth white snow, snow covered with windblown sand, blue ice, sastrugi, and fractured ice blocks. I was feeling grumpy, wishing that I wasn't so old and feeble, which generated even greater grumpiness, wondering what happened to my equanimity, wishing that I wasn't wishing that I was so old and feeble.

I pushed on in this manner, only because we had a goal for the day and because Boomer was ahead of me anyway, out of earshot, so there was no choice. At about quitting time, when we were almost exactly at this magic line of 80° N, I saw Boomer's kayak parked near a large block of ice, but no Boomer. Curious, maybe even a little alarmed at his disappearance, I stopped, closed one eye to see better, and scanned the horizon. Ah, yes, there he was, on a nearby hillside, silhouetted against the sky, highlighted in light and shadow, carrying our .17 rifle, hunting for a nice fat ptarmigan to supplement our meagre dinner.

Relieved that everything was okay, I waved cheerily and he waved back, but with a lot more animation than was warranted by a casual "Hello." Boomer was not the kind of guy to greet me with such a show of enthusiasm after only an hour of separation. Then he was yelling something—but since he was far away and I'm half deaf anyway, his words dissipated into the great sky. I waved again, and shouted, "Calm down. I see you." But he became even more animated, agitated even, pointing behind me. Finally, I turned and.... Woops. There, right behind me, now right in front of me, staring at me with beady-eyed intensity, I saw a great white wolf, silent, motionless—paw prints set firmly in my ski tracks, not more than 20 meters away. Instantly, my think-too-much-know-it-all brain decided that its double-vision-I'm-tired-tantrum was no longer allowable and I focused clearly, as if I were a young man.

I braced for a flying ball of fur with fangs reaching for my jugular. But instead of attacking, the wolf sat down slowly, deliberately, looking like another block of pressure-ridge ice strewn across this frozen ocean—a chunk of ice that had once been part of a wave, but was now locked within a long peaceful pause.

We made firm, unwavering eye contact and gradually my fear dissipated into the great polar void, like dandelion seeds in the wind, leaving only silence. The wolf is the great ancestor of dogs, and we are all accustomed to communicating with dogs, so I searched for the voices of body language. The wolf was clearly not an exuberant stick-fetching Labrador retriever, but it wasn't a snarling junk-yard Rottweiler either. It was much calmer, infinitely more regal and patient than either of those domesticated relatives. He or she sat on the ice, looking right at me: two dark inscrutable eyes and cute, almost rounded ears, set in a white face, with just a tint of brown fur under the chin. I did my best to remain as calm and as regal as I could muster, maintain eye contact, and say in body language, "Good afternoon, wolf. I am a creature of the ice, too, potentially lethal, like you, but currently friendly. We are fellow travelers, sharing this space."

I waited, watching the wolf while the wolf watched me—two

dangerous predators choosing not to be dangerous at this instant in time.

After five or ten minutes, I turned my back, slowly, deliberately, as a lover would turn to lead a partner into her bedroom. Without looking behind me, but feeling absolutely confident that the wolf was trotting along in my tracks, I continued my journey. Boomer ran down the hill and I envied that he had so much energy spilling over the top that he could waste it at the end of the day by running for the sheer joy of motion when there was no more forward distance to travel and no need to hurry. If we lived in the Stone Age, Boomer would be hunting polar bears and whales with weapons made of stone and bone and I would be dead long before I reached the ripe old age of 65.

The wolf sat and watched patiently, as if it had nothing else to do in the world, as we pitched our tent behind a block of pressure ridge ice for wind protection, as we always did in this wilderness, which at the moment was still and quiet, not wild at all. I cooked dinner, on that calm, peaceful evening, and nothing actually happened, but everything happened because the wolf became woven into a tapestry of all the animate and inanimate forces around us, forces that could turn violent in a gale, or friendly and embracing in moments such as this.

At bedtime, the wolf curled up in a cozy ball not five meters away and I snuggled into my sleeping bag, dozing off peacefully, resting tired muscles that were repairing themselves, as best as they could, molecule by molecule, cell by cell, within the limited span of eight short hours. I imagined reaching out and stroking its fur, scratching it behind the ears, and at the same time wished that my sense of smell was acute enough to sense the wolf more intimately, know when it had eaten last, and what its prey had been. In the morning, when we opened the vestibule door to permit some ventilation for our cooking stove, the wolf was standing at front of the door, watching us. At the alien sound of the zipper, it jolted briefly, hid behind a chunk of ice, then re-emerged and stopped, front legs almost crossed, head lowered, ruff flowing in the breeze like summer wheat in a Montana field, looking thinner in the shoulders than I imagined an arctic wolf to be.

Scientists have studied wolves near the Eureka weather station for thirty years, and one photo that I pulled up on the internet showed a white wolf that looked remarkably similar to our companion. So you could argue that wolves in the area have been habituated to people for generations and it should come as no surprise that this individual decided to pay us a visit. Maybe it was begging for food. Ahhh. Now we run smack-dab-head-on into that fuzzy line between logic and magic, coincidence and synchronicity. And ultimately, it's not a matter of fact versus fiction; it's about how you choose to view the world—or perhaps more appropriately—how you choose to *feel* or to *communicate* with the world around you. If you feel that the wolf was an annoyance, inappropriately adapted to humans, begging for food, then that's how you live your life; there's no argument. But, to me, life becomes so much more glorious if you align with a Crow elder who famously remarked, "You know, I think if people stay somewhere long enough—even white people—the spirits will begin to speak to them. It's the power of the spirits coming from the land. The spirits and the old powers aren't lost, they just need people to be around long enough and the spirits will begin to influence them."[9]

Boomer and I were crossing from the High Arctic to the Polar Zone. All we had was the gear in our kayaks and a GPS coordinate where we hoped to find the next food cache. We were alone, vulnerable, and, yes, subliminally scared. Yet, all those fears, in all their rawness, had incorporated us into the landscape in the most intimate manner. Then the wolf paid us a prolonged visit. If you accept the aboriginal worldview, it came to talk to us.

Does that mean that Boomer and I were special, like when God communicated with Moses through the burning bush? No. Don't be ridiculous. That's missing the point.

Was it the fairy godmother wolf promising us safe passage onto the north shore of Ellesmere? No again, don't be ridiculous. There is no fairy godmother wolf to relay comforting assurances that nature will be "kind" if we are "good." Benevolent Gods that reward good with good and fairy godmother wolves are just the product of slippery philosophical reasoning—or downright deceit.

All I know for certain is that out there on the ice, in the cold and aloneness, in some deep, visceral, aboriginal way, this particular fur-and-blood wolf visited us as a representative of nature in general. It said to me, or more precisely, its presence caused me to say to myself, "Welcome to the Polar Zone, Jon and Boomer. You will assuredly be hungry, cold, strung out, and exhausted. You might die out here. Enjoy. It is good to see you."

It's not as if I actually heard the wolf speak, in any identifiable and recordable way, either in English or in some universal creature-language that is embedded into our DNA, with cherubs flying overhead and harps playing, or with wolf packs howling into the wind like a Greek chorus. Those images are simplistic, inaccurate, open to ridicule, and, again, totally missing the point. I looked into the wolf's eyes and saw another mammal, who loved its children, feared, found joy, and sadness. And I was deeply honored that this flesh and blood wolf had taken the time, for whatever reason, to spend fifteen hours in our company. Closely on the heels of that emotion, I felt absolutely certain that this visit occurred because, in some undefinable way, Boomer and I had become integrated into this landscape, traveling alone in the vastness. It made no difference whether this was a Spirit Wolf that was talking to me, or if it was a Real Wolf whose presence triggered me to talk to myself. Whatever mysterious mechanism was going on here, and however that was manifest, the communication was a synchronous oneness with "the power of the spirits coming from the land."

That's why we were here, wasn't it? To jolt awake on a sleepy afternoon and stare eyeball to eyeball into the spirits of the land.

To accept the obvious reality that I can't play the charade that I am master of the Universe. To understand that we might die on this mission to walk around a big chunk of land for no particular reason. And to thank the wolf for relaying that message, because all that was just fine. Accurate and liberating. We weren't running the show here; we didn't have the power.

Am I a hopeless, irrelevant, and marginalized crackpot for contriving a long expedition, to travel around an island that most people haven't heard of anyway, for no other reason than to embrace the hardships, danger, and travail of our brutish, savage, hunter-gatherer ancestors? Didn't we discover agriculture to free ourselves from the vagaries of nature's cycles, and assure abundance, prosperity, and health?

I believe that this Real or Spirit Wolf, and this whole journey, contrived or not, was conveying an essential message for all of us in this über-technological world.

In my childhood, along with the dangerous myth that biblical Abraham was heroic when he threw the Earth Gods out of the temple, we learned that agriculture was the greatest invention of all times, because it freed humanity from the vagaries— vulnerability—of nature—of life. But stop right there. Can we question that? In an essay, "The Worst Mistake in the History of the Human Race" Pulitzer Prize winning author Jared Diamond argues that "in actuality, human health and welfare took a huge and catastrophic downturn when people started farming."[10]

Diamond starts his essay by pointing out that modern hunter-gatherers don't work very much to support themselves. For example, African Bushmen devote only 12 to 19 hours a week to food gathering and the Hadza nomads of Tanzania "work" about 14 hours a week. One Bushman, when asked why he hadn't emulated neighboring tribes by adopting agriculture with its long hours of toil, replied, "Why should we, when there are so many mongongo nuts in the world?"

When people made the transition from their leisure-time-rich lives in the forests and savannahs to tilling the ground, not only did they lose their leisure, but their health took a dramatic downturn. According to Diamond, "Skeletons from Greece and Turkey show that the average height of hunter-gatherers toward the end of the Ice Ages was a generous 5' 9" for men, 5' 5" for women. With the adoption of agriculture, height crashed, and by 3000 B.C. had reached a low of only 5' 3" for men, 5' for women. By classical times, heights were very slowly on the rise again, but modern Greeks and Turks have still not regained the average height of their distant ancestors."

Skeletal analyses show that when people shifted from hunting to maize farming in the Western Hemisphere, the combination of hard work, reliance on a few starchy crops, risk of starvation when these crops failed, and concentration of pathogens caused by the aggregation of people into crowded societies all combined to cause skyrocketing prevalence of tooth decay, malnutrition, iron-deficiency anemia, infectious diseases and degenerative conditions of the spine. Average life expectancy at birth plummeted from 26 years to an almost unbelievably young 19. How can you grow up, have children, and care for them, if you die before you reach the ripe old age of 20? Well, clearly, some people lived longer, but nevertheless, the onset of agriculture seriously threatened the survival of early agricultural tribes.

What were the ten plagues that devastated biblical, agricultural Egypt? Blood. Frogs. Lice. Flies. Dead cows. Boils. Hail. Locusts. Darkness. Death of the First Born.

The paradox of all this is that even though agriculture was a "bad idea," leading to higher workloads, more disease, and shorter lifespans, agriculture also created a non-nomadic civilization that was conducive to producing a lot of babies. And even though a majority of these infants died horrible and early deaths, enough survived so that the population, after stalling for a while, eventually exploded. Soon farmers organized massive and efficient armies that quickly conquered the remaining hunter-gatherers and stole their land.

Let's jump quickly to the early 17th century, when René Descartes ushered in the "Age of Reason" by arguing that conclusions should be built logically on observation and experimentation, rather than on belief and spiritual dogma. In the hundred fifty years following his death in 1650, the Western world became drunk on discovery, invention, and political change. Electricity and steam engines improved people's lives beyond their wildest imaginations. People built factories with the first rudimentary assembly lines; they churned out clocks, microscopes, flush toilets, and fountain pens, paving the way for modern WalMarts. Doctors performed the first appendectomy. The American colonies, and later the French, threw off monarchies, replacing the white-wigged aristocracy with democracy, Enlightenment, and then the blood-filled, head-chopping-off Reign of Terror. All this led to the belief, reasonable up to a point, that mastery of nature would lead to freedom, comfort, and security. Throw out the old Wolf Gods; bring in agriculture and monotheism, followed by science and technology, and everything will be rosy. And that is where we are today, opulent beyond the wildest imagination of 17th century philosophers, scientists, or even kings. In Canada today, life expectancy is not 19 years, or 26 years, but 80 for males and 84 for females.

So, what's the scorecard here? I'm one of the lucky people on this planet, wrapped in technological luxuries, 70 years old, and still skiing and riding my mountain bike aggressively. What can be the downside to that? Well, for one, there's a billion fellow humans just hanging on, in abject poverty, or actually starving. That's a lot of misery, which just isn't right or good for everyone. And then, we got so good at controlling our environment and creating long life and opulence that we have gotten addicted to control and opulence, and forgotten about the wolf, about oneness, and vulnerability. And somewhere along the line a potentially good thing has turned against us, generating overpopulation, global warming, and other environmental catastrophes that threaten our civilization.

Thirty-five years ago, in 1980, the average American had approximately half the wealth that she or he had in 2015[11]. In other words, if you or I were willing to scale down the amount of stuff we own, the size of our houses, the number of miles we travel, and so on, to the lifestyles we lived in 1980, we could all work half time and make half the impact we now make on the planet. I was 35 years old in 1980. I had a loving wife, two cars, telephone, TV, warm house, lots of food, and good health. As far as I can remember, I had everything I needed. Have I really doubled that? It's hard to imagine. Going back to 1980 isn't like going back to the Stone Age.

So what are we buying with all this money? Freedom, comfort, and security? Ecstasy? Openness to synchronicity? Many of us in the environmental movement believe that while our political leaders and corporate CEOs are trying to convince us that this phenomenal increase in purchasing power is improving our lifestyles and increasing security, there is ample evidence that we have reached a tipping point where just the opposite is happening. Let's go down the line.

On average, are we buying more health? Nope, sorry, not that. Over the past 35 years, despite incredible developments in medicine, the health status of people in the United States, the richest nation on Earth, has declined. According to a recent report issued by the US National Research Council and Institute of Medicine, the United States, "is last among peer nations in health status...at almost every stage of life...adverse birth outcomes, heart disease, injuries from motor vehicle accidents, gun violence, sexually acquired diseases, and chronic lung disease. Americans lose more years of life to alcohol and other drugs. .. [they have] the highest rate of infant mortality among high-income countries and the second highest incidence of AIDS and ischemic heart disease [as well as]...the highest rates of obesity and diabetes in children and adults."[12]

Okay, if we're not healthier, then surely all that money must be buying what the first farmers and political leaders were striving for so many years ago: an urban-agricultural infrastructure more secure than the old hunter-gatherer reliance on nature. At the moment, my life is pretty good. But are we approaching a tipping point here, too? In a recent article in the prestigious scientific journal, *Nature,* the author states, "Today's strongly connected, global networks have produced highly interdependent systems that we do not understand and cannot control well. These systems are vulnerable to failure at all scales, posing serious threats to society, even when external shocks are absent."[13]

What about our financial systems? Raise your hands, please. How many people out there feel cuddly-teddy-bear secure in the global banking infrastructure? Nobel Prize winning economist Paul Krugman writes in *The New York Times*, "In recent years the intervals between [financial] crises seem to be getting shorter, and the fallout from each crisis seems to be worse than the last. What's going on?"[14]

And then of course there's global warming, overpopulation, water scarcity, thermonuclear bombs, and the looming threat of energy scarcity that threaten all of these man-made systems.

My argument is that we've reached a cosmic paradox: For our civilization to continue in a smooth, uninterrupted fashion, we must cheerfully reduce our physical opulence and embrace vulnerability to assure security. Joy. Contentment. Wholeness. That is what Tundra, and Wolf, and our little contrived modern adventure can tell us.

In a fascinating TED talk, "The Power of Vulnerability," Brené Brown starts with the argument: "Connection, the ability to feel connected, is—neurobiologically that's how we're wired— it's why we're here."[15]

Then she asks, what is the difference between people who feel connected, and those who do not? And she concludes that people who are connected (and content with life) have "fully embraced vulnerability. They believed that what made them vulnerable made them beautiful. They didn't talk about vulnerability being comfortable, nor did they really talk about it being excruciating… They just talked about it being necessary…that the way to live is…to stop controlling and predicting."

While Brené talks mainly about social connectivity and vulnerability, the same arguments and conclusions apply to our reciprocal relationship with our environment. Ten thousand years ago people tossed out the bear spirits, wolf spirits, and storm spirits—and replaced them with a single God who controlled the cosmos in an absolute, hands-on manner. They told us that if we embraced the new technology and, incidentally, if we were good, and got down on our hands and knees and beseeched this God to take care of our problems, everything would be hunky-dory. Well, sorry to rain on your parade, but it doesn't work that way.

Out there on the ice, it was obvious that Boomer and I were two tired, hungry men, with heavy loads and painful feet. We were alone and fragile, in an environment generally hostile to humans. Wolf was telling us that to survive, we must joyfully accept the possibility that we would not survive. I have taken the liberty of expanding that message into a broader, global metaphor that, to me, is just as obvious. To survive, humans must first reject the worn-out worthless paradigm that we are in control of the situation (because we're not), or that technology will eventually place us in control (which it does, to a point, but then gets us into trouble). Then we would be wise to reinstate critical, vital elements of the old cooperative, reciprocal relationship with nature, with all its inherent chaos and unpredictability, and all its creatures, great and small.

There is a movement in Western civilized countries today called Deep Ecology, which is the belief that everything is inter-connected and therefore the entire environment, all the plants and animals, as well as the inanimate ice, should be honored with the inalienable right to live and flourish, independent of its direct, immediate, provable usefulness for humans. Aboriginal people never needed a Deep Ecology movement because all of those fancy words were so integrally woven into their spirituality, functionality, and physical survival that Deep Ecology just *was*.

Boomer and I finished our breakfast and broke camp. The wolf wandered off. We hitched our heavy kayak-sleds to our harnesses, and headed across the ice, toward the feared and potentially fearsome north coast.

THE NORTHWEST COAST

For the past few weeks, we seemed to pass back and forth between spring and winter, like watching the sunrise several times in a single morning, by walking up a hill and to catch the orange globe on the horizon and then back down the hill, into the shadow. Some days the temperatures were well above freezing and we waded through deep slush pools that floated on the ice, and on other days the seascape locked back into frozen winter. Through it all we doggedly maintained our 15 mile per day mandated average.

On the night of June 3rd, we dozed off to sleep listening to the ever-so-soft sound of wet snow falling on the thin, nylon walls of our tent. Within an hour we were enveloped in deep white silence as the accumulated snow muffled its own voices. In the morning, we waded through the soggy, calf-deep snow, dug out the buried boats, and hooked up our harnesses. I jerked my boat free of its resting place, traveled a few meters, and stalled out. I jerked against the traces again, moved fifteen centimeters, slipped, and jerked again. Boomer took the lead, but even with his incredible, youthful strength, breaking trail and pulling the kayak-sled through the deep, sticky, mush was agonizingly difficult and slow. After fifteen minutes, Boomer stepped aside to rest and I took over. As the day wore on, we evolved a pattern, Boomer would break trail for half an hour and then I would break for fifteen minutes. Repeat. We made eight miles that day, seven miles short of the 15 mile per day average we needed to complete the expedition in 100 days. "Lost time" is one of those civilized phrases implying that there is something critically important to accomplish at every instant, and if we watch the sunset, or take a nap, or go fishing, that time has become misplaced, darn it, like losing your car keys. But "lost time" had meaning for us here, because we had a finite amount of food and also a finite distance to the next resupply, and if the two didn't match up, we would starve. So "lost time" was akin to "calories burned," and was, in fact, a real and persistent concern. In addition, even though we were traveling on a frozen ocean right now, the temperatures were relatively mild. Soon the air would get even warmer and ice would melt. And then, presto, shortly afterward, winter would return with full polar speed and ferocity and the ocean would settle into a deep, dark, frigid, silence, offset by pulsing, shape-changing, glowing aurora and we could not possibly survive with the clothing we had with us. Throughout those natural rhythms, we had created an artificial reality where distance was survival, because we were racing to circle away from civilization and then back to that land where coal and oil, wrested from the earth, sustained us in a way that we could not sustain ourselves as our ancestors had.

Over the next few days, temperatures warmed and the snow became even heavier, wetter, and stickier. It was melting, but watching 40 cm of new snow melt is not a high-action spectator sport. On shore, rocks absorbed the heat of the June sunlight, so that the snow on the hillsides was melting faster than it was on the sea ice. Rivers broke up and began to flow. In turn the flowing water melted the sea ice near the deltas. Geese sensed, or knew, or learned, that this open water had just appeared, and they flew from somewhere in the forested southland, across a desolate land-scape to land here, seeking a home to raise their young, relatively free of predators and fed by an abundant bloom of polar aquatic life. Boomer and I sat on our boats for a snack break, watching the geese glide in for their end-of-the-journey reunion and listening to their joyful honking. Then we started fretting again about the sticky snow, our slow travel, and the possibility of rough ice and even slower travel on the north coast.

Oh, I count coup on me. How could I be so fickle—once again—making a solemn pact with the Spirit Wolf about embracing vulnerability and then, barely a week later, allowing myself to get stressed out by a spring snowfall in the Polar Arctic, a totally normal act of nature? Oh, it's devilishly tricky being a big-brained human some days.

Our snack break over, it was my turn to break trail, so I jerked my kayak into motion and concentrated on skiing forward at a steady pace, without hurrying or stopping.

By the first week of June we had moved north out of Nansen Sound into the Arctic Ocean proper. Here the sea ice never melts completely, even in summer, like a glacier, and over the years, it is buffeted by melt-thaw, currents, and wind. The ocean locks up into solid immobility, then it breaks up into massive chunks that float around, break and smash, get tilted, ground down, partially melted and refrozen. It's like an old mountain range, compressed and torn by tectonic forces, with some rock removed by weathering and erosion, and new rock added by slow intrusion of magma or volcanic eruptions.

As I write this, I pull up a photograph of Boomer near Lands Lokk, where we finally turned eastward along the north shore. He is trudging along on his skis, leaning into his harness, dressed in base layers only, with no parka or hat. His beard has grown, and his sandy blond hair is frazzled, but somehow he still looks tidy, as if on a weekend camping trip. He's moving through a small opening between two blocks of multiyear ice, each about three meters tall. The new snow that had given us so much trouble for the past week had now passed through enough freeze-thaw cycles so that it had consolidated. During this consolidation process, hard windblown snow had filled in the spaces between the jagged, angular ice, creating ramps and bridges that made travel easy once again.

Even though travel had become easier, we worked as hard

over favorable snow as when the snow was wet and sticky. Every day, no matter what the conditions, we forged onward until we were utterly exhausted; we just traveled farther over "good" snow than over "bad" snow. I wrote in my journal:

"I start seeing double earlier and earlier every afternoon. Feeling faint, disoriented, half-hallucinating, on the edge of falling, but not really because I don't fall. I stare into Boomer's tracks, trying to sort out the blurs, and oblivious to the wild glaciated peaks of Ellesmere to the south. We have 177 miles remaining to our food drop and our half-way point for the entire journey. Then we'll be heading home and I can start 'gliding gracefully into geezerhood' because this is my retirement party. I'm not strong enough to do something like this ever again."

Thinking about that passage now, five years later, from the comfort of a warm house, I see that journey not as a retirement party, but an accelerated experiment into the unavoidable process of finally growing really old, when I hope to find joy and contentment and when I will perpetually be 'faint, disoriented, half-hallucinating, on the edge of falling.'

Reading onward in my journal, *"By an hour before quitting, time ends for me completely, but as Boomer calculated from GPS coordinates, in my fatigue-infused dream state, I actually speeded up. I have no idea how I kept moving one foot in front of the other. I was running on empty, like the proverbial chicken dashing around the farmyard without its head."*

The next entry reads, *"Boomer's Chinese piece-of-shit spoon that he stole from McDonalds is even more mangled than it was before, if that could conceivably be, and he borrows my superior spoon to stir the dinner."* Obviously I needed to change the subject and avoid a meaningless contemplation of my own mortality. The spoon, at least, was real, tactile and mildly humorous.

My next photo, from the following day, shows Boomer shirtless among multiple blocks of three meter fractured ice. Most of the windblown snow ramps have melted, so the angularity of the ice is exposed. One of Boomer's skis is shorter than the other, because he broke one ski stepping over the sharp edges of naked ice. Then he moved the binding forward, off the center point of the ski, which would be awkward if he tried to make turns, but we were just trudging.

On the airplane flight north, I had sat next to a scientist who told me that the ice was likely to be roughest at any exposed cape on the north shore and that Cape Colgate would be our first test. Following his failure to reach The Great Nail in 1906, Robert Peary sailed along this stretch of coast in the ship *Roosevelt* and "discovered" Cape Colgate. He went to shore and climbed the adjacent 700-meter mountain and reported that he had sighted distant land to the north. Following the flow of money, he named the mysterious (and nonexistent) island Crocker Land after one of his sponsors, San Francisco banker George Crocker. As it turns out, Peary not only lied, but he admitted his lie in his own journal, like Nixon admitting the Watergate scandal on tape, and then not destroying the tapes. Anyway, Crocker was not sufficiently vain to be impressed by the glory of having his name plastered on an imaginary island, and failed to support Peary's next expedition.

The Capes spread out before us: Bourne, Armstrong, Woods, Alfred Earnst, Mitchell, Hansen, Evans, Egerton, Bicknor, and so on, each with its own obscure bit of Arctic lore, all named after white men who had either discovered the place, died there, or coughed up money for others to go or die there. Day after day, our journey was charmed. Mostly, we found easy routes through the jumbled ice. In a few places where the sea ice was particularly rough, we hiked up on land and scooted quickly across nearly flat, featureless glaciers, which we called "ice toes" because of the way they jutted out into the sea.

Boomer and I were living in a world of frozen water, which appeared in many forms: snow on ice, snow on land, one-year ice, multiyear ice, glaciers, and ice toes. We walked on this frozen water, slept on it, and melted it for cooking and drinking. Our progress and hence our survival depended on our relationship to it. Snow and ice were everything, everybody, and everywhere. We talked about it constantly. How fast will the snow consolidate? What will it consolidate into? Will our travel speed up or slow down? When the snow melts on top of the ice, it cannot percolate downward, because ice is impermeable and it cannot flow away; because the sea ice is flat, so it sits there and turns to slush or shallow fresh-water lakes that lie on top of ice.

Boomer and I spent a lot of time and expended a great deal of interest and thought on watching the snow melt. When I get old, nearing death, and all that advertising becomes so meaningless because more stuff won't change my fate, and I hope I won't care anymore about politics, maybe I can find fulfillment in watching the snow melt, or spring blossom. And the greater point, which Moolynaut tried to teach me, is that at any stage in life, if I can enter into a reciprocal relationship with the earth, then environmentalism will become part of me, glorious, meaningful, life-sustaining, not some outside and tedious sacrifice.

Although we had experienced twenty-four-hour daylight from the beginning of the expedition, with the proximity to the solstice and our far northerly location, the sun remained high in the sky perpetually. It would rise in the east, as it does in temperate latitudes, travel across the sky toward the west and then turn north where it would complete its lazy circle back to the eastern horizon. Nights were bright, but somewhat cooler than days so Boomer and I took advantage of the firmest snow and traveled in what civilized people would call the "wee hours of the morning."

Following is a chronicle of the last nine days to our food cache in the manner that I recorded it, image snippets from my journal, extracted from Dream Time:

> *June 13: I feel tired waking at 3:00 AM, which is silly, because it is just a number on an electronic device... Boomer's bindings pull out of his skis and he Rube*

Goldberg's it back together. Stupid fucking bindings. My skis crack.

June 14: We are only 85 miles from our food cache at Ward Hunt Island. There's an emergency airstrip there as well. If I broke my leg now, I could crawl there if need be, but it would suck.

June 15: We have had information from many sources that this combination of slush and polar pack, can form nearly impenetrable barriers where we will be forced to take off our skis and work together, two men to a single boat, to lift it over closely spaced parallel pressure ridges, making a mile or less a day. This has not happened yet. Made 13.3 miles today, just a smidge below our required average.

June 16: There's rough ice all around us, but we keep finding a path, sometimes on the ice toes, other times right against the shore, occasionally out a mile or more from shore. Adventure involves making a decision, a guess, a hunch, based on incomplete information, and then being so confident that you put your life on the line. So far, so good.

June 17: Smooth ice, some cracks all the way down to deep, black, salt water, but nothing we can't jump over. Made 15.4 miles, like the old days.

June 18: The snow is becoming increasingly rotten with lots of melt-water pools floating on the surface. Our feet are swelling from constant immersion in cold wetness. We cut holes in our shoes to make a little extra room for the swollen feet and to let the water drain out faster when we hit dry snow.

June 19: It's hard work dragging these kayaks through the slush. Skis sink. Tips get stuck in the muck. My feet have been soaking in ice water for so long that the skin is shriveling up like a prune and peeling off. My feet

hurt. It's too warm. Before that it was too cold. I'm tired.
Hungry. Wimpy. Whining. Poor me.

June 20: Hooray. We made it to the Ward Hunt
Ice Shelf—somehow. Our food cache is close. We have
completed nearly half the expedition. We were either very
lucky or very clever. I'll never know. Maybe a wee bit of
both.

PRINGLES AND RUM

In the temperate and even the equatorial regions, glaciers form
on high mountains where the temperature is consistently low
enough and the precipitation high enough, so winter snow never
melts completely in summer and therefore accumulates. In the
Arctic and Antarctic, temperatures are consistently cold enough
so glaciers flow right down to the sea, and then keep going. An
ice shelf is an extension of a land based glacier that has continued
flowing out into the ocean and is now floating on seawater.
Today, the largest ice shelves are found along the Antarctic coastlines but there are a few smaller ones on Greenland, and to a lesser
extent, Ellesmere. The Ward Hunt Ice Shelf is the last remnant of
a nearly continuous ice shelf that formed on the north coast of
Ellesmere 3,000 years ago, and then began gradually breaking up
as the temperature rose and precipitation declined. This break-up
accelerated dramatically starting in the spring of 2000 under the
influence of human-caused global warming.

Because an ice shelf is much thicker than sea ice, fractures
created a new potential problem of having to cross crevasses in
the ice that would be too wide to jump across and too deep and
precipitous to climb into and out of, without proper climbing
equipment. Fortunately, the first crevasse we encountered was old
enough so the edges had melted into a rounded valley, rather than
an abrupt cliff. Boomer jumped on his boat, with his butt in his
cockpit and legs spread out in front of him, like a bronc rider out

of the chute, and slid down the ice hill, splashing across the deep freshwater lake at the bottom. I chickened out, lowered my boat in a controlled manner, and then paddled across. Then we helped each other drag the boats up the ice hill on the other side.

On June 21st, we reached our food cache that was sitting on the ice in three steel barrels. Coincidentally it was also the summer solstice, the turn-around point in the sun's northward journey. We had bought that food in a multi-shopping-cart binge, when Tyler was still one of us, before he broke his back. I had packaged this huge pile of food into small baggies, so we could accurately ration individual meals. Then I had stuffed the baggies into many small cardboard boxes and mailed all the boxes to Resolute. After a large number of emails and phone calls, expenditure of $6,000, and considerable hair-pulling, some pilot, whom we never met, flew over this place, found flat ice, landed, unloaded the heavy barrels, and wrote down the GPS coordinates on a piece of scrap paper. At the last minute, Boomer had tossed in a few non-essential goodies. We opened a box of Pringles and Boomer held two of the perfectly formed chips between his lips, so he looked like Donald Duck. Feeling giddy and silly we shared a nip of rum. I felt like crying but didn't want to show my emotion.

In a sense, this expedition had started in 1988, when Chris and I dragged and paddled our kayaks along the east coast of Ellesmere. I was 43 at the time, older than Boomer but considerably younger than I was now. I was a late bloomer in this expedition business. When I was Boomer's age, I was still in graduate school. And then I bumbled around for fifteen years, being a nomad, being married, getting divorced, raising kids, and working as a carpenter, raising chickens, doing a wee bit of horse logging, spending a few seasons as a commercial fisherman, and, oh yes, writing books. Looking back at it all, it was madness, but perhaps understandable madness—and a fun madness. Once I realized that I couldn't spend my life in a lab, with a secure salary and a respectable position in society, I stared into the void, with no models to follow, trying all the lifestyle experiments simultaneously, jumbling the responsibility of being a father with the irresponsibility of running away from an urban society that I could no longer accept. I hurt people along the way and I apologize.

My early expeditions were all disasters. When I tried to kayak around Cape Horn, on the southern tip of South America—solo—I got caught in a storm, washed into the surf, dislocated my shoulder, lost my boat, and swam through the Antarctic Ocean to shore. Then I hobbled back to a Chilean military base—cold, wet, half starved, and defeated. I failed again on an attempt at rowing the Northwest Passage, and then turned back, when I could have kept going, on a winter dogsled passage on Baffin Island. But on the first expedition to Ellesmere Island in 1988, two powerful teachers, the landscape and Chris, joined together to help me shed that frenetic escape mentality. At the end of that expedition, the narwhals paid us a visit, the first time a wild animal came to speak to me, or, more likely, the first time I stopped to listen to the wild animals who had been trying to speak to me all along. And the narwhals "brought us the magic that we had traveled so far to find."

There are a zillion other ways to make this journey of discovery. My friend Eloise once told me, with a playful smile, that I am seeking what many others seek, only I make a big deal about it, and then hit myself over the head with a heavy stick. Fair enough. I'm just using the tools I know how to use.

We broke the food packages down into bags that could fit into the kayak hatches, and filled the boats until they were overloaded and too heavy again. But there was no alternative. We had no more food drops. I had contacted the military base at Alert, on the northeast corner of the island, but they had never responded and we were unsure of our reception if we stopped by to beg a shower and dinner. So, with a half a day's rest and a few more shots of rum, we headed east, across the crumbling remains of the Ward Hunt Ice Shelf, a visual reminder of civilization's inroads into the most remote landscapes on the planet. There is no Deep Wild, really, because we are all ensconced in the Anthropocene.

ECSTASY

June 23: "Woke at 2:30 AM and looked out of tent. Snowing. Felt like going back to sleep. My turn to cook and the stove quit. That sort of morning. Followed a convenient ice toe around the next cape, then we went back onto sea ice. Smooth ice, then rubbly. Traveling over the rough, angular ice, Boomer's ski breaks, for about the third or fourth time, I can't remember, so we move the bindings around again, until the set-up looks downright silly. Over pressure ridge ice and then onto smooth ice. All this involves a lot of huffing and puffing. Boomer announces, 'This is fun. Finally I feel like I'm really on the North Coast. When it was easy, back there, I felt that we were cheating.' I smile and agree—halfheartedly—because I am too tired to really agree but because it would be too much work to disagree. In the afternoon, Boomer's ski breaks yet again and we decide that skis are sort of useless in this terrain anyway—jagged blocks of ice, interspersed with melt-water pools."

Chris and I built a marriage around skiing. We skied on our first date. And on our wedding day. We were married 24 years and 11 months, before Chris and Will Crljenko died together in an avalanche on the East Face of Mount Tom, in the high Sierra. We all made mistakes and no one needed to die that day. I've written about the accident a few times already, and I don't have the energy to do it again, trying to explain, explore, or rationalize the innate danger of big-mountain skiing, interwoven with our own mistakes, our own frailty, and the natural chaos of existence. Two years after the accident, I married Nina Maclean, Chris's best friend. Now Nina is my partner, lover, ski buddy, best friend, and teacher.

One of the disadvantages of growing old is that you live to see others die. I always knew that this journey around Ellesmere was, in part, a memorial to Chris and our 1988 expedition, the shared danger, the day the narwhals visited us, her quiet appreciation of wilderness with no complex explanations or goals. She had no need to write books to explain herself. I crossed the ice this far on the blue Atomic OT Telemark skis that we married in, and now that summer was here, and the snow had melted, I set the cracked and useless skis against an ice floe, took a picture, and said goodbye, embracing and accepting grief once again, because grief will never go away; it can only be acknowledged now and again, or more precisely, every day of my life. In a few weeks, the ice would melt, and the skis would sink to the ocean floor, to be encrusted in rust and barnacles. So the first and present Ellesmere expeditions were bookends for me—the beginning and end of my adventure career. The marriage and final goodbye to Chris. But only as bookends that are created by the storyteller, because in reality it is all a continuum.

With the skis behind us, and ragged, tilted, slippery ice ahead, we strapped on lightweight crampons and forged onward.

> *June 24: "Travel into heavy rubble ice early in the day. At times, there is just too much resistance to pull the loaded boats forward while standing on two feet. So we crawl. There's more power that way. Both of us do it. Even Boomer. When you've got 750 miles to go and you're crawling through saturated slush and frigid meltwater pools, soaked to the skin, you've got to shut the mind off. Stop thinking, stop calculating miles versus food remaining. Don't even suffer. Just crawl. It's clean. Fundamental. Cathartic. Then we find smooth ice right against the shore and we stand up and walk again, as if we have just evolved from knuckle-walking apes to humans. Most of the snow has melted off the land and in the*

afternoon we find purple flowers lying low to the ground. No, I don't know what species they are; it is just wonderful that they are purple. We run out of smooth ice but find some melt-water pools a few hundred meters offshore that are so extensive that we sit in our kayaks, float along and push with our ski poles. Luxury. At river mouths, the sea ice has melted for a short distance and we paddle. It's warm today so melting and breakup are happening quickly. Boomer says that this is, 'The best day yet.' That's fine. Again, I just agree. My small toes are quite gnarled and bloody. They hurt with every step. Throb when I go to sleep."

June 25: "Snow. Ice. Melt-water pools. Actually paddled a little. Drag, paddle, pole, paddle, drag, crawl. Rubble to the north is scary in its impenetrability. If we ran into that, it would be a show stopper. But we find flat ice near shore. We've always found a way."

June 26: "Very hot today and everything is melting. But there is a lot of ice to melt. A whole ocean of ice. Rubble, open leads. The pressure ridges are so formidable that we help each other, two men to a boat, walk back, and get the other one. Yet somehow we made 11 miles today. Is my GPS broken or did we really do that? My toes are oozing blood and pus but for some weird reason, I think they will be ok. I am fine. My toe is just a small part of me."

June 27: "At one point during the day I dragged my kayak onto the top of a chunk of ice, and then walked down into the melt-water pool below. My kayak slid down, speared me in the left calf, and knocked me into the icy water. Splash. Full, spread eagled immersion. Now I'm wet from head to toe. I strip naked, wring out my garments so they will dry faster against my skin, dress again, and continue onward, doggedly. My calf aches and

I am limping. When I catch up to Boomer, he is cheery, oblivious to what happened. 'Hey buddy, if you just drag your boat onto that pressure ridge, over there, even though it is out of your way, I'll get a great photo. It's all set up.' We laugh about it in the evening, but at the time I wasn't amused."

June 28: "Embrace the crawl. When you're trying to drag a 250 pound boat over a dune of ice and snow, and you're sinking crotch deep into slush, don't try to preserve your dignity. Dignity is a foreign concept from another cosmos. Crawl. The boats tip over a lot. Lots of walking back to direct the boat into the correct slot between ice chunks, because we are weaving around obstacles all day. We made eight miles, half of what we did on flat ice. That still seems a lot, given the conditions."

June 29: "I got nailed hard in the right calf today when the boat slid out of control. A moment of carelessness. This is the foot with the bad toe. I'm limping on both legs now, which should cancel into a non-limp, but it doesn't. I sit down on an ice block and cut a bigger chunk out of my boot to relieve pressure on my toe. But it doesn't seem to do any good. I have to leave some remnants of boot on my foot or the boot will simply disintegrate."

June 30: "We've been traveling and camping on the ice for 55 days, this solid, seemingly permanent but impermanent floating world. Lately, the ice has water floating on top. No big deal. The continents have water floating on top, but they're still solid continents. But now you look into opening leads and the water between the fractured ice is a deep dark blue, extending all the way to the ocean floor. We always knew that this continental-sized expanse of solid sea ice was impermanent, but now, somehow it is unsettling that it is fracturing and melting—disappearing before our eyes—even though it should be comforting because that is the way it is meant to be. We're camped on a flat pan of dry ice and during the night we hear a rumbling of great magnitude. I wake with a start, because I fear that our ice pan is breaking apart, but in reality it is a landslide from Cape Joseph Henry. So, tonight, the solid continent is moving and the melting ice is stable, which is vaguely upside down, as it should be.

July 1: "Very rubbly ice. No linear travel more than a boat length. So we decide to go to land and look for some snow, or a little bit of open water right against the shore. But there is a seven-meter near-vertical ice cliff adjacent to land. We're standing on a pan of ice, about as long as my kayak. Boomer climbs the ice cliff and I hand him a few bags, so we can get some weight out of the heavy boats and then lift them up and over. Suddenly, Boomer is sliding away from me. Why is he running away? Wait a minute. He is standing still. The ice is moving. No I am moving. Everything is moving. The whole ice pack has cracked into pieces and is moving. Did that just happen? This moment? The ice wasn't moving five minutes ago. I drift to a place where the ice cliff is less formidable, and we haul the boats out. Then the ice stops moving again. What's going on here? It doesn't matter. We find a narrow lead of open water, and paddle."

July 2: "We are close to the military base at Alert. Maybe they will feed us, give us a rest day. I am spent, done, finished. My toe looks and feels horrible, mangled and showing the meat that lies beneath the thin and fragile layer of skin. I make a conscious decision today not to pretend that I am above the pain. Just endure. I am good at enduring; I've done it before. Count the miles. Open your heart to this pain. Accept it. Embrace it. My only rule to myself is not to get so grumpy that I say something unpleasant to Boomer that I would later regret and have *to apologize for. I've done that already and don't need to repeat it."*

That day there was no energy left in my brain for subterfuge or posturing. I did what was necessary to drag my kayak across the ice. The first of the Four Noble Truths in Buddhism starts with the observation that in life, pain is unavoidable. We stub our toe when walking into the bathroom, get old, watch loved ones pass away, suffer economic setbacks, and eventually each and every one of us dies. No one escapes this reality. But suffering, which is an emotional response to pain, is a decision we allow ourselves to make, and is absolutely and unequivocally avoidable.

I'm not a Buddhist acolyte or scholar. But, from my own experience, suffering occurs when that pesky think-too-much-know-it-all brain takes a simple event—which started out maybe slightly negative, or maybe even positive or neutral—it doesn't matter—and twists that event up into knots, invents side-plots and intrigue, runs it around and around in feedback loops, like a puppy chasing its tail, until it grows, explodes, matures, over-runs the castle, and emerges triumphant as true misery. Suffering. We've all done it. But out there on the ice, there is no room for that bullshit. No energy. Life is on too thin a line to allow the brain to indulge in its favorite pastime—the luxury of extraneous emotional misery. So a sore toe is just a sore toe. It hurts. Nothing more and nothing less. So simple. So liberating.

Jesus, Moses, and Buddha all wandered off into the desert to fast and find awakening. Most, perhaps all, aboriginal cultures embrace some intentionally induced pain, such as fasting or self-mutilation, as part of their religious and cultural rituals. The great Inuit shaman Igjugarjuk, once said, "All true wisdom is only to be learned far from the dwellings of men, out in the great solitude, and is only to be obtained through pain."[16] I would disagree that this is the "only" way, but agree that it is one way.

Thus, counterintuitive as it may seem, pain can lead to ecstasy, not suffering.

Ecstasy is one of those complex words with seemingly contradictory meanings. The party drug *Ecstasy* makes you feel good, which is the usual connotation of the word, to slide into a state of great rapture. But rapture is so much more complicated than dancing all night and joining sweaty bodies in the wee hours of the morning. The word *ecstasy* is derived, in part, from the Latin *extasis*, for "terror." Of all the many definitions of ecstasy, the one I like best is, "It is a subjective experience of total involvement." You are in an ecstatic state when you are terrified, enraptured, or otherwise "totally involved" with something, whether it is music, prayer, meditation, painting on cave walls, sex, skiing, or even pain.

All those words aside, July 2 was a hard day. But Boomer and I made our miles. Pitched the tent. Cooked dinner. And as I wrote in my journal, *"For one more 24-hour period, we escaped total, complete, and irrevocable disaster because Boomer's piece-of-shit spoon didn't break."*

THE WARRIOR AND
THE POLITICIAN

On Sunday, July 3rd, we woke up with two miles of medium-rough ice separating us from the communications towers at Alert. There was a rhythm to our travel now. I had an intuitive knowledge of when my boat would catch on a piece of jagged ice and flip over, when it was most efficient to stop and adjust the boat's position to work around an obstacle, when to muscle over, or when I should turn or shorten the rope connecting me to the boat—all those mini decisions. So there was a choreographed dance encompassing me, the ice, and the boat. And our speed reflected that, because we were moving almost as fast as we had traveled on much smoother ice.

We reached land, left the boats on the beach, and walked

along a good dirt road, parallel to an aircraft runway, past numerous communications towers, hobbling along on those bloody feet and bruised calves. After a mile, we reached the base, a collection of industrial, rectangular, unfriendly buildings, set incongruously in this remote wilderness, so far north that no one actually lived here permanently. We met a few men, dressed too warmly for the summer day, because they spent so much time indoors that they really didn't know what clothes to wear when they stepped out of their metal, heated, electrified, cocoons.

"Holy fuck! Where did you guys come from?"

A man pulled his cell phone out of a pocket and we posed for photos. Then the civilian-clad soldiers ushered us into the main reception and dining area, dominated by several large flat screen TVs, with a bowl of potato chips and another bowl of fruit on a central table, all to assure us that we were no longer, actually, in the Arctic. I slipped an apple and an orange into my pocket and munched on some salty, greasy chips—free calories and yummy fruit that we hadn't dragged across the ice. A cook appeared with a plate of pastries, which I tried to eat slowly, but gobbled down anyway.

Then someone announced with a clear order, "You guys wait here until the commanding officer arrives." It sounded threatening, but no worries. We sat on chairs for the first time in weeks, and ate another plate of pastries. A very fit looking guy with a weather-beaten face appeared—the kind of man who could do 500 push-ups before breakfast if he wanted to. By the way he carried himself, and by the deference other people showed, he was high in the command hierarchy, although no one at the base wore uniforms or insignia. I nicknamed him immediately, The Warrior. We exchanged a brief account of our journey so far and then I asked him if he could spare some Neosporin and some fresh bandaging materials, because, right now, my toes were more important than my stomach. Before he could answer, an older, slightly pudgy guy with a permanent scowl, like Dick Cheney, walked in. The Politician.

Without so much as a "How do you do?" He started right in, "This is a secret military base. How did you find us? How did you penetrate our perimeter? You are not welcome here. We cannot host you."

Secret? Huh? On every map of Canada I've ever seen, there is a little red dot on the northeast coast of Ellesmere, with the label, "Alert." And if you were a Russian military expert, in charge of programming missiles with target coordinates, you could Google, "Alert Military Base", and you would be directed right to Wikipedia, which will give you the GPS coordinates (82°30'N; 62°19'W) and the mission, "Canadian Forces Station Alert, also CFS Alert, is a Canadian Forces signals intelligence intercept facility located in Alert, Nunavut on the northeastern tip of Ellesmere Island." I decided to keep this valuable information to myself. The Politician didn't want to hear it. Instead he went on to complain that the only reason we were able to "penetrate the perimeter" was that it was Sunday, and the sentries had the day off, with the implication that we had planned our Sunday arrival as part of some nefarious invasion or spy strategy.

While The Politician started to rant that if he relented to help us, soon the whole polar zone would be inundated with veritable crowds of hippie nutcases who would also demand assistance, The Warrior tapped me on the shoulder and silently guided me out of the room, down the hallway, and into a medical treatment facility, where a physician's assistant asked me to take off my shoes. I joked self-consciously that my feet were really yukky: Dirty, smelly, and bloody. She smiled kindly and explained patiently, "Look, I've been a combat medic for two tours in Afghanistan. Just take off your shoes." So I took off my shoes and socks and she luxuriously bathed my feet in warm water with Epsom salts. While I sat there, seemingly floating in a painless ether, The Warrior explained that, although he was actually only second in command, "This is my base." I wasn't at all surprised when he continued that he was a commando eco-challenge racer, and a trainer of Special

Forces units, from all over the western world, in the art of Arctic warfare.

According to some rule that someone devised, in some city far away, the personnel at Alert were allowed to help Arctic adventurers only in "extreme medical emergency." Clearly a sore toe didn't fit this definition, so The Politician wanted us off the base and on our way immediately. But The Warrior argued that without treatment, I could get gangrene two days from now, and then they would be legally required to order a helicopter evacuation, which would cost a quarter of a million dollars. Therefore it was a good business decision, as well as a humane thing to do, to invest ten dollars in Band-Aids and Neosporin now, and therefore to reduce the probability of a much bigger commotion later.

While the argument continued, the kindly medic worked on my toes, silently and efficiently. One of the kitchen staff walked in and surreptitiously stuffed some small bags of instant oatmeal and a jar of peanut butter in my coat pocket, which was hanging on a hook behind The Politician's back.

Alert is a tiny spaceship of human beings so far north that it is closer to Moscow, traveling over the North Pole, than it is to Ottawa, the capital of Canada. Its motto is "Inuit Nunangata Ungata" which means in Inuktitut, "Beyond the Inuit land," beyond the land of the most northerly people on this planet, beyond the habitable land. Two guys show up. Maybe in your opinion, they are irresponsible, stupid, goofy, dirty, and unshaven. Hippies. Maybe in your opinion they don't belong here. But one guy has a sore toe. He asks for a Band Aid. You have an infinite supply of Band Aids. You don't think you should give him one.

Excuse me if you think I am being too critical, but The Politician was totally off-the-wall. He didn't like Boomer and me because we represented a class of human beings that for some reason he had chosen, way back in his youth, not to like. Why didn't he start off by shaking hands first, and saying: "How do you do? My name is…"

It's the *us* versus *them* again thing, albeit on a small scale. Oh well.

To me, it's all about connection and compassion. I don't know which comes first. Does connection breed compassion or the other way around? Or do they come bundled together—indistinguishable and inseparable? It doesn't matter. Once we lose one or the other, or both, the world becomes a much less pleasant place, and a more dangerous place, to live in.

Enough philosophy. With a little food stuffed in our pockets, and a freshly bandaged toe, The Warrior and The Politician bundled us into their pick-up truck and drove us down the hill to give us the bums rush out of Alert.

TIPPING POINT

The Arctic Ocean is almost completely surrounded by land, with only a few narrow straits connecting it to the Atlantic and Pacific. There's the Bering Strait between Alaska and eastern Siberia, wider waterways between eastern Greenland and Europe, and the Nares Strait, just southeast of Alert, where Boomer and I were heading. Here, Ellesmere and Greenland pinch together into a 20-kilometer-wide constriction, like the neck of a giant hourglass separating the Arctic Ocean from the Atlantic.

The short Arctic summer was in full bloom as we trudged along the coast, first east and then southeast. On shore, most of the winter snow had melted by now, exposing bare rock and thin patches of soil. A few sedges and some flowers hugged the ground, nothing taller than an inch or two, tucked behind rocks or nestled into tiny undulations of the land to escape the relentless northerly gales. To the east, we could see the coast of Greenland, hazy in the distance, while the Polar Ocean lay north of us, a perpetual sea of floating, fractured, moving ice. On July 4, Independence Day in the United States, when people down south were charging around in shorts and bathing suits, waterskiing, drinking beer, making love on beaches, and shooting off firecrackers, we started our morning with the old ice dance, pulling and dragging around broken pressure ridges—a dance that I had embraced and vilified ad infinitum. After a few miles, we came to the mouth of a small river, where fresh water had melted the sea ice and had left a narrow channel of open water. Our kayak cockpits were still crammed with food and gear, leaving no room for our legs and feet, so we plunked our butts into the seats, with our cramponed, cut-up boots hanging on the deck. It's a potentially dangerous position to paddle in, with our bodies squeezed into an awkward V, and no spray-skirt to repel water that might wash over the deck, but the lead was narrow, calm, and close to shore, and this goofy paddling position was ever so much faster, more efficient, and more fun than the ice dance.

The moment I sat down, my throbbing toe squeaked up to me, like the mouse to the lion, "Thank you, Jon," said the toe. "I've done my best, all that I can do. I'm just a little toe, after all, and you've been putting so much weight on me." And the lion roared back, "Grrrr. I weigh 80 kilos. Okay, maybe 70 by now. And you, little toe, you weigh only a few grams. You certainly are a big bundle of trouble for just a tiny little thing." And the toe just whimpered quietly and squeaked meekly to itself. But now that I was seated in the cockpit, paddling, the argument between my toe and me subsided and the world looked brighter, as my toe commenced the long process of healing, molecule by molecule, cell by cell.

On the map, Cape Sheridan is a tiny, almost imperceptible dimple on a smoothly curving coastline, barely worthy of a name—a pile of windblown rock, battered by ice and wind. Yet, as we turned our course a few compass degrees from southeast to a little more southerly, in what seemed like barely more than an eye-blink, after 60 days, and 800 miles, I looked out into the Strait and saw a ragged jumble of ice that was more rubbly than anything we'd ever seen—too rubbly to even consider dragging our boats across, as there were no level surfaces anywhere. It was beauty and fear wrapped together into glistening silent whiteness, like a deadly horizontal avalanche frozen into immobility. As a scientist, I could explain how the ice was crammed into this place by a global current, driven by temperature and salinity differences and the spin of the earth. But the feeling was one of instant smallness, as if I were now the mouse, squeaking pitifully into the inscrutable Arctic vastness, as if it could listen and had consciousness, "I've done my best, all that I can do. Mentally and physically. I'm just a little human after all. I am honored to be here. To experience this. It would be nice, in a way, if you didn't kill us."

We paddled until our open water lead closed out, and then dragged the boats onto shore to decide what to do next. And then, as if someone clicked off the pause button on a cosmic video, the entire icepack began to move. This frozen ocean, that we had walked over and camped on, that had been our own private continent for two months, stable and secure underfoot, had now, in this instant, morphed into a dynamic maelstrom of independent chunks that were moving: mushing, grinding, smashing and smearing together. We stopped and listened to the whooshing, cracking, and tinkling that sounded like rumbling thunder choreographed with breaking wine glasses and melodious lullabies. This was the Nares Strait, which Tyler and I had feared over laptops and lattes in Hood River Oregon on that bright, warm, lazy summer day seemingly so many eons ago. This was the icepack that had crushed the stout oaken ships of the western navies during the great Age of Discovery.

It almost made me seasick, as if an earthquake had occurred and solid rock was undulating in a wave, as if reality itself, which had been solid and predictable for so long, was now, suddenly, in chaos. I blinked in disbelief and asked Boomer, "Did the entire ocean of ice just now jostle free and begin to flow? This second? Or had we been so unobservant five minutes before that we hadn't noticed this massive and critical change in our world?"

Boomer didn't answer. He just stared out to sea, hands uncharacteristically hanging loosely by his side, useless appendages that they now appeared to be.

Tipping points occur because systems, of all sizes and compositions, usually don't change in a linear manner with perturbation. They are so common in everyday life that we have popular sayings to describe this concept: "the straw that breaks the camel's back", "pushed to the edge", "the match in the powder barrel".

The atomic foundations of life, itself, were created in the fiery explosions of stellar tipping points. Our sun has been around for 5 billion years or so, shining brightly, and more or less constantly, in the heavens. Look up into the night sky and you see billions and billions of other stars all glowing away, seemingly unchanging—forever. But inside each star, from the smallest to the largest, atomic fusion reactions are changing its composition, day by day, minute by minute, and nanosecond by nanosecond. When the tipping point is reached in a massive star, the entire core—ten times as massive as our sun—can collapse within the incredibly short time span of *one second*. And then the star explodes. Inside this cosmic cataclysm, small elements fuse into larger ones, creating the nuclear crucible for life.

Boomer and I were witnessing the breakup of the arctic icepack, a tipping point that is huge on a human scale but smaller than an exploding star. The Arctic is like that. The World is like that. Temperatures had been above freezing for a month, yet the sea ice was still two meters thick, unmoving and inscrutable. Half an hour ago, we had marveled at how jumbled the ice was, but it was still stationary. Even now, the ice hadn't melted—it was still out there. But within an incredibly short time of five minutes or so, the little fractures and cracks that had been slowly developing for all this time, suddenly interconnected to the point where the pack ice broke free under the influence of underlying currents, and began to float around as independently moving pieces. Thus, the slow, steady, ever-changing march of the seasons, the inexorable rise of the sun's angle and the month-long above-freezing temperatures, had combined to suddenly set an ocean of ice into motion.

Many scientists argue that the effects of global warming will manifest like that. We've heard about it for decades, read increasingly alarming scientific reports, but so far the effects, although increasingly significant in recent years, have been relatively manageable. Then one fine day, it's very possible that we will wake up in the morning and look out the window.... And the earth will have changed, hugely, and irreversibly. If a catastrophic global warming tipping point occurs, it will be exacerbated by many feedback loops, one of which was clearly visible to the two of us, standing on this remote beach. When the Arctic sea ice melts or breaks up, open water becomes exposed and the albedo of the Arctic Ocean decreases dramatically and instantaneously. In turn, this decrease in albedo causes the entire earth to warm even more rapidly.

Around and around, like a tornado, complementary effects spin the system out of control. In the past dozen years, the earth has been warmed by the greenhouse effect. During this time, the Arctic has warmed much more dramatically than the temperate or equatorial regions. In turn, this warming has caused oceans to freeze later in the fall and the breakup of the Arctic icepack to occur earlier in the summer, leading to a cascade of interconnecting meteorological events on distant parts of the globe: changes in the jet stream, increased frequency and intensity of tropical hurricanes or droughts, alteration of ocean currents, and so on. And then one day, poof, there is a really good chance that it will all get much, much warmer.

I don't *want* to sound alarmist, or to be alarmist, but *I am* alarmist because the scientific evidence in compelling. In the past 40,000 years, extremely rapid climate change, much greater than anything humans have seen in the past 10,000 years *has* happened—repeatedly. And it could very well happen again, very soon. This warming, in turn, will assuredly lead to coastal flooding, decreased food production, water shortages, and a host of other real and tactile calamities, probably including further human-induced catastrophes such as war and strife.

Right here, watching the ice move, I felt that I was in the planetary clockworks, holding on to the big second hand and flying around in great arcs, legs spun out by centrifugal force, gears spinning behind me. The clockworks of a planet. The ice had become an emotion. My own frailty had become an obvious and glorious emotion. This is what the Spirit Wolf was trying to explain, which we now call Deep Ecology—a fundamental, innate empathy for the "living environment as a whole," and a tactile appreciation for the interconnectivity of nature.

You don't have to go to the Arctic to see and feel the Earth's changing moods. Changes in the seasons, at any latitude or in any ecosystem, occur in abrupt fits and starts, less dramatic than the breakup in the Arctic icepack—to be sure—but real and observable nevertheless. I believe that the first step in reining in our headlong rush toward human-induced climate change is to watch spring unfold and realize how quickly the Earth systems can change. Once we internalize local weather and seasonal change, as an emotion, once we love it, as family, then perhaps we can grasp the less visible changes in our larger systems. And then, maybe—hopefully—we will be motivated to implement the concrete political, economic, and technological initiatives do something about it. Even if it means reining in our opulence a little bit.

Boomer and I looked up, and our whole world had changed into something we had never experienced before. That's why we were here. To feel this change within the marrow of our bones. The Spirit Wolf had assured us that we would become vulnerable, that we wouldn't be in control of the situation. But that was the glory of it all, because the difference between success and failure, between life and death, was how well we would adapt to this marvelously intricate, incomprehensibly powerful, chaotic infinity of moving ice. We pulled to shore. Right now it would be suicidal to venture another millimeter toward our goal.

HANG TIME

There's a saying I learned way back in my youth: "When the going gets tough, the tough get going." That's a reflection of the industrial-agricultural mentality—that if I am gnarly enough, mean enough, and drive a big-enough bulldozer, then I can "control the planet." Sorry, that mentality was patently ridiculous here. And anywhere else for that matter. No, we weren't going to "get tougher" than the Arctic icepack, squeezed together between Ellesmere and Greenland. No, it doesn't work that way. It's a dangerous lesson to teach our children.

Let's try, "When the going gets tough, the tough drink tea." Doesn't that sit more comfortably in the pit of your stomach? Sit down. Observe. Relax. Embrace and enjoy your vulnerability.

Boomer and I made camp. I slept for fifteen hours. When I awoke, I had diarrhea but couldn't pee. My toe hurt even more than when I was on the move. Amazingly, all my bodily functions had held together for all those weeks of hard travel—until the ice called a rest day. Then the body shut down, but it was too tired to make a coherent plan, so it turned switches on and off at random, told me that I was hurting more when I should be hurting less, forgot how to poop and pee—a prelude to what was to come. I wrote in my journal, "*Go body! And thank you for what you have done for me these past weeks.*"

As a continuous parade of ice flowed with the current, the power of moving water began to fracture the two meter thick chunks of floating ice into smithereens, so that the ocean was now packed with ice fragments as big as a baseball, a basketball, or your kitchen table, packed tightly around the larger pans of stronger, more cohesive ice, some as big as a football field and others a kilometer or more across. I had once written that the kayak and the nuclear-powered ice breaker were the two best boats in the Arctic—because, while an icebreaker can crunch through the ice, a kayak can dance around it. But that was just wise-guy journalism. We couldn't go out into that powerful chaos and dance around anything, no matter how agile we were. We were trapped.

Boomer went for walks, while I sat against a sun-warmed rock, absorbing the photons, feeling every muscle in my body relax, willing my toe to heal, and watching the ice, which paraded back and forth with the tide. The entire pack compressed and relaxed, compressed and relaxed, like a pulsating jellyfish. Sometimes huge flat pans would float offshore, moving stately along at a knot or less. These were composed of gnarly old multiyear ice from the Polar pack that had already survived multiple seasons of collisions, fragmentation, and refreezing. Occasionally thick ice ran aground against the beach, just below me. Then, pressured by the current and moving ice, the grounded pans might rear upward into unstable cliffs and towers, ten meters high, which generally collapsed soon after, with a large cracking sound and a shower of fragments. Occasionally the precariously tilted pans remained poised and unstable for an hour or even for a day or two, like a child's tower of blocks, ready to crash down to squeals of joy and faux terror. Frequently, moving ice would collide against grounded ice with enough compressive force so the pans stacked on top of one another, like a tower of dinner plates, as if I were watching a time-lapse movie of a continental collision and the rise of a mountain range. I watched for hours at a time, partly because it was the most exciting show in town, and partly because every observation and bit of information about the ice behavior might turn critical in the days ahead. In any case, my toe was grateful for the rest.

My relationship with my brain is like a marriage between two people who bicker all the time, but for some reason can't quite decide to divorce. I was exhausted, hurt, half starved, trying to heal and now I had the opportunity to sit back, relax, and enjoy the unspoiled Arctic landscape that I had struggled so hard to reach. So what did my dumb brain do? It ruined the entire vacation by fretting, being bored, and reminding me that it was time to get up out of this comfortable seat in the warm sunshine and keep moving.

In a classic Zen story, the Master is hoeing his garden, when a young acolyte walks by. "I see you're working," the acolyte comments. "No, I'm resting," responds the Master. The next day, the Master is sitting on his front porch, cross-legged and stationary. "I see you're resting," the young man observes. "No, I'm working."

The point is that our bodies are trained by evolution to do something, and our minds are trained to keep thinking even if we think drivel that can become a pain in the neck, or downright detrimental. If there is nothing to do, we do stuff anyway, or think about the stuff we're not doing, or should be doing, or have been doing. According to this lesson, hoeing your garden, while hard physical work, is restful because it gives your busy-body arms and legs something to do and also gives your hyperactive, annoying brain something to concentrate on. Now, sit cross-legged on the porch and try to meditate, and the untrained human will want to fidget like a first grader in church and the brain will come up with a whole barrage of worries, stuff to be grumpy about, and stories that have no basis in reality. Hanging out, doing nothing, is harder work than you think. Our DNA seems to be hardwired for something other than contentment.

"Free time" is elusive, simultaneously the most expensive and the cheapest commodity on the planet. You can't buy it for cheap at Walmart or for a lot of money at Neiman Marcus. Prisoners are forced to endure decades of "free time" as punishment. Rich pilgrims pay big money to go to ashrams where gurus will teach them how to sit and do nothing. Back in the 1960s, we had a saying, "You can work all your life, retire, and go to the beach. Or you can go to the beach." But most of us, myself included, keep working long after we have the means to "go to the beach."

In a recent clinical experiment, participants were asked to sit still in an undecorated room for 15 minutes, just to relax. They could think, tell themselves stories, sing songs, or meditate into a thoughtless nirvana. Their choice. But, if they got really bored, they had the option of delivering painful electric shocks to themselves, just to break the "monotony." And, guess what? 67% of men and 25% of women zapped themselves to avoid being in a situation where nothing was happening, including one nutcase who pushed the button 190 times, about once every five seconds, until he was jittering and shaking from the flow of current.[17]

Perhaps there have been half a dozen humans in all of history—Jesus, Buddha, and a handful of others—who could actually sit in that room for fifteen minutes and meditate totally. Well, maybe there are a few more than that, but nearly all of us fall somewhere in between the true ascetic and the nutcase. Boomer and I talked about the need to groove out, but all too frequently we slept, fretted, and got bored, now that we were forced (or given the opportunity) to do nothing.

Finally, we pushed the metaphorical electrical jolt button and expended a great amount of energy, suffered pain, and risked our lives to venture out in the moving ice and travel for a measly 2½ exhausting and hair-raising miles. Then we got really scared and made camp on a beautiful platform against a small rock outcrop that blocked the wind and absorbed the sun. Frustrated, I turned to our crumpled and weatherworn pages of the *Tao* for some tips on how to *learn* to relax, but the *Tao*, in ever confusing contradictions, chided me, "Banish learning and there will be no more grieving."[18]

Despite the *Tao*'s warning, I sat and watched the ice, trying to *learn*—or more precisely, to internalize its moods, so that when the moment came, I could respond on a subconscious visceral level. Our society does not train us to observe the subtleties of nature. When I was in Siberia, my friend Lydia explained that when she was a young girl the Soviets took all the children out of their skin tents, away from family, reindeer, and language, and imprisoned them in dank school rooms where they sat behind desks to learn their ABC's. As a result of this education, or deprivation, depending on your view, she could never, ever, no matter how hard she tried, see the natural world with the same precision as Moolynaut saw it. I started my education in a funky old wooden school building that looked like a house, which wasn't so bad. But midway through first grade, they lined us up, shortest to tallest, marched us into an orange bus, and drove us to a brand-spanking-new, built-to-last, brick-and-concrete-block school. As we all walked down the hallway, being careful not to talk or fidget, I looked at the silent, geometrical gray lines of block, reaching out seemingly to infinity, through time, from youth to old age. Understanding my fate, like a gulag prisoner who just can't take another step, I fell out of line, curled up on the floor, and cried. Without being able to articulate it, I knew, at that instant, what was happening. They were stealing, forever, my aboriginal heritage. Now, over sixty years later, I appreciate that my education has incorporated me into this society and given me a good life. I can't complain. But out there in the Nares Strait, in the sunshine, sitting against a rock, with the polar icepack streaming by, I was trying to reach back to find a sensibility and awareness that has been obfuscated by my upbringing, but is still hardwired into my DNA—because, right then, my equanimity and even my life depended on it.

So we sat. As the days passed, my little toe was no longer stuck to its neighbor with dried pus and blood. There were moments during those days, where I did actually find true contentment—moments when I felt a glorious peacefulness beyond anything I have ever felt before or since. Moments when "me," "myself," and "my ego" lost all separateness from the wondrous, all powerful, and yes deadly world around me.

Moments when there was no boredom, only completeness. There was no fear because there was nothing to be afraid of— not even death. No thoughts, because thoughts simply dissipated into the power and wonder of the ice. Perhaps, although I can never be sure, I subconsciously understood that negative or hassled thoughts eventually lead to wasted energy. And, out here, we didn't have the luxury of diverting excess energy into bad shit.

There were moments out there, watching the ice, watching the sun, feeling the world spin, when I approached a contentment that was so complete that I can only barely recall the glory of it. And then the clarity would fog over and I would begin fretting and worrying, becoming bored and then stressed. Because, the fact was that here on the northeast coast of Ellesmere, hanging out was dangerous in the long term. Clearly, if we ventured into the moving ice, we could be crushed to death within seconds. But if we waited on this warm, protected, nourishing tent platform long enough, we would run out of food and then winter would descend, and we would slowly starve and freeze to death.

How long were we going to have to wait?

In 1881, First Lieutenant Adolphus Greely assumed command of the Lady Franklin Bay Expedition with a mandate to travel north along the east coast of Ellesmere, establish a semi-permanent camp, and conduct astronomical and meteorological observations, as part of the First International Polar Year. The expedition members traveled north that summer on the *Proteus*, a large steamship fitted with three masts to assist her engines in periods of favorable wind. That summer, the channel between Ellesmere and Greenland was relatively ice-free, and the *Proteus* steamed along the coast to establish a winter camp just a few miles south of where Boomer and I were now. As it turned out, the winds that summer were predominantly from the west and southwest, pushing the ice offshore, toward Greenland, and leaving an open water passage. The *Proteus* dropped off the 25-man scientific team. Then, with a wave, a promise to return the next year, and, I imagine, a hearty "Cheerio," the ship's crew motored back south. However, for the next *two summers*, the wind blew predominantly from the northeast. As a result, relief expeditions could not penetrate the pack ice either in 1882 or 1883. As reported, in typically dry military language, in the Proceedings of the "Court of Inquiry on the Greely Relief Expedition."

"The steamer, *Proteus*, St John's Newfoundland, Captain Pike, chartered by the United States Government, to carry relief expedition under my command to Lady Franklin Bay, was caught in ice pack six miles NNW, ½ W from Cape Sabine, and was crushed, sinking at 7:30 PM on 23 July, 1883. The crew and relief party all saved, and also about 40 days provisions for all hands, together with a lot of fur and other clothing...."

The shipwrecked sailors proceeded in lifeboats across the strait to settlements in Greenland where they found shelter and provisions. The account closes with, "Everybody well and in good spirits. With God's help, we all hope to reach port in safety in good time. E. A. Garlington. 1st Lieut., 7th Cav., A. S. O. Commander."[19]

Meanwhile, back in camp, Greely and his men, after having waited in vain for two years for resupply, took off on foot in August for Cape Sabine, looking for the relief ship, which was by now collecting barnacles on the bottom of the sea. (For some weird reason, that arctic historians and adventurers can never understand, Greely didn't decide to high-tail it to settlements in Greenland, as Captain Garlington did.) As a result, that winter, 18 of the original 25 man crew died from starvation, drowning, and hypothermia. Greely shot a 19th for stealing food. After their eventual rescue in the summer of 1884, a 20th expedition member died of complications on the way home.

The point is that the ice distribution, and hence our fates, were inexorably linked to the direction of the wind, which could be unfavorable for the next two years, or perhaps five minutes.

Whatever the future held for us, at the current moment, the wind was pushing the ice against the northeast coast of Ellesmere, where we were camped.

Over the past 30 years, the overall extent of the Arctic sea ice has declined by 50%, globally. This decline is of great concern for the approach to planetary tipping points and long-term climate. It is of great concern for native people of the North who depend on sea ice for transportation and hunting, and also to bears, seals, walrus, and all the smaller animals who live here and who have adapted their survival to historical ice conditions and distribution. But, right now, our survival was not linked to any of these global phenomenon, no matter how critical and even catastrophic they may be to humankind and Arctic ecosystems in general. Our fates were inexorably linked to wind direction—in this specific place—and thus to the position of the icepack—at this instant. Right now, an awful lot of ice was stacked right up against the shore, just 100 meters from our tent. Furthermore, if Greely's misfortune was any indicator, we might have to wait for three years for conditions to change appreciably.

As I've said before, Boomer and I didn't have that much to say to one another. Long wilderness trips are like that. The void wrings the words out of you because most of what we say in normal daily life could be safely left unsaid anyway.

> *But it is on the space where there is nothing that*
> *The usefulness of the wheel depends.*

But of course, we did talk. It was Boomer's first long, totally committed expedition and my last. He was trying to figure out how to enter the adult world with some semblance of relevance, grace, and equanimity, and I was trying to figure out how to become an old man with the same relevance, grace, and equanimity. Unless you are born a trust-funder or a criminal, everyone has to contribute to society, so society will return the favor and supply you with food and whatnot. For most people, contribution means a job, and for some—or many—jobs represent an unpleasant, but acceptable compromise in exchange for the joys of owning a home, raising a family, and so on. Boomer was trying to balance that compromise within the reality of his deep passion for freedom, manifest by love of wilderness and extreme outdoor adventure. And I was trying to figure out how to adapt to the reality that, very soon, like next month, my body would no longer allow me to travel into Deep Wild at the level we were involved in at the moment. Soon, I would have to generalize what I was learning from the ice and the danger in Deep Wild and take these lessons into less extreme environments, such as the garden of an old folks' home. Boomer asked me, repeatedly, to tell stories of past adventures, and together, we planned the most ambitious passages imaginable, passages I knew that I, for one, would never attempt. So we talked, covering the same ground over and over, rehashing endless details and possibilities, with a relaxation rooted in the knowledge that we would never verbally resolve our problems, but that the discussion bonded us to each other and passed the time.

Meanwhile, out in The Real World, people were worrying about us. We were in regular satellite phone communication with Nina, who was posting our progress on my website, available to anyone who cared to look. In turn, she was in regular email contact with Dr. Humfrey Melling from the Canadian Institute of Ocean Sciences, Trudy Wohlleben from the Canadian Ice Service, and the Canadian Coast Guard, all of whom were feeding us as much weather and ice information as they possibly could. Every once in a while, a military two-engine propeller plane flew overhead, dipped low over our camp, wagged its wings, and then zoomed off, leaving us again alone in silence. Although I can never prove it, I believe that this plane was evidence that The Warrior had become our fairy godmother in need and was looking out for us, should Big Trouble arise. In sum, our situation was sketchy, and no one wanted to close this expedition out in an inglorious rescue, but this was the 21st century, and we weren't going to sit out here, starving in total isolation and darkness, for three years, before we either died, ate one another, or reunited with civilization.

On the afternoon of July 12, we climbed up on a bluff and watched the ice, for the umpteenth time. A floe the size of a football field drifted slowly toward the cliff below us, rotated, and buckled. The air filled with a human-like groan, followed by a sharp crack that echoed off the nearby mountain. Ice crystals exploded and danced rainbows in the sunshine, while two-meter thick chunks rose out of the sea like a whale's tail, and then smeared against solid rock.

Neither of us wanted to be rescued. We discussed the unpleasant option of walking to Grise Fiord, overland and half starved, after the ocean froze again in the fall. But when we tried to plot a course over the mountains, with no climbing gear and not even adequate backpacks, we realized that it was impossible. We had to get through the ice.

Every day the sun settled lower in the sky, reminding us that even though we still enjoyed 24 hour daylight, winter would soon descend upon us with polar speed and ferocity. Our food supply dwindled. Boldness or caution? Caution or boldness? Just a smidge too much on either side would kill us. The line between courage and foolishness is drawn only after the fat lady sings. If you make it, you were courageous. If you die, all the Monday morning quarterbacks can puff up their chests and proclaim that you were foolish.

Think out of the box. There must be a way. Dr. Melling reminded us that the main current flowed north to south and suggested that we risk a treacherous passage across moving ice onto one of the large floes. In theory, this floe would be strong enough to withstand collisions with the rest of the ice—and we could ride it southward with the main current. All the way to Newfoundland if we wanted to. The problem was that in addition to the underlying current, water in the strait flowed southward with the flood tide and north with the ebb. Eddy lines and tidal shears would complicate our drift, but all the scientists assured us that the net drift was south.

On July 13th, a large floe, a few football fields in size and consisting of thick, multiyear ice, floated to within 100 meters of shore. We reasoned that this floe would provide a safe "ship" to carry us south. The current slowed at slack tide, giving us a narrow time window to cross from shore to the floe. The intervening distance was choked with small pieces of ice floating in a watery matrix. Some of this ice was large and stable enough to stand on, but other floes were small and tippy. We attached a long line to the boats and jumped from one tippy floe to another, until we reached the safety of the first large chunk of ice. Then we pulled the boats across to join us. But now our continued passage was blocked by a small open channel wider than we dared jump across. So, Boomer bridged the gap with his kayak and crawled across the deck, in a gymnastic tightrope act. I followed. Next, Boomer slipped his boat into the water, launched into an even wider ice-choked passage, and then paddled a few boat lengths through the daiquiri-like slush.

I clicked a photo as he scrambled out of his boat, back onto an ice floe that was large enough to stand on, and I refer to the photo now, to relive the moment, as I write about it. He had been sitting in his kayak "goofy-style" with his butt in the kayak and feet on the deck. In attempting to climb out, onto the ice, his left leg was knee deep in the icy water on the left side of the boat, and his right leg was knee deep in icy water on the right side of the boat. The boat, itself, was listing so severely, that a tiny stream of water was flowing into the cockpit. His ungloved right hand was resting on a chunk of ice that was precariously balanced at the edge of the floe. It is a still photo, 1/1,000 of a second in time, preserved now as an array of bits and bytes. But the trajectory is clear. If the boat had listed another degree or two, or even if it had just remained as it was for a few more seconds, it would have filled completely with water. Boomer had no footing, so he launched himself out of the water, across that boat, onto the ice, on the strength of one arm stretched out past his body, well beyond his center of gravity, like a gymnast on a set of rings. But, if a gymnast fails, he or she gets a poor mark on a score card. Disappointment. No medal. End of story. If Boomer had failed he would have fallen into the icy Arctic Ocean, where moving ice could have squashed him until blood ran out of his nose and his eyeballs popped out of his head. He didn't fail. And then, I followed.

Moving in this manner, going all out, we traveled 100 meters in three hours.

Once we reached the large floe, we high fived, and relaxed in the new-found security. This was old, thick, multiyear, ice that was born and raised in the Polar Ocean. Under tremendous compression, two-meter thick ice-pans had been forced on top of other pans, layer upon layer, forming a huge pressure ridge on the south edge of our floe. Over time, this ice had melted and refrozen, and the pressure ridge had been blasted by wind and plastered with snow. If our strategy was sound, this mountain of ice would be our battering ram to propel us southward, unscathed, through the smaller, thinner, less formidable ice floes all around us. We set up camp in a sheltered valley on our island of ice, our own private Shangri-La, adjacent to a small lake of fresh melt-water. My next photo of Boomer shows him stretched out on the ice on his sleeping pad, napping in the warm sunshine.

Our GPS told us that we were heading south at 0.3 to 0.4 knots. That's not real speedy, but if sustained, it would multiply to 7.5-10 miles a day, which is significantly faster than nothing. I felt happy to be doing something—but at the same time, I was wracked by an uneasy, indefinable concern that this ice pan, as formidable as it was, could break apart at any moment, spilling us into the ocean. I tried to draw assurance from the Spirit Wolf, or the *Tao*, or to draw energy from my transient, fleeting equanimity back there on shore sitting against a sun-warmed rock. But reality laughed at me with a wry grin, because brave words and noble thoughts are easy, but also so fragile and ephemeral.

Boomer woke from his nap brimming with his characteristic childlike enthusiasm. He climbed to the highest point of our iceberg, and pretended that it was the bridge of a massive diesel-munching icebreaker. He grasped an imaginary steering wheel, grinning with joy, and shouted into the silent sky, "Get out of our way, *Ice*, here we come." The orange and white military aircraft flew overhead again, jauntily wagging its wings, amplifying Boomer's enthusiasm.

At the next slack tide, the floe stopped, and we crawled in our tent and went to sleep. In the middle of the night, Boomer woke me with a gentle tap on my shoulder, looking uncharacteristically concerned, with his GPS in his hand. We were drifting north with the ebb at 1 knot, traveling the wrong way at more than twice the speed of our earlier southward passage. We dressed and crawled out of the tent to stand in the semi-twilight of the Arctic night. Somehow, the massive compression had relaxed and our pan was floating free, like an island, all alone with open water stretching all around us. There was no noise of grinding ice, no wind. For a brief moment, everything seemed so peaceful and quiet, as great forces became great serenity. I don't know if I have ever felt such a peace, floating, like a sleeping polar bear, in a world that itself seemed to have gone to sleep. We stood there, in the semi-twilight, shoulder to shoulder, surrounded by this great nothingness. Then, the ice started squeezing together again. I couldn't tell whether we were continuing to drift north and the ice to the north of us was stationary, or if we were stationary and the ice to the north was crashing into us. Or both. In any case, the open water surrounding us became smaller and smaller as if space itself were being sucked into a black hole. The collision occurred with a slushy, wooshy sound, not a metallic clang. Then our cosmos changed as edges of our floe crumpled and fractured, shooting ice splinters into the air, while the center, where we huddled together in awe and fear, rippled, as if it had been impacted by an earthquake. There is no metaphor to describe what was happening. This wasn't *like* anything. It *was* the arctic icepack compressing and fracturing into rubble.

Fear is a universal and necessary emotion, hardwired into our system for its obvious survival value—to run away from that lion lurking in the bushes. I've often argued that I'm blessed with the ability to subdue my fear, to rely on it when necessary, and exorcise and control fear when it threatens to drive me toward bad decisions. Barry Blanchard, a world-class extreme alpinist, disagreed with this analysis and told me that in dangerous situations, fear is inevitable. To function in these situations, you can't subdue fear; instead you must make friends with it, embrace it, and hold it close and dear. The alternative, to let it run amok, unwanted, unfettered, and uncontrolled, leads to panic, which is disastrous and potentially deadly. But it's all just words, the tools that writers use to fill pages. All I know for certain is that, out there on the ice floe, in the hazy soft midnight of arctic summer, I was terrified and desperately wanted to get back to dry land—but the ice was moving too fast and too unpredictably, so we had to rely on patience.

We waited till full daylight and the next slack water and then reversed our tenuous and terrifying passage across small floes. By mid-morning, we once again stepped on *terra firma*, having survived a Grand Adventure, and in the process, traveled a net distance of one mile northward—away from our goal.

For the next week, we inched southward, averaging 0.7 miles a day. In places where the shoreline was still covered with winter snow drifts or avalanche debris, we dragged overland, sometimes over snow, and sometimes over rock. Occasionally we paddled short distances between giant pressure ridges, and once we tediously carried our boats and gear over talus and rock. Several days we waited, going nowhere. Finally we reached a zone where steep cliffs dropped sharply into the sea. We could no longer travel a mile or two and return safely to land. Boomer and I had to somehow paddle for ten miles through this ice-choked compression to the next safe harbor. But, in the process, if we were trapped against the cliffs, if the ice closed in on us, we would be crushed. Maybe all the ice will melt in 40 years, when global warming becomes even more pronounced. But, for now, that was useless information.

A good friend and accomplished endurance athlete, Paul Attalla texted us, "Be patient. Don't do anything stupid." We broke our bags apart, counted our food, and then grimly packed everything up again. "Don't do anything stupid?" Fine. It would be stupid to paddle into the ice and get crushed and equally stupid to wait and starve.

THROUGH THE GAUNTLET

On July 20th, a mild wind blew from the northwest, pushing a significant amount of ice offshore, but still not enough to risk our passage. The following morning, the wind veered a little more westerly and the ice relaxed even further. We had eaten a lot of our food, which was a concern, but also a positive, because now there was enough room in the boats to actually sit inside the cockpit, with both feet, like real kayakers, and pull our spray-skirts tight. We had been resting, floating backwards on our ice floe, or moving in tiny increments for 17 days, 2½ weeks, during which time we had moved forward a total of 17 miles, one day's travel under decent conditions. A month from now the sun would be setting and the Arctic would begin to turn seriously cold. We had to break out of this prison, somehow.

With resolve, mixed with trepidation because the ice was only marginally cleared out, we broke camp, packed, slipped into our kayaks and pushed off the beach. As soon as I felt buoyancy, I rocked my boat back and forth with my hips, to loosen up my body and to communicate with the craft, as if it were a living, conscious creature. It felt good. The Wilderness Systems Tsunamis that had survived being dragged across the ice, and occasionally across rock and dirt for countless hours, remained robust and uncompromised. Now, finally, that we were asking them to do what they were designed to do, they felt perfect: the right balance between speed and stability, tracking and turning. I felt focused and ready for the sea, the floating ice, and the storms that lay ahead of us. Thirty meters offshore, two towering bergs bobbed gently in the channel, and I followed Boomer into the narrow space between them. For a brief moment, I felt the almost effortless glide of the kayak, the coolness of the ice that was barely a paddle-length away, and the glistening purity of a surreal ice-walled slot canyon that would be our escape route into the more open deep water, beyond. Then, even before my stern-wake had dissipated, I heard a cracking sound, followed by a swish, and turned to watch one of the towers collapse into the channel with a loud splash. If I had launched five seconds later, I would now be dead. Boomer looked back with alarm on his face, then said nothing, which was a more powerful statement of alarm than a simple platitude. "Okay," I told myself, "No worries. Nothing bad actually happened." But of course I couldn't "not worry."

In whitewater, the current is flowing, but at least the rocks stay still. Here, everything was moving—the water, the ice, and the wind. Our open water channel slammed shut, so we dragged our boats onto a large floe, and started hiking on the floating ice toward the south edge where a remnant of open water remained. Boomer was ahead and urged me to move faster so we could launch into this channel before it, too, closed out on us. I tried to run, but in rushing, my boat tipped over in a pool of water, and I was forced to race back to turn it back right-side up. Although I didn't see it at the time, my precious case of maps slipped out of the boat, into the water. Hurriedly, I grabbed my line and started off again, screaming down into my nerve endings to force my legs to move faster, but sheer will-power was not powerful enough.

Like the older gulag prisoners who lay down in the snow to die on their long trek to Siberia, there was simply no "faster" left inside me. I stopped. Sat down on my cockpit. Noticed that the map case was gone. The victim of inadequate lashings. Carelessness. Stupidity. Blind panic. Poorly managed fear. I looked back over the jumbled cacophony of ice and water behind me and realized that I could never retrace my exact steps to find it. I would have to proceed for the next month or more without my maps. "Oh well," was the only pathetic, half-hearted emotion I had the power to summon.

I watched Boomer reach the edge of the floe, ahead of me, searching for a way onward. The next large ice floe jutted farther out to sea, away from land, toward the uncertainty of the open sea. A week ago, when crossing rough brash ice, we had managed 100 meters per hour. What if we were caught five miles out to sea in compressing, chaotic ice and had to return to land? Had I lost my fighting edge? Or was I wise, with enough innate, gut recognition of impending disaster to save both of us? There was no way to know then, no way to second guess myself now. But in that moment of decision, I felt deeply that we were drawing too thin a line for ourselves if our survival constantly depended on split-second timing in a fast-moving, lethal and unpredictable environment.

I called out to Boomer and after a brief discussion we reluctantly retraced our tenuous and dangerous steps to our old camp, simultaneously elated to be unscathed and saddened to be defeated. Then, we crawled into our tent and slept peacefully for a few hours to let the adrenaline drain away. By afternoon, even more open water presented itself, so we paddled out for a second time that day. But after about a half a mile, the ice started to close back in again. You could hear the compression and feel it, a low level rumble, like the cosmic background radiation that infuses all space, from the beginning of time, from the Big Bang itself, powerful enough to sprinkle galaxies across the Universe like fairy dust. Ice collided against ice; ice smeared against the cliffs; and our open water channel again got narrower and narrower—so we retreated and pitched the tent for the second time that day. It seemed as if we would never leave this place. I closed my eyes with the unrealistic hope that sleep would vaporize our predicament.

The magic of our partnership, and, I believe, the reason why we were eventually successful, and, more than that, returned home alive, lay in the messy, ill-defined, unplanned balance between youth and geezerhood. While I slept to replenish my waning energy and to allow the adrenaline to go wherever adrenaline goes when it has finished its work and is free to leave the bloodstream, Boomer charged off, up the nearest hill, because he still had faith that we could journey south today, if only he were vigilant enough to capture the fleeting moment. He returned breathlessly.

"Hey, Jon. Wake up. Looks good out there. We gotta go for it. Right now."

I don't know why I believed him and trusted him. I don't know why I trusted the ice, or fate, or luck, or whatever I decided to trust. Perhaps it was the stupidest thing I have ever done. Or the smartest. What do I know? "Banish learning and there will be no more grieving." Or the *Tao*'s corollary, my words now: "Banish thinking, or second guessing, or self-recrimination, and there will be no more grieving."

For the third time that day, we broke camp and packed the boats. It was 9:00 PM and except for two short naps, we had been going flat out: making and breaking camp, or paddling, or dragging, or sprinting—for twelve hours. I was exhausted. I poked my head out of the tent. A gentle wind blew out of the southwest. It was just a tiny puff, barely discernable on my face, like a lover's feather brushing across my skin. Yet, in this channel where a global current was driving an ocean of ice southward— this gentle puff had managed to push a quazillion tons of ice several miles offshore, now hazy in the distance, as if it never existed. Nature is like that, mysterious, chaotic, prone to tipping points, sometimes delicately responsive to seemingly minuscule forces.

We packed our boats quickly, picked up our paddles and slid off the beach into the water. Perhaps we said something to each other. But, if I remember correctly, I looked into Boomer's eyes and he just nodded. Words, left-brain thinking, or futile attempts at mathematical certainty, were so totally and obviously useless. A few broken pieces of pressure ridge ice floated by, torn out of the main ice pack to bob about peacefully in the calm water, away from the main herd. The summer sun was so low in the northern sky that it reflected off the top of one of these small bergs, diffusing its light into scattered rays, like you see in medieval paintings of the Madonna and child. And we were paddling. Actually paddling. After all these miles and months—skiing, crawling, dragging, pulling, walking, sitting, I was in a the familiar world of a kayak, feeling buoyancy, and gliding almost effortlessly over calm water.

This is the moment you live for as an adventurer. It is comparable to any great wilderness challenge: pulling out of an eddy, heading for that big rapid. Or turning skis into the fall line and dropping into a steep, snaking couloir. It is the moment when you must trust yourself and your partner absolutely and completely. A trust earned by traveling across the Arctic, alone together. It is the glorious moment when fear metamorphoses into rapturous beauty because you have committed to that space beyond fear. This is ecstasy with all its seemingly contradictory definitions and roots, both rapturous and terrifying.

A major league baseball player reaches the Hall of Fame if he connects once out of every three times at bat. An NBA basketball player draws a multimillion dollar salary if he hits 50 percent from the floor. An adventurer must have a lifetime batting average of 1,000. Nothing less. I had a gut feeling that we would make it, but don't remind me how much we were depending on blind luck.

And then the ducks showed up, out of nowhere it seemed, and they appeared to be as overjoyed as we were by the sudden appearance of open water. They swooped and tilted playfully until their wingtips skimmed the sea, and then they soared above the scattered icebergs. The sea was a mix of dark shadows, interspersed by the ever-changing sunlight now reflecting off the ice, now turning the ocean orange. On our right we passed the imposing cliffs of Cape Union, its soft, rotten rock, too shattered by eons of freeze-melt to maintain verticality. To our left, on the eastern horizon, the main icepack was several miles away, now compressed against the Greenland side.

For us, this was the first day of summer, the day the ice finally floated away, up here in this forgotten land. And, in true Arctic fashion, it was the first day of winter as well, because as we were battling the fatigue of our all-night ordeal, as the ducks frolicked overhead, the temperature dropped and a thin film of ice formed on the sea, emitting a tinkling sound as our kayaks crunched southward, toward home.

It was the glory of knowing that every decision in my life, from the stupidity of getting myself in trouble in Jerusalem, to the assurance of walking out of my chemistry career, from dumb little things that I have forgotten to clever little things that I have also forgotten—all of this—had combined to put me here, in this calm evening: exhausted, hungry, vulnerable, with the ducks flying overhead, paddling resolutely through the wall of unfathomable fatigue, racing past the shadowed cliffs to reach a sheltered bay before the ice closed in again.

Once again Paul Attalla's wisdom resonated within me. He once told me that when you bump up against a "wall of unfathomable fatigue" you cannot cross it through willpower alone. You cannot talk yourself into pushing onward, tough it out, or rely on words or resolve. Instead you must find a way to enter into a blissful state that is "beyond willpower," where you are just existing and paddling, "in the flow," where the pain dissipates, where reality dissipates, but it doesn't. It just changes.

And if indeed there is a place beyond willpower, where pain

stops, the glory is that this secret valley is guarded by pain itself, the gnarly old trickster troll under the bridge with a wry smile, a peaked rumpled green hat, dirty underwear, and rotten teeth. So you must endure, or cross over, or worm your way through, or suffer through pain before you no longer need to endure anymore because the pain evaporates into something that we don't have a word for in the English language—perhaps because it is not a sufficiently significant part of our heritage. It is not bliss or contentment. That is way too foo-foo romantic. Maybe ecstasy comes close, if we seek its roots and not its modern connotations and the party drug that aligns with that mentality. The word doesn't matter. All I know for certain is that I came all this way to bob around on a flat sea, in a prolonged polar twilight, with icebergs here and there, while my flesh and bone arm became an abstract extension of my carbon graphite paddle and the most memorable image or thought or feeling—the one that I will carry with me to my grave—is those ducks skimming over the water, tilting their wings, because they were ducks and that is what ducks do sometimes.

About 3:00 AM we paddled into a small inlet, called Lincoln Bay, where a river had eroded a path through the cliffs and created a small beach. We had completed our passage through the narrowest neck of the hourglass—broken free. South of us, the channel widened, eventually into Baffin Bay, eventually into the Gulf Stream, to Montreal, Boston, and New York. As a result, the ice would never again be forced against the shore with the same relentless power. The urgency had dissipated and we were safe—sort of. A few boat lengths from shore, I stopped, set my paddle on the deck, and stretched my cramped fingers.

I see the world in physical terms and all my metaphors are based on tactile experience. Even when I ate the amanita with Moolynaut and was on a mission with an ancient shaman to journey through Dream Time into the Other World, I saw myself as a physical entity, walking through a dark, enclosed, confining labyrinth leading to a shining portal, which I never could quite reach.

Once, when I was in the South Pacific, I attended a ceremony, where a Polynesian chief built a huge fire pit, and invited all of us to walk across. "If you are willing and able to step across the white-hot stones," he assured us, "you will never go hungry." The fire walk has become a cliché in our world, but when I took my first barefoot step from the cool, damp, soil into the glowing pit, surrounded by the darkness of a jungle night, there was no cliché about the hot embers beneath my bare feet and the stifling heat that rose into my nostrils, threatening to steal my breath and resolve. On the other side of the fire, the chief's daughter, a young Polynesian princess, waited with mythological beauty—long hair and dark shining eyes, full breasts, torchlight reflecting off bronze skin, the promise of fertility. After I crossed the stones, set foot on cool soil, and stood breathlessly in front of her, she smiled a simple but embracing welcome and brushed my face and the soles of my feet with healing leaves.

We don't always have nubile princesses waiting for us on the other side of our passages. Or maybe we do, if we can only recognize them for what they are, in what otherwise might appear to be chaos, tragedy, or mayhem.

I picked up my paddle again and punched through the last few feet of this ocean that had just turned from ice to water and back to ice, all in the space of one exhausting, memorable day. A decade ago, I had promised Moolynaut that I would try to fly with the mysterious ancient wisdoms that rode on Raven's jet black wings. I had made that promise again when I washed my face in a muddy river to acquaint myself with a five-meter, man-eating, sharp-toothed, grandfather crocodile. I can't tell you why I was so driven to honor those promises. I can't tell you succinctly, in the scientific terminology I grew up with, why it was so important for me to put my life on the line so I could feel earth-rhythms in this remote, frozen ocean. But as I stiffly climbed out of my boat and took the first few awkward steps on the gravel beach, cranking my aching joints into some semblance of verticality, I knew that in my own way, with the DNA my mother and father gave me, this was the best I could do.

We set up the tent, brewed ourselves a hot cup of tea, and then finally, cooked dinner. The ice had moved even farther east toward Greenland, and although we had passed the crux, another stretch of dangerous shoreline guarded by steep cliffs lay to the south. We had to use this stretch of favorable weather to maximum advantage, but we were too exhausted to continue safely right now, so we resolved to sleep for two hours and then continue onward. As I pulled the hood of my sleeping bag over my head and just before I finally surrendered to my bottomless fatigue, I reminded myself to absorb this place and this feeling because it would be the last time I would push my body this hard on such a playing field.

The next great journey would be even more difficult, although much less glamorous—the passage into old age.

KAYAKS ON THE BEACH

Driven by some wondrous energy, beyond willpower and perhaps even beyond survival, we awoke after two hours, cooked a quick breakfast, and then slipped back in our boats and paddled past the Black Cliffs. With every stroke I tried to concentrate on power and speed, because every millimeter forward brought us that much farther out of the potential danger. Favorable conditions persisted, and the ice remained far out to sea. We reached the safety of a gravel beach by late afternoon, but with inertia on our side, and conditions still favorable, we continued southward. A few hours after we had begun to follow this gentle, welcoming beach, the wind suddenly shifted to the northeast. It wasn't a ferocious gale, or anything dramatic like that, just a gentle pressure against the back of my left ear: a zephyr, a breeze for ducks and seagulls to play on. But this nothing of a wind was enough to move the ice toward us, closing the gap of open water. Suddenly, house-sized bergs rocked on gentle swells a few meters out to sea, and the intervening opening of shallow water was filled with a congestion of smaller chunks, as if some evil witch doctor had zapped them into existence from electric fingertips.

Now, the ice posed no danger because we could go to shore and camp anytime we wanted, but if that had happened an hour ago, we would have been fighting for our lives. I didn't need to be afraid, and I was too tired to speculate about that razor thin tightrope of skill, daring, and luck that had, so far, kept us alive. If anything, I felt relief, because now that we had passed the cliff zone and the ice was impacting against the shore, and we could no longer paddle, we could stop, cook a hot meal, and sleep, without feeling that we were being wimpy.

But Boomer was all revved up. Without even a transitional rest stop, he jumped out of his kayak and charged through the calf-deep, ice-choked water, dragging his kayak with mighty splashes through a tiny channel between grounded ice floes and shore. It was 7:00 PM. I'd been pushing my body as hard as I could for 34 hours, with only two hours of sleep tucked in between extreme exertion. For the past twelve hours, I'd been cramped in the cock-pit, paddling resolutely, with only a few mini-breaks for snacks and an occasional gulp of water. That bowl of oatmeal at breakfast had long since been metabolized and turned to carbon dioxide and water. I saw no reason to sprint right now, so I sat in my boat for a while, doing and thinking nothing, watching Boomer grow smaller in the vast landscape. After only a few minutes, I realized that I couldn't sit here forever, so I wearily lifted myself out of my kayak and stepped into the shallow water. But as soon as I tried to stand, the blood rushed out of my head. Slowly the rocks, ice, and ocean all turned fuzzy and ethereal, and I felt myself falling.

To land in a 50cm deep pool of ice water now wouldn't kill me. The temperature outside was slightly above freezing, not forty below. My clothes would dry after a few hours of vigorous shivering. I would recover. But in expedition vernacular, it would suck. Yet, despite my best wishes to remain vertical, I just could not command the necessary nerve-muscle response. My body was screaming, "I just need thirty seconds to stop, rest, and regroup." My mind screamed back, "You can have thirty seconds. Take sixty if you need it. But not while lying in a pool of ice water."

Whatever internal dialogue was actually going on, I was definitely falling. No doubt about it. Brain fuzzy. One leg collapsed, the other soon to follow. A half a second to do something, anything. Use your weakness as your strength. I pushed off my bent leg with one desperate lunge and landed—kersplat—on the dry, soft gravel beach, centimeters from the water. Boomer hadn't seen me and continued charging south. I lay there on the beach and the stones felt so sun-warmed and comfortable that I wanted to take a nap, right there, but meanwhile my partner showed no signs of stopping. So painfully, reluctantly, I stood and followed. When we finally regrouped, I told Boomer as calmly and firmly as I knew how, that I needed to stop, set up camp, eat dinner, and sleep.

Over the next few days the ice continued to pulsate—relax and close in, relax and close in. We had scary moments and serene moments. But we were paddling, and could make 20 or more miles in a day, and thus make up for "lost time." On July 25, just north of Greely's camp, which was established in 1881 at Fort Conger, we met three men walking along the beach, Alex, Doug, and Steve, rangers for the Canadian Quittinirpaag National Park, which we were traveling through. They gave us each a Pro-Bar, which seemed extravagant and delicious enough. But then they jotted down the coordinates for an emergency food cache at Fort Conger with the invitation to "take anything we needed." Alex, the park manager explained that it was his resolve that Adolphus Greely and his men would be the last people to starve in this place.

We rested at the cache for a day, gorged ourselves, and then loaded the boats with as much weight as we dared carry. From now on, we would be paddling. Our boats were too small for this project, and overloading them would be as dangerous as going hungry.

As July slowly morphed into August, the sea ice was fractured, moving, and sometimes thick, but never again impenetrable. On most days, we paddled in narrow channels through an infinite maze of glistening floes. Occasionally the floes compressed together and blocked our passage, but after the Nares Strait, these compressions were short-lived. When we could go no farther, we hauled out on land, or a large floe, and waited, usually only an hour or two, for a change in tide or wind. Sometimes we dragged on the closely packed ice, jumping across small tippy floes. At other times, when the ice compression was particularly fierce, we set up camp, slept, and then moved on again when conditions improved.

On the afternoon of July 31, we were closed in by ice and pulled to shore. A chill wind was blowing, so, to keep warm, we took a short walk up the beach. Suddenly, we stumbled onto ancient, bleached kayak ribs that were the silent remains of people who had survived on this land, hunting with pieces of bone and ivory tied to the ends of long sticks. Our ancestors. Moolynaut's ancestors. On my previous expedition to Greenland with Chris, in 1988, I had the opportunity to sit on the beach and watch modern Greenlanders hunt narwhal, using spear launched with an atlatl, a primitive throwing lever that preceded the bow and arrow. The spear point was steel, ground down from an old screw driver, but aside from that little bit of sophisticated metallurgy, the hunter was using fundamental Neolithic technology—a lone man, in a fragile, tippy, wood-ribbed kayak, in a primordial encounter with a small whale.

I looked down at the kayak ribs at our feet—just a few weathered pieces of carved driftwood. I never knew that humans had lived and traveled this far north. What led them to abandon their valuable kayaks? Had the entire band perished of starvation? The kayaks looked so flimsy and vulnerable. But if Greely had adopted even a small fraction of that "primitive," "vulnerable" Inuit technology, he could have survived three winters, or a lifetime of winters.

Initially, I was motivated to initiate this Ellesmere expedition to appreciate the wisdom, perseverance, strength, and ingenuity of the South Pacific Island navigators, and by extension to learn from our Stone Age ancestors, in general. And now I stood on a frozen gravel beach, peering down at the remains of a boat-building culture, 70 degrees latitude north of the Solomon Islands, in a land of ice, rather than palm trees. The boats were different, of course, because the environments and available materials were so different, but the spirit was identical.

For some reason, the lure of open water travel lies deeply within the human psyche. About 800,000 years ago, well over a half a million years before our species, *Homo sapiens* had evolved in the savannahs and semi-deserts of Africa, even before pre-humans developed sophisticated language, tool-making hominids in Southeast Asia built boats and paddled across the open sea. These earliest seafarers left only a few stone artifacts and butchered animal bones, but archeologists have found skeletons of *Homo floresiensis* on a remote island, Flores. These skeletons belonged to small-brained Hobbit-people, barely more than a meter tall, who were either direct descendants or evolutionary offshoots of the original migrants.

Over the eons, watercraft became such an integral part of so many diverse cultures that it has become one of the defining characteristics of our species. The history of seafaring parallels a history of human civilization. Just south of here, archeologists found pieces of chain mail and old rivets from Viking seafarers. In 1999 and 2000, I paddled a kayak across the North Pacific Rim from Japan to Alaska, following the 10,000-year-old migration of ancient navigators to North America. In a book about this expedition,

In the Wake of the Jomon, I asked, "Why would people leave their home in northern Japan, with deer in the forests and salmon in the bays, to journey across the High Arctic during the tail-end of the Ice Age?" Answering my own question, I concluded that the migration was so difficult that—paradoxically—it must have been undertaken, not for practical reasons, but for the raw, romantic spirit of adventure.

Anthropologists attacked me with vehemence. They argued: We are a practical, survival-oriented species, are we not? In Paleolithic and Neolithic times, life was so tenuous that evolutionary pressures left no room for frivolity. As a result, people undertook difficult migrations to escape powerful enemies or seek new food sources.

I looked down at the weathered scraps of wood at my feet. Certainly, for the Inuit, a kayak was a pragmatic hunting tool—not a sport—an essential technology to harvest life-nurturing food from the sea, in a harsh land. Along the same lines, the Polynesian *wa'a kaulua* double-hulled voyaging canoes were used to move tribes from island to island, to alleviate population pressure and again, to assure survival.

People with stone tools built boats and went to sea—one of the most dangerous, unpredictable, and chaotic environments on Earth. They hunted whales and walrus along Arctic coastlines and journeyed vast distances across untracked ocean in the South Pacific. They fished in the Mediterranean and migrated from Asia to Alaska. Those are the facts. To me, these voyages conjure an image of romanticism, but in actuality, the difference between pragmatism and romanticism may be just semantic mumbo-jumbo.

According to the dictionary definition, romanticism involves "heroic or marvelous achievements, colorful events or scenes, chivalrous devotion, unusual or even supernatural experiences, or other matters that appeal to the imagination." Doesn't any oceanic voyage in a small boat qualify according to this definition of romantic, even if the adventure results in dinner or escape from enemies? Humans are too complex to categorize their actions as A or B. Whale hunting brought food, but it was also a test of bravery, skill, and fortitude, a means of seeking approval of potential mates, and who knows what else.

Today, there is a popular movement to adapt a paleo-diet; to eat the food that our ancestors ate, because, according to this argument, that is the diet that our DNA and our physiology is adapted to. I suggest that we adapt a *paleo-attitude* to our modern culture, because that is the mind-set that powered humans to survive for two million years, against stronger and faster predators and competitors, through multiple and dramatic climate changes. It is the mind-set that brought our ancestors out of Africa, across deserts, steppes, oceans and tundra, to settle in every habitable environment on Earth.

This journey that I was undertaking with Boomer, around Ellesmere, was a contrived experiment, an elaborate personal allegory, to explore that mind-set. Yet, when told through the powerful, silent voice of these abandoned kayak bones in this harsh and frozen landscape, this *paleo-attitude* of pragmatic-romanticism is the best, perhaps only mind-set that can carry us into the future in a sane, compassionate, and peaceful manner. Yes, technology provides the tools to move a complex society toward sustainability, but technology becomes effective only if supported by patience, acceptance of vulnerability, a recognition of the survival value of a reciprocal relationship with nature, and joy in simple pleasures even in the face of danger and adversity.

POLAR BEARS AND WALRUS

On August 7th, we saw two polar bears, a mom and a cub, walking along the beach. When the mom saw us, she splashed into the water heading in our direction. Boomer grabbed the shotgun, and I felt alert, of course, but not overly adrenalized. There was a few hundred meters of water between the bear and us and, as I correctly surmised, she was warning us, scaring us away, and not actually charging. Anyway, if she had been charging, we probably had a chance to escape in the water, because a kayaker can sprint-paddle about as fast as a bear can swim. Yet, even though I acted calmly, as if I weren't frightened, an underlying fear has imprinted a memory of the bear, with its torpedo-like head and neck, broad shoulders, and huge, powerful paws moving purposefully beneath the clear water, forming a bulging bow wake as her body drove toward us.

Three days later, we were paddling along routinely, on a flat calm day, in half-open water and half-floating ice when I saw a sudden flash of motion under the bow of Boomer's kayak. It didn't register in my brain as animal, vegetable, or mineral, just light and motion, electromagnetic waves traveling at warp speed, as if it were an underwater aurora. The motion doubled back on itself, seemingly almost silvery, like a tiny flying fish, although it was too big for that. And then, an instant later, a giant walrus rose out of the water like an apparition, on the left side of Boomer's kayak, just behind the cockpit, a ton of gracefully awkward skin, blubber, and muscle rising and rising out of the depths, revealing ever more of its improbable bulk, wrapped in brown wrinkled skin, as if it would soon leap entirely out of the water, like a breaching whale.

Inuit hunters, from all over the Arctic, have told me that an angry rogue walrus will hook a kayaker with its tusks, tip him over, and then, not eat him as a crocodile would, but suck out his intestines, as if to savoring the gooey flesh of a giant clam. While this image hovered in my mind, the massive ivory tusks hovered over Boomer's shoulder, protruding out of the bulging jowls, scraggly mustache, and almost cat-like inverted V of a mouth. As Lewis Carroll noted, the walrus's face not only evokes power and danger, but also, paradoxically and mysteriously, silliness and improbability woven together with sage wisdom:

The time has come, the Walrus said,
To speak of many things,
Of shoes and ships and sealing wax
Of cabbages and kings.

For an instant, power, danger, humor, beauty, and mystery were poised in space at that apex between the top of the lunge and the moment when gravity drags everything back downward. I knew that Boomer was dead. I was twenty meters away, too far to react in any meaningful way. And even if I had time, what could I do? The shotgun was on Boomer's boat, but it would be useless anyway because you can't shoot when your partner and an attacker are locked in mortal, hand-to-hand swirling combat. Boomer was dead, and there was no other possible outcome. In that moment of non-time, I realized how much I loved the man. A flash image passed through my brain about Antarctic explorer, Douglas Mawson, who traveled onward after both of his companions had perished, across a landscape where "loneliness was in the vast wasted land outside in the soughing wind, in the corners of his mind, in the anguish and in the fear for his own safety."[20] But hopeless as it was, I had to fight back, so I dipped my paddle in the water to race forward and do battle.

I don't think that the walrus's shoulder actually touched Boomer's kayak, but the upwelling water tipped the boat dangerously on edge. In retrospect, I am so glad he attacked Boomer, and not me, not because I wish him any harm, but because his reflexes are so much faster than mine that he survived when perhaps I would have perished. Boomer reached his paddle out on the right side to stabilize himself with a quick aggressive brace, and then in one fluid, continuous motion he brought the paddle flying back, *whack*, to smack the walrus on the nose. Quickly, another sharp *whack*, and with his paddle almost tangled in the massive tusks, he pushed hard against the sea monster's face, using the force of this thrust to propel him out of immediate harm's way. I must have been frozen momentarily because Boomer glanced over his shoulder with a look of terror, mixed almost with a wry grin. Then he shouted one command, "Paddle!"

The walrus settled back into the water and serenity spread, once again, across the seascape of ice and ocean. Danger and then non-danger. As if it were all a chimera. Peacefulness on a calm ocean with white ice floating in a patchwork mosaic and channels that we could follow, like the labyrinth in the amanita journey with Moolynaut, toward The Other World.

We reached Cape Faraday that afternoon and visited the ruins of tiny stone igloos used by the Stone Age migrants in Qitdlaq's party, in 1853. Like the bleached bones of the kayaks we had found earlier, these humble habitations were another silent reminder of our ancestors on their improbable, treacherous migration across this landscape, huddled by the light of blubber lamps, through the interminable darkness of a polar winter. I had visited this Cape with Chris on our expedition in 1988, before we had veered east, left Ellesmere, and crossed over to Greenland. At that time, as young lovers, we had spent an afternoon wandering through this sacred site. Now I walked away from Boomer to be alone for a moment, to think about Chris's strength and bravery, and the wondrous marriage that we had shared. It was a time to grieve, again, but I was too fundamentally exhausted, down to my core, too close to the razor-thin edge of the near disaster we had faced earlier in the day, to reflect deeply on Chris's untimely death six years ago. My journal entry for the day read, "*Boomer attacked by walrus. Got to Cape Faraday. See old ruins. 26 miles. Tired.*"

Suddenly there were polar bears everywhere, every day. My laconic journal entries record their passage: "*Polar bears on floe, but no hassle.*" "*Saw two young bears, probably litter-mates, hunting on broken ice. They checked us out. Boomer got out the gun but no problems.*" "*Saw two bears while paddling. Then a bunch more. Then a mom and two cubs at camp. If I remember correctly, that makes 11 for the day."*

On the night of August 15th, day 98 of the expedition, I wrote, *"The sun is losing its power and I am cold a lot. Above freezing but wet. Rashes on hands. Feet swollen."* Then I crawled into my damp bag and dozed off. The tent was swaying in the wind, a movement that registered peacefully in my sleeping brain, as sailors know the motion of their boats at some deep subliminal level that pervades sleep. Around 1:00 AM, the gentle undulation became a sharp jerk. I awoke abruptly, knowing in my heart to scream, "Go away bear!" I reached for the shotgun that lay between us, but Boomer, quick as he is, had already grabbed it. Then the world went silent again, except for the wind. We sat shoulder to shoulder, the barrel of the gun swaying ominously back and forth, as we looked and listened apprehensively, waiting fearfully for the seemingly inevitable paw swipe that would shatter our little nylon home. When the anticipation became unbearable, holding the loaded weapon in one hand, with the safety off and his finger on the trigger, Boomer cautiously zipped open the inner tent door to peek inside the vestibule. There, not more than an arm-length away, he came face to face with a polar bear—two curious eyes and a long black snout that protruded incongruously, curiously, almost comically, into the hole in the vestibule that the bear had just torn.

From previous experience, Boomer and I had decided that tough-talking profanity was the best first line of defense. We had to somehow communicate to the bear, "You're bad. But we're just as bad. Or badder."

"Fuck you Bear! Fuck your Mother! Fuck the Horse You Rode in On!"

The bear backed away. Boomer unzipped the outer door of the rainfly and peering over his shoulder, I saw two additional males, along with a mother and two cubs, all hanging out among the nearby rocks, while the Bad Boy Bear who had entered our abode was sulking away, his nose to the ground, like a child caught with her hand in the cookie jar. And then—nothing happened. The bears moved off slowly, sideways, telling us with body language, "Well, we'll leave now, because you are making such an awful racket, saying all those naughty words. We'll leave, but we're not really afraid of you, just respectful—as long as you respect us."

Once again, I was faced with the question that I had asked on the second day of the expedition, "Why didn't The Bear, or more precisely, this small tribe of bears, eat us?" If Bad Boy had charged, or if they had all made a coordinated attack, as if attacking a seal, moving fast and resolutely, swiping with their powerful paws, snapping their ferocious canines, surely they could have killed us before we had the time to grab the gun. To understand their restraint you have to assign motives, emotion, or even human-like thought processes to these wild animals, which is dangerous ground, open to criticism or even rebuke in this urban, scientific, us-centered world we live in. But I've been here before, with the Spirit Wolf, and before that, with Moolynaut on the wings of the Black Raven. I believe that this Bear, all bears, have a unique and wondrous consciousness, just as we have. Oh, it's different, of course, and perhaps unmeasurable. But it's there. And in that bear's consciousness, it recognized, in some electromagnetic way, that Boomer and I also have a unique and wondrous consciousness. That, even though we were potentially edible, we were different than a seal. Maybe it was fear, maybe respect. Maybe something I can't define. Those are just words. But in those moments, when Boomer and I sat shoulder to shoulder, in the waning twilight of the Arctic summer—with the loaded gun because sometimes bears do eat people—we communicated—mammal to mammal. Restraint, fear, respect, oneness, unity, solidarity—words again. But I am convinced that we both understood that we were equally powerful, potentially fearsome, blobs of DNA and protoplasm. Certainly, we smelled different than a seal, and it's perfectly reasonable to argue that the bears were just afraid of us. But I like to think that in addition, we shared a unique and bonding higher level of mammalian consciousness; that together we were sharing the beauty and hardships of this frozen landscape. And once you cross that line and recognize the sentience out there in nature, once you stare face to face with a living, breathing polar bear and negotiate a détente—you don't eat me, I won't shoot you—then your relationship with the planet changes.

John Vaillant's excellent book, *The Tiger*, is about such a détente. In this true story, Vaillant documents that, traditionally, the hunters and trappers of the Siberian taiga respected a long-standing truce with the tigers. Hunters didn't kill tigers; tigers didn't eat people. When the hunters broke that truce, the tigers returned the violence with calculated vengeance, carefully, patiently, and lethally stalking their human prey. Humans and tigers both suffered and the taiga became a less pleasant, more vulnerable, and more dangerous place for all. By extension, on a global scale, if humans nurture a cooperative, harmonious, reciprocal relationship with nature, both will flourish, whereas if we "kill the tiger" we threaten our own existence.

Faulkner again: "You mean he (the bear) already knows me, that I ain't never been to the big bottom before…So I will have to see him, [the boy] thought, without dread or even hope. I will have to look at him."

"So I will have to see him." Seven words to sum up Deep Ecology. In my interpretation, when the boy says, "I will have to see him…I will have to look at him…" he is clearly talking about a much deeper interaction than mere vision, it is about *feeling* the environment at a deep visceral level. It is about smelling the polar bear's stale, seal-meat breath, and telling him to Fuck Off, even while you are honoring the Bear Spirit that has paid you a visit. Deep Ecology is about real and metaphorical passages through the Nares Strait, ducks skimming over the water, walrus attacks— embracing our own powerlessness—the cold, the sore toes, and swollen feet—passing into the zone beyond willpower—striving individually to survive, while at the same time revering the Bear Spirit and the Ice Spirit that might easily kill you in an instant. There is no other way.

Even though we had only slept a few hours, Boomer and I skipped breakfast, packed up quickly, and paddled southward. That evening, when the adrenaline had been reabsorbed into our bloodstreams, and we had a moment to relax before sleep, I texted Nina: "Bears scare us. We scare bears. Wind scares us. We don't scare the wind."

GRISE FIORD AND HOME

As we continued south, huge waterfalls cascaded off towering ice cliffs formed by land-based glaciers on Ellesmere, while equally awe inspiring ice islands, calved off the even more massive Greenland glaciers, floated in the sea. The sun was so low against the horizon now that the sky had a perpetual purplish hue, embracing us in its pastel glow. We talked too much about home and the end of the expedition, clean sheets and showers, friends and girlfriends, ham sandwiches and potato chips, until one or the other of us would repeat the obvious, "Stop this meandering, weak-willed complaining. We need to be here, now. Enjoy this place, because we will never be here again."

And then, for a while, I would be here, in the moment, with a paddle connected to my hands as if it were a living appendage. I would be here, a creature of the ice, watching the landscape drift past, the ice continue to melt, the wind blow, and the waves rock the boat, while the sun dipped ever lower, ever so slowly, toward the long night of a polar winter. I would be here, paddling my orange plastic kayak like those ancestors before me paddling their craft of driftwood, seal skin, and sinew. I would be here, blissfully hyperaware of this infinitely complex, infinitely beautiful, ever-changing environment—Moolynaut's world, the world of the

Nares Strait with its shifting ice. And then my pesky think-too-much-know-it-all brain would decide that I am bored, because the empty spaces in Lao Tzu's wheel were lacking something, not strengthening, because there were no billboards or newspapers, because I couldn't conjure up a big plate of broccoli, complete with mayonnaise-rich Hollandaise sauce.

On August 16th, our 101st day, the pack closed in again, and for one last, weary time, we battled through a maze of ice that was so tight we wedged pans apart with our paddles and kayaks, to find open passages. The following day as we crossed the mouth of a fiord, a strong arctic gale, called a williwaw, dropped off the icecap and threatened to push us out to sea. We battled to shore, rested briefly, ate a handful of nuts, and continued onward, hugging to the lee of the rocks, like bedraggled muskrats. A few miles later, we rounded King Edward Point, the southernmost extremity of Ellesmere, and turned northwest toward Grise Fiord and home. We may have celebrated with a brief high-five. Maybe not. It didn't matter, we were focused mainly on finding a hunter's cabin that Raymond had told us about so long ago. By the time we reached the shack, our weakened bodies were shivering from the cold, so we started up our main stove, and then also ran our auxiliary stove, to provide as much heat as we could generate—because we were close to the finish now and had a little extra fuel to spare.

On Thursday, August 18th, we decided to make a long open-water crossing to shortcut across a bay. I started off strongly, over a flat, calm sea, but as we neared the far shore, I was overcome by a fatigue that struck with the ferocity and suddenness of the williwaw we had encountered yesterday. One instant, everything was just fine, and then an instant later, I could barely lift my paddle. A serene fog descended. "Of course you have another layer of reserve," I told myself, "that layer, beyond willpower." But then I didn't—and it was all so peaceful, because both the wall of fatigue and the fog were absolute and impenetrable. I had no power left, there was only the Arctic, wrapping me it its opaque dampness, and I knew now, without words—again—why Moolynaut had urged me to do this thing.

Meanwhile, Boomer was disappearing into the mist, so I called out for him to wait, and then, from somewhere, the energy mysteriously overcame the non-energy. My paddle felt light, the smooth cadence of stroke after stroke, through wrist, arm, and torso, felt natural, like breathing, and the landscape felt like home. The fog lifted just as we reached shore and we dragged the boats onto a protected grassy meadow, so lush it seemed as if it were some uber-green golf course in an almost forgotten land. I lay down on the soft vegetation and felt heat radiating from the earth, which was paradoxical because on this day the sun actually set for the first time, although we would never have known, because it was already hidden behind a nearby mountain and it didn't get dark enough for the stars to twinkle.

I turned on my satellite phone and read a text from Nina that another storm was imminent, so we slept briefly and woke at 4:00 AM. As we broke camp, I felt miraculously young and strong, as if my body were toying with me, as if this were the first day of a weekend outing with the grandchildren. We slipped into our boats, pulled the spray-skirts tight, crossed our last open-water fiord over a calm sea, and rounded our last exposed rocky point, watching the storm clouds build to the west. At around noon, at low tide, we paddled through a shallow bay, slaloming around exposed rocks, back toward the small hamlet of Grise Fiord where we had started with my skins screwed on backwards over a frozen ocean 104 days before. I joked to Boomer that we should grab a little food at the local store and make a quick victory lap around the island, trying to break 100 days this time. With houses and the huge blue fuel tank dominating the horizon, a few locals gathered on the beach as our bows crunched against the gravel. I handed my camera to one of the men and he snapped a photo.

I look at it now. The hull of my boat and my body are reflected in the mirror smooth water, with the reflection seemingly double-exposed over the rounded rocks of the ocean bottom. In the distance, you can see an unnamed mountain, its reflection slightly blurred by a wisp of wind in the fiord. This had been our first landmark at the start of the journey. In the photo, Boomer is red-faced and smiling. My eyes are closed with my head half resting on my life vest and neck hidden, as if I am a turtle about to recede into the shell of an indescribably deep fatigue.

We pulled our boats above the high tide line, leaving everything behind except our cameras, memory chips, passports, and money, and walked back up the hill to Raymond's for a much-needed shower. After I had washed off the layers of sweat and grime in abundant and luxurious hot water, I put on clean cotton clothes and sat at Raymond's 1950's Formica kitchen table, with its patterns of green and gold. With a cup of bitter, stale, previously-boiled and now lukewarm, watery coffee in one hand, I wrote in my journal:

>August 19
>*Warm today.*
>*Feet very swollen and sore.*
>*Very.*
>*Complete circumnavigation.*
>*Yahoo.*
>*Now to get home.*

There was a scheduled flight out of Grise the next day, but the anticipated storm rolled in and grounded all aircraft. Boomer and I hung out, talking now of home, and the moment when we would separate into our individual lives—lives separated by a generation. We bought what fresh produce was available, and cooked a scrumptious meal of potatoes, onions, cabbage, and carrots. Then, for lack of anything better to do, we binged on chips and salsa.

That night, around 3:00 AM, I woke to pee, but when I got to the bathroom, no urine would flow. Over the next few hours, I continued to have an intense, painful, and seemingly uncontrollable urge to pee, but when I returned repeatedly to the toilet, nothing would come out. I've been sick before, and I know what it feels like to have the flu. I've been hurt before and know what it feels like to sprain an ankle or break a bone. Not being able to pee is different. Your basic metabolism has broken down. Wastes accumulate in the bloodstream. The ratio of sodium to potassium ions in your blood goes haywire and your muscles don't know how to operate. I lay down on the thin, worn, red, mite-infested carpet in Raymond's living room, and my muscles trembled, as if shivering in my sleeping bag as a blizzard raged outside.

Raymond drove me to the nursing clinic in the big diesel sewage truck that he managed for the hamlet. Wendy, the kindly nurse, determined that my blood pressure was off the charts and other vital signs were "life threatening." Then she inserted a catheter and we both hoped and expected a stream of yellow fluid to seep down that clear plastic tubing into the bag. No luck. My blood pressure went even higher. In a stern, authoritative voice, Wendy ordered, "Your vital signs are life threatening because you are worrying too much. So, stop worrying."

I looked at her wanly. How could I explain that I was too drained of all energy to worry? Or, maybe she was right. Maybe I was worrying too much. Whatever. How was I supposed to know? For the past 104 days, I had pushed the limits of control and endurance as far as I could. Maybe the other day, in the fog, when I had lost all power to paddle, and then found it again, maybe that was the last burst of energy I could summon. Now I simply could not will my blood pressure to lower, or my body to release the wastes that were clearly accumulating in my bloodstream. It seemed to me that all systems were acting—or failing to act—on their own accord, without central management.

When yelling at me didn't work, Wendy thought I might

calm down if she gave me some morphine, so she inserted an IV, set up a saline drip, and added the narcotic. I slipped into a pleasant-enough drugged haze.

I have a medical evacuation insurance policy with Global Rescue, so Boomer called them and reported on my condition. Wendy fed the data to a medical team at Johns Hopkins hospital in Baltimore, and the doctors confirmed, "Yup, he's dying. Find an airplane and go get him, right away."

I heard what they were saying, but I didn't believe them. Through the morphine haze, I thought, "Gimme a break." After all I had gone through, I wasn't going to just slip off into oblivion now that I was in this warm room with all the food I could eat, no Bad Boy polar bears, and lots of people making a big fuss over me.

The storm persisted and all aircraft were grounded.

On the morning of August 22nd, after being unable to pee for around 55 hours, my older daughter Reeva, who is a veterinarian, called and became uncharacteristically professional, as if she were talking to the owner of a prized, pet poodle. "Dad, I know a lot about mammalian metabolism. You are a mammal. This is very serious." I hung up and told Wendy what Reeva had said. Wendy told me not to worry so much. Then she took away phone privileges because she didn't want me to discuss my condition with any more potential troublemakers. Perhaps, because she didn't know what else to do but felt that she had to do something, she gave me another shot of morphine. I zoned out. Boomer came and went, being cheery and friendly. Even though he seemed to be vaguely out of focus, floating in a separate reality, he remained a foundation of familiarity in this sterile clinic that didn't smell or feel at all like my old friend, the tent.

Meanwhile, back in civilization, Global Rescue chartered a twin-engine jet air ambulance to come and get me. The pilot, saying that he would go no further due to bad runway conditions and inclement weather at Grise Fiord, flew with a flight medic named AJ to the northern coast of Baffin Island and landed at

Arctic Bay. AJ convinced a skilled and heroic bush pilot to make the dangerous crossing to Grise Fiord and land under the fog bank, between the ocean and the mountains. Wendy packaged me up and someone came by with a pickup truck to take me to the dirt airstrip. Boomer asked if he could hitch a ride south along with the evacuation.

I felt a huge wave of relief when I climbed painfully into the airplane, happy to be moving toward medical attention, and, at the same time, bummed out that I was heading home in such an inglorious finale, in a standard white hospital gown with my ass sticking out into the Arctic morning.

We flew to Arctic Bay, transferred into the jet, flew again, and then landed in Iqaluit, on the south coast of Baffin, to refuel. Boomer's girlfriend, Sarah, an accomplished Arctic explorer, lives in Iqaluit and she was waiting on the tarmac. As soon as he saw her face, Boomer excitedly grabbed his duffel. I knew, intuitively, that he was gone forever out of my life. Oh, of course, we would see each other again, and we would always love each other for those days on the ice with the danger and the easy-going rambling closeness, but due to our generational difference, this was, in essence, goodbye.

Hunched over in the cramped space, Boomer reached the doorway to the aircraft, where he was in shadow, back-lit by the brilliant summer sun. I wanted to make some sort of speech, to hug him or something, but the medics, the pilot, and the refueling crew were bustling around, and the morphine made concentration, words, and action impossible. Words were irrelevant, anyway, as they had been so frequently over the past months. And then, in this now-rapidly changing world, Boomer waved, turned toward Sarah and disappeared. AJ closed the door, the pilot revved up the engine, and we taxied onto the runway.

Once we were airborne, I was, again, alone with my thoughts in this sterile alumascape zooming quickly and improbably through the heavens, an environment so alien from the sea and ice-scapes that had been my reality for so long. I think that AJ must have cut down the morphine because, for the first time in a few days, I shook off the haze and felt like Jon Turk again. Compromised, in pain, unable to pee or control my muscles, but recognizable as myself.

"Good, that's a start." Out there in my kayak, pushing myself beyond limits, I had made life and death decisions every day. I don't think that Wendy appreciated my will to survive, and I felt that she had endangered my life when she drugged me into near oblivion, bypassing my best opportunity to remain alive.

"Good, thank you AJ, I have a better chance now."

In a methodical manner, as if I were evaluating ice movement rather than the thin thread of metabolism that kept my heart beating, I tried to move my arms and legs, to evaluate how much control I had left over the muscles. That experiment was compromised because I was tightly strapped to the gurney, but still, I couldn't do basic isometric exercises. Not good. If my blood chemistry was so wacko that my arms and legs weren't working, how was my heart hanging on? I listened to the rhythms of heartbeat and breathing and decided that things were running rough, but that my body was smart enough to keep the heart going, as a last resort, even when everything else had turned off. I would make it to Ottawa. AJ later told me that as soon as people ask, "Am I going to die?" then poof, off they go. I must have understood this intuitively, because I still had faith in my own strength down the stretch. I hope that when it is finally time to die, I will know that I am about to pass the threshold and give in peacefully, and the doctors will back off on the drugs so I can truly experience this last grand journey.

Perhaps because I was concentrating on living, I didn't experience any near-death revelations. As Oleg told me so many years ago, "Jon, you are a lousy traveler in The Spirit World. You are a hunter like me. You must make your journeys on the tundra." It wasn't time for me to journey into The Spirit World, and on that airplane I pushed through the drugs just as I had pushed through willpower to continue paddling, to remain in a hyper-tactile communication with my body and everything else around me.

With AJ's face and stethoscope hovering over me, I reminisced about all the obstacles Boomer and I had overcome: rough ice, pressure ridges, crawling through slush, and that night of ecstasy when we paddled through the hourglass in the Nares Strait. In the end, I felt a great and enduring pride in our accomplishment, mixed with a recognition that I, at least, had been foolish to push my aging body so far. But a foolishness I was proud of. Foolish, as there is foolishness in most of the grand things that we do. Because journeying around Ellesmere was secondary. I had followed my deepest passion into the rawest depth of my strength and endurance. Forever, in my life, when I am tired, cold, hungry, or just plain grumpy for no reason at all, if I can step outside of my momentary travail for just a second, I can remind myself that I had the power—I have the power—to paddle to the portal of death. And return.

But it was more than that. When I am not just a little bit old, but really, really old, perhaps, if I am lucky, I can remember sitting on that hillside and watching the ice melt. Perhaps I can find joy in that elusive space between the spokes in the wheel.

Then, with clarity, grinning through all the confusion, I reflected one more time that to reach the starting line of this expedition I first had to walk out of the expectations of my society—so many years ago—which in retrospect involved determination and risk, but no foolishness. No foolishness at all. My awakening, or rebellion, if that is what you care to call it, had led me on an improbable wayward journey to a gypsy wagon, and then, decades later, to a small village on a sand-spit in Kamchatka, the east coast of Siberia. And now, I finally comprehended the commitment I had made to Moolynaut when I stood naked on one foot and told her, "My mother never taught me how to talk to Kutcha the Raven. But I will try." With Moolynaut, I had journeyed through the dark labyrinth of the amanita, and now with Boomer I had journeyed through the white labyrinth of the ice, and through all of that, I was privileged to know that the Black Bird was out there, cawing from telephone lines, ready to carry messages to The Woman Who Lives on the Highest Mountain, if we will only take the time out of our busy lives to seek this level of communication. Now all that was left was the flow of ice, representing both the Earth itself and my own fleeting mortality, churning, grinding out of the North Pole, southward toward the equator. Melting. Because if anything significant happened to Boomer and me out there, it was that we were honored to feel the ice—the planet—as a living, breathing entity. Perhaps it was only for a few moments in time, but it was there, we touched it, wrapped up in our own obvious and glorious frailty.

The whine of the jet engines softened and the radio cackled. The pilot talked to the control tower, then to the hospital staff, where a team of specialists was waiting for me. AJ read off my vital signs and the pilot repeated them. A doctor came on the aviation frequency and asked the control tower to give us landing priority over a string of commercial passenger liners, carrying vacationers home and business executives to and from work. "Whoa," I thought, with an almost unreal detachment, as if watching the final minutes of a close basketball game.

If I had any clear thought, it was that I just wanted to live, and to do that, I needed to pee, a simple bodily function that we take for granted every day, yet is so critical. The wheels rotated out of the underbelly of the aircraft, and clicked into place, and then we touched down softly onto the runway, masking the speed and the forces involved. I was relieved to be returning to this wondrous civilization that had the power to save my life.

The jet taxied to a halt and the door opened into a summer evening. Warm fresh air from the outside, even airport air infused with jet exhaust, feels so much more nourishing than warm air from inside the alumascape. Wondrous, soft, embracing. Life-giving. Attendants rolled the stretcher out of the airplane. Guards stood by and gates opened. They raced me into an ambulance, another constricted tube full of whiteness and gadgets. Again, smiling but intent faces hovered over me. Their job was to keep me alive until we reached the next team of specialists. We exchanged pleasantries. A siren turned on and the red flashing light reflected across the tarmac. We were on the freeway and it was evening rush hour. People were driving home from work, thinking of their families and dinner, listening to the radio perhaps, maybe fretting over problems at the office. Nina and my younger daughter, Noey, were waiting at the hospital. It would be good to see them.

CHAPTER 3

BIKE RIDE TO
THE DALAI LAMA'S BIRTHPLACE

The massive red Dong Feng truck passed so close that I could feel it vibrate as it downshifted, as if I were astride it, like Dr Strangelove riding the atomic bomb to oblivion, waving his cowboy hat in the air. In Chinese, Dong Feng means "East Wind", inspiring images of mating cranes taking flight—idyllic and pastoral—not a diesel-belching 22-wheeled monster carrying re-bar onto the Tibetan Plateau, to build roads, skyscrapers, and factories in the Himalaya.

MISTAKES HAPPEN

When the ambulance screeched to a stop at the Ottawa Hospital at the end of the Ellesmere expedition, I figured that I was going to survive this commotion. But I had heard rumors that they were going to put me on dialysis, a fancy medical word that I knew was bad, without fully understanding the details or ramifications. I was too young, and there were too many fun things left to do, to be hooked up to a machine for the rest of my life. Okay, we'll worry about that later. Right now, I wasn't dead.

After all the rush and expense of flying me there on a private jet, I ended up stuck in the hallway on my gurney for a seemingly long time while aides bustled around importantly filling out paperwork. Nina and Noey were standing beside me, smiling, and holding my hand, which made me feel as if I were already back home in the Bitterroot Mountains, and drinking my morning coffee while watching a red-headed pileated woodpecker hammering for bugs inside tree trunks. Finally they wheeled me into the treatment room where the portable dialysis machine was already revved up, humming softly, friendly and threatening, like a purring tiger, lights blinking. I thought, "It would be hard to ski with that fucking thing strapped on my back."

A small army of men and women in white coats poked, jabbed, and measured me, connected me to devices for more measuring, and then retreating to a corner to talk quietly among themselves. When they returned to my bedside, a nurse removed my catheter, which wasn't doing anything anyway because there was no urine in the tube or the attached bag.

She raised her eyes and looked at the lead doctor. "That came out easily?"

The doctor turned his head, looked at me thoughtfully, then at the computer print-outs in his hand. "If I look at these," he said, shaking the papers and speaking to me, but also thinking out loud to himself, "You appear to be a very sick man." He paused. "But if I look at you, you appear to be a very healthy man who needs to be jump-started." The doctor then turned to the nurse, and spoke softly, "Insert a new catheter." She did. It seemed that she pushed a little harder than Wendy had pushed in Grise Fiord. There was just a tiny bit of dull pressure, like an accidental elbow jab on a crowded subway—nothing at all like being bashed over the head by a polar bear's paw—and suddenly a deluge of dark yellow urine flowed into the bag. And kept flowing and flowing. The pressure on my abdomen released instantly and through the morphine and the general haze caused by a chemical imbalance in my system, I watched the bag fill up. Nina's hand tightened on mine; I squeezed back and when I looked into her eyes, I started to cry softly because I saw our old life returning, full of wonder, mountain biking among spring wildflowers, skiing on snowy ridge-tops, picking strawberries in her garden or huckleberries in the forest. Everything was going to turn out fine.

Later, the urologist in Missoula explained that my urethra had been blocked by an enlarged prostate. Then, although no medical professionals were willing to say this outright, I am certain that the kindly, well-meaning nurse in Grise Fiord was too frightened and inexperienced to force the catheter past the blockage. Consequently she didn't drain the bladder. So, a condition that is fairly normal for old men, and that should have been diagnosed and treated routinely, that should have been no big deal, nearly killed me. The rescue insurance company incurred an unimaginably huge cost to charter a private jet into the High Arctic.

In retrospect, I shake my head that this incredible error-induced-near-death occurred in a medically advanced nation. She was an experienced nurse who had been in charge of an Arctic clinic for decades. How could she have been so incompetent? Didn't they teach her how to insert a catheter during the first week of nursing school? Having my life in her hands was like hiring an auto mechanic who doesn't know how to change the oil.

Anyway. Mistakes happen. I'm not dead. All is long past—forgiven.

My kidneys had been through a bit of a shock, and the enlarged prostate was still an issue, so it took some months, one more hospital stay, a surgery, and some anxious weeks before I could walk out into the woods, unzip my fly, casually watch the clouds drift lazily past, and piss against a tree.

There's one more question: Unanswered, and unanswerable. In all the great span of days and years, why did my prostate just happen to become inflamed 36 hours after we had completed the expedition, and not at any other time? If the same thing had happened 36 hours before the end of the expedition, a rescue would have been much more complicated, perhaps so much more complicated that I would have died. If it had happened a few days later, it would have precipitated a routine visit to the emergency room in Hamilton, Montana. The urologist told me that it was coincidence, nothing more; don't make a big deal of it. Fine. That's his opinion. With the caveat that I never went to medical school, (but I do have a free and universal degree from the Google School of Fine Medicine) I disagree. I believe that during the expedition, my body was so intent on performance and survival, that, among a host of other complex functions, it was pumping massive doses of natural anti-inflammatory hormones, such as cortisol, into the bloodstream. These natural hormones kept a marginally enlarged prostate from exploding to the critical point where it stopped me from peeing. Once the journey stopped, and my body and I were in what I imagined to be a safe environment, these natural homeostatic controls shut down. Essentially, my body said, "Whew. It's been a lot of work getting you around that stupid island. But I'm done now. Exhausted. Can't I relax now?" And, with a mouth full of chips and salsa, I said, "Sure. Mission accomplished. Relax away. We can both relax now."

But we relaxed just a bit too much, causing the cortisol levels to drop off, and then, *pop*, the prostate, released from the chemical restraining order, zoomed out of control, which rapidly cascaded into the medical emergency that I endured. If you accept my amateur interpretation, rather than the urologist's professional view of things, then you can only marvel at the intense and powerful relationship between thoughts and chemistry—between willpower and that place beyond willpower.

Fine. I was 65, almost 66 by this time, had accomplished a physical journey of great magnitude—whatever that means—been successful on some measure of those things—again, whatever that means—and then skated away from my own folly, and the folly of others, emerging alive, at the end of the labyrinth—and still able to pee. Enough already, right?

UNUSUAL TRAVEL SUGGESTIONS ARE DANCING LESSONS FROM GOD[21]

After Chris died, in 2005, I found it impossible to live alone, hermit like, in that house-cabin in the Montana forest. So I moved into my Ford Ranger pick-up truck for a couple of years, staying briefly in Boulder, CO, and Taos, NM. In both places, I had the opportunity to live a rural-urban lifestyle, surrounded by nature, yet close to a vibrant intellectual and artistic community. Both times, I walked out the door, and drove back home to Montana. I can't explain my feelings in a five paragraph essay, with a proper beginning, middle, and end. All I can tell you is that the mountainside above that simple, half run-down house in Montana had become my silent, faithful companion, like a conscious, breathing, living friend. Like the Spirit Wolf who had come to say hello—and incidentally to remind me of my own vulnerability. In addition, I missed my Montana friends and neighbors, both the white-haired, ex-hippie, unemployed, semi-derelict skiers and mountain bike riders and the ultra-conservative rednecks who would disagree with me vehemently if we were ever stupid enough to enter into a senseless, unresolvable political discussion, but who would also come over to share a beer and deep friendship, and who would gladly stop by to help if I needed to move my refrigerator.

And then Nina moved into my life. She expanded the garden, and when Boomer and I were off in Ellesmere, she solicited her thin, white-bearded brother Don to come over, cut a big hole in the south side of the house with a chain saw, and tack on an attached greenhouse.

When I walked out of my last hospital stay that fall, away from all those sterile life-saving gadgets, needles, dials, and machines, along with the smiling nurses and abundant sick people—when I stepped into the blinding sunshine and took the first tentative, unbalanced, painful steps across the parking lot toward the plate of green broccoli smothered in mayonnaise that I had dreamed of and lusted after, I thought, "Now, as an old man, can I please just sit on my rocking chair, drink a soothing cup of chamomile tea, and live in my home in true contentment?" I told anyone who wanted to listen that I was done with foreign expeditions in remote places. Maybe I would start tilling my own small patch of snow peas.

Several months later, in mid-winter, when I turned on the computer after a hard day of skiing soft powder, an email showed up from my friend, Ma LuBin, who lives in Xinjiang Province in northwest China:

> Dear Mr Turk (old man):
> It has been too long that you are not visiting in China.
> Come now and we will ride bicycles across the mountains
> to the Dalai Lama's birthplace.
> Ma LuBin (also old man)

Luckily, I'm not a politician. So I can say dumb things and then change my mind without hiring a crisis team to convince everyone that I didn't say that dumb thing in the first place. I hit the "reply" button and fired off a short note:

> Dear Mr Ma LuBin:
> What a wonderful idea. When do we start?
> Your Friend, Jon Turk

As Kurt Vonnegut famously said, "Unusual Travel Suggestions are Dancing Lessons From God."

If I went halfway around the world to view His Holiness's birthplace, you could argue that I was launching on a religious pilgrimage. But actually, that's way too pretentious, overblown, and self-aggrandizing. The truth is that I was only pretending to be a pilgrim. I'm not a practicing Buddhist and I know very little about the Dalai Lama, other than what everybody else knows: that he has become a global spokesperson for tolerance, peace, compassion, and environmental ethics. Furthermore, that short stint in the interrogation room in Jerusalem so long ago had permanently cured me of any desire to join any organized religion—ever.

So why did I decide to go, almost immediately after the electrons had come to a screeching halt after their long journey across the ocean from China and even before they dried on my computer screen? The answer to that question is uncomplicated. Ma LuBin was a good friend and an interesting travel partner, a philosopher-comic and Falstaff-like commentator on the monochromatic Chinese society. Tibet and the Himalayas are exotic destinations for an addicted traveler like myself. A bike ride is always fun, even though—or especially because—we were guaranteed to get cold, hungry, worn out, and out-of-breath along the way.

But that is an oversimplification, too. Ever since I had stood naked on one leg while Moolynaut had chanted us into the Other World—perched precariously, wing-tip to wing-tip with Kutcha the Raven, wavering in the wind on a thin branch—I was, in my own weird, unplanned, chaotic way, perpetually seeking not only adventure but also pilgrimage, if you want to call it that. And I felt that I had come a long way, interacting so intimately in the Wild of Ellesmere, talking with its ice and storms, and drinking coffee with its animals. But, actually, I had only opened the door and peeked timidly inside. I hadn't even come close to completing the journey that Moolynaut had asked me to undertake. I could have continued my journey without making any physical journey at all, in that garden with those snow peas, 10 meters from my front door. I just didn't happen to choose to do it that way.

A VERY BRIEF HISTORY OF CHINESE-TIBETAN RELATIONSHIPS

Over the millennia, Chinese-Tibetan relationships have been complex, and, as is true for most of Central Asian history, frequently bloody. At various times the two nations have been allies or enemies, at peace or at war. There has been honesty, subterfuge, prevarication, signed treaties, broken treaties, trade, peace, war, treachery, feasts, murder, rape, ceremony, poisonings, unity, and schisms. A long time ago, Tibet conquered China for a brief period, but more recently, and much more frequently, China has conquered Tibet or chunks of Tibet. According to historian Sam Van Schaik, China often assumed the role of benevolent patron to the Tibetan priest-state.[22] In the 18th century, the Chinese conquered the eastern and northern regions of the Tibetan homeland, incorporating them into the provinces of Sichuan and Qinghai, respectively. But up until the middle of the 20th century, the Tibetan mountainous heartland was an independent, physically and culturally isolated Himalayan nation-state, presided over, politically and religiously, by a Buddhist Lama.

According to a tradition dating back to the early 15th century, when the ruling, or Dalai Lama, died, a team of learned acolytes would search the kingdom for a young boy who was the reincarnation of the deceased Holiness. After the 13th Dalai Lama, Thubten Gyatso died in 1933, and was lying in state, the head of his embalmed body, which initially faced south-east, mysteriously turned to face the northeast, indicating that his successor would be found in that direction. Two years later, an infant boy, Tenzin Gyatso, was born to a Tibetan peasant family in the small hamlet on the eastern border of the Tibetan region of Amdo, in Qinghai Province of China. A team of searchers located the boy and showed him various relics, some of which had belonged to the 13th Dalai Lama and some of which had not. As the story is told, he correctly identified all the items owned by the previous Dalai Lama, exclaiming, "It's mine! It's mine!"

The young boy moved to the Potala Palace in Lhasa, but because he wasn't old enough to rule, the senior Lamas did not immediately and officially crown him. Meanwhile, to the east, Mao Zedong led the Chinese Communist army to military victory over the Nationalist government under Chiang Kai-shek and thus brought Communist rule to China. On October 7th, 1950, shortly after the end of the Chinese civil war, the victorious and powerful communists invaded Tibet. The Tibetan forces along the border had no radio, so they sent a runner to the nearest town that had communication equipment. Five days later the messenger managed to alert Lhasa that the country was under attack. There was no response. The leaders in Lhasa were enjoying their annual picnic and not tending to matters of state. A month later, as the invasion raged on and gunfire rang across the high, semi-desert mountainous plateaus and steppe, Tenzin Gyatso, at the age of 15, was formally recognized as the 14th Dalai Lama. Obviously, the young peasant-boy Lama-Ruler had a lot on his plate. On July 7th, 1951, the government in Lhasa ceded to China.

The Dalai Lama summed up the situation in his own, simple, understated words, in the Preface to the book, *Ethics for the New Millennium,*[23]

> Having lost my country at the age of sixteen and
> become a refugee at twenty-four, I have faced a great
> many difficulties during the course of my life. When
> I consider these, I see that a lot of them were insur-
> mountable. Not only were they unavoidable, they
> were incapable of a favorable resolution. Nonetheless,
> in terms of my own peace of mind and physical health,
> I can claim to have coped reasonably well.

After the shooting stopped, Chinese rule was, by and large, peaceful, stable, and for the most part, more or less welcome, or at least well-tolerated. The Chinese helped modernize the country by building roads and hospitals, installing an efficient postal system, and introducing modern banking. A popular saying at the time was: "The Chinese communists are our kind of parents; their silver coins fall like rain."[24]

In 1954, the teenage Dalai Lama traveled to Beijing and met with Mao. After the meeting, Mao personally opened the door for the Tibetan Holy Man and said, "Your coming to Beijing is like coming back to your own home. Whenever you come to Beijing, you can call me. You can come to my place whenever you want to. Don't be shy."[25] As the Tibetans drove back to their quarters, the Dalai Lama told his aides that "Mao was a great and unique person," and that he believed that the situation would unfold favorably.

It did not. The Chinese tried to collectivize Tibetan agriculture. They destroyed monasteries and killed monks and lamas. As a result of these intrusions, injustices, and murders, guerrilla factions formed in eastern Tibet by 1958 and they began to fight the PLA (People's Liberation Army). The Chinese answered with overwhelming force. The Dalai Lama fled to India. Thousands of monks were sent off to labor camps to die under torture or forced labor. Over the next three years, 97% of the 2500 monasteries in Tibet were demolished, and an uncounted number of cultural artifacts and holy books were destroyed.

Jump now to the early winter of 2011, when I received the enigmatic email from Ma LuBin. Despite the fact that hippies had been plastering "Free Tibet" bumper stickers on their cars for 50 years, Tibet had become an established province of China and independence appeared to be a chimera. Tensions had flared up again, in the early 21st century, and over 100 Tibetans had poured gasoline over themselves and lit their bodies on fire, as a gruesome protest. In turn, the Chinese had shut the border to most foreign tourism into Tibet. But Amdo, where Tenzin Gyatso, the 14th Dalai Lama was born, was not in the political boundaries of Tibet, but in Qinghai, which had been part of China for so long that most people have forgotten about the initial invasion and thus, there were no travel restrictions.

MA LUBIN

In September 2012, Nina and I packed our clothes and some lightweight camping gear for ourselves and our friend, and flew to Urumqi, a bustling city of 2.3 million in northwest China, the capital city of Altai Province. Mr. Ma was waiting for us at the airport. He is a small man, tiny even, 60 years old at the time, with short dark hair, just starting to recede, a warm, almost whimsical smile, and a leanness honed first by childhood starvation during the Great Famine, and now by a passion for long distance bike riding. And I was, as least partly, responsible for that passion.

Five years earlier, in 2006, before we met Ma Lubin, Noey and I were riding mountain bikes across the Altai Mountains in central Asia, with inadequate maps and a "guide" who spoke no English, had never been in the area before, and was notably displeased with our agenda. We were tired, hungry, and more or less lost, pedaling along a rutted dirt track that rambled across the broad steppe in Xinjiang, which was once the East Turkistan Republic, the traditional home of Kazakh herders and horse warriors who had been both enemies and allies of Genghis Khan. Late in the day, we descended into a small valley with worn pastures, too many sheep, and dun colored yurts that matched the parched hills. In the village, we met a Kazakh woman who was carrying water in pails swinging from a stick that was balanced across her shoulders. She shyly, but graciously, invited us to dinner in accordance with the Asian nomad's etiquette that anyone who has already pitched their yurt is honored to offer shelter to weary travelers. The men returned from their herds and we all sat cross-legged on colorful carpets to eat mutton and noodles cooked over a cow-dung fire on an open hearth.

The next morning, we rode across rolling grassland, grazed to stubble, under a sky too broad to hold thoughts inside. By late afternoon, we passed irrigated fields and then rolled into the city of Altai with glistening modern buildings and wide avenues, where well-dressed business people hurried along spacious curving sidewalks, past tidy sidewalk-gardens of white, red, and yellow flowers.

Traveling without language is interesting in a way, but you miss a lot, so now that we were in the city, Noey and I located a small college perched on the third floor above a fashionable boutique. We found the head of the English department, who was a pretty young woman dressed in tight jeans and high heeled sandals that revealed glittering purple toe-nail polish.

I knew that the Chinese had wrested this land from the indigenous Kazakh and Uyghur people, just as they had conquered Tibet, and that they had imported agriculture and urbanization into a land traditionally belonging to the nomads. But, even though we had been riding and camping on the landscape, and sharing meals with its people, in our world without language, we witnessed no direct signs of internal discrimination, dissent, or violence. The herders we met were kind and compassionate towards us, and as a result, the conquest and tragedy remained strangely sterile, as if humans weren't involved.

After formalities, I foolishly put on my journalist hat and tried to extract some information about the turmoil and injustice that I knew was lurking behind the pastoral landscapes of Xinjiang.

"What is the relationship between the Han Chinese and the Kazakh people here in northwest Xinjiang Province?" I asked.

"Yes." She smiled.

"Did you understand my question?"

"Yes." Another coquettish smile.

I reworded my inquiry, using simple syntax.

"Oh. We are all very happy."

We chatted, congenially, in this manner until Noey and I thanked the woman and retired to go shopping. When we stepped off the escalator in a large department store, two Philippine women mysteriously approached and suggested that we might want to talk with a local resident named Ma LuBin, who spoke excellent English.

The women arranged a meeting for us in a posh hotel. Ma LuBin approached, a short man, pale, frail-looking, but confident, smiling through bad teeth, and wearing large eyeglasses that made him look like an academic, or maybe an aged Harry Potter. We sat down for tea and he explained in very serviceable but self-taught

English that he was a retired bank clerk, 54 years old, had been married twice and had three children, but was now divorced, living as "a free bird." After the introductions, I asked about the political situation here in northwest China, but our new-found friend waved his hand dismissively, explained in a whisper that he couldn't answer these questions in a public place. Then he invited us to his house. That evening we discussed Hemingway, the Bible, and Joseph Conrad, but Ma LuBin deflected all inquiries about politics, social interactions, or history. Three days later, well-rested but defeated in our quest for information, Noey and I decided to continue our bike ride across the steppe, still with our useless and grumpy guide.

Ma LuBin asked if he could join us.

"But you have never bicycled farther than to the market, you have never camped out, you have a $25, piece-of-shit Chinese bike, no tent, no sleeping bag, and no raincoat. I'm sorry my friend, you can't come."

Ma LuBin, for all his apparent physical frailty, wasn't deterred. In a quiet, but determined voice that assumed no rebuttal, he replied, simply, "But I want to ride with you guys."

"No you can't," I responded firmly, looking hard into those sad eyes behind the oversized glasses.

We shook hands and parted company. And then Noey and I returned to our hotel.

When we woke early the next morning and walked down to the hotel lobby to pay our bill and retrieve our bikes from the storeroom, the clerk told us that a man was waiting outside. He had been there since before dawn, and he had a bicycle.

I looked out the window.

Ma LuBin was sitting on the cold stone steps, with his bike. He had wrapped up a few clothes and a cotton blanket inside a blue denim duffle and tied the load to his bike with some plastic rope-like stuff. The load listed so dangerously to the left that I wondered how he had even made it across the city from his apartment to the hotel. An empty wire basket was clamped to the front handlebars. Ma LuBin was wearing baggy Chinese blue jeans, a gaudy red shirt, and a gray woolen vest that once had been part of a three piece suit, in Shanghai perhaps, or Hong Kong, where businessmen wielded power and pulled financial strings. A blue baseball cap shielded his eyes and those ubiquitous wire-rimmed glasses.

I stepped outside and when he saw me, without exchanging pleasantries, Ma LuBin announced, "I'm coming with you guys."

This was a calm, measured, statement of fact, not a question or a polite inquiry.

"Okay, then," I replied. "We must eat a healthy breakfast before we go."

As we ate and drank our tea, Ma LuBin explained that he had asked his mother for permission to join us and she angrily replied, "How are you ever going to find a suitable Chinese wife if you are out riding with those two Americans?"

The journey began with a long, slow, grind up-hill, on a rutted road, suitable only for four-wheel drive vehicles and high-clearance trucks. Noey and I had been bicycling for a month, had just rested for several days, and we felt fit and strong. The hill was relentless, under a hot sun, and after a few hours, my legs were tiring. But Ma LuBin was pedaling right beside me, staring resolutely ahead, eyes fixed on the ruts. I said nothing. When we reached the summit of the pass, we all stopped and after a moment to catch my breath, I asked, "Hey, Ma LuBin. You are riding an old broken-down bike. You have never in your life ridden on a steep mountain road. How do you ride so strongly?"

Ma LuBin smiled thinly. "In my life, I have suffered more than you have. I am strong in my basically."

"I'm sorry, I am not certain I heard correctly. Did you say that you are strong in your bicycling?"

"No, not so strong in my bicycling," he replied patiently. "Strong in my basically."

In the decade I have known him since that day, I have never questioned or doubted Ma LuBin again.

Ten days later, we stopped at a remote road junction, sat down for a drink and a snack, and I took out my map. Ma LuBin leaned over to get a better look, until his head was almost resting on my chest. Then he looked back and forth, in front of us and behind us, moving his head furtively, as if being watched by a hidden assailant. I followed his gaze, now nervous myself, but we were on the broad brown overgrazed steppe, covered intermittently with low-lying bunch grass, with rounded hills in the distance. A few apple trees clustered around crude irrigation ditches. The wind was calm, the sky blue and there were no people, structures, animals, or vehicles in sight.

Ma LuBin pointed at the map representation of the valley below us, and rested his finger squarely on the label, "Many irrigation ditches." Then he pointed to these features in the landscape.

I looked up, wondering what the problem was.

"Yes?" I asked.

"My father dug those ditches with a shovel."

Then he began to cry. I sat back on my haunches and looked to Noey, who was nearby, wondering how to react.

After a few moments Ma LuBin continued, "You are a writer. Sometimes you ask too many questions. Remember, this is China. There are many stories about the Han Chinese, the Kazakhs, and the Uyghurs. Stories about wars and the Cultural Revolution. Some of these stories may be true, while some may not. It is very hard to know. All the time you ask too many questions. You will talk to me and then go home and say now that you understand China. You will write stories about us. But, remember, you know nothing about China. Nothing. Do you understand me?"

Starting from that day and continuing for the next decade, in bits and pieces, around campfires and in restaurants, in Da Wu, Qinghai and in Canmore, Alberta, Ma LuBin told me the story of his father and his own life. As it was told, the story was fragmented and disjointed, with some sections repeated numerous times, and others whispered only once. Carefully, I filled in the transitions and added dates in my notebooks to form a chronology.

Then, one day, in 2015, in Canmore, Alberta, after I had gathered all my skeletal scribblings and consolidated them into a single, coherent, chronological narrative, when I realized the value of this story, I set my pen and paper aside, and asked: "Ma LuBin. We are friends now. We have bicycled together in China, the US, and Canada. You know that I am a writer. We both know that China is not a free and democratic society. So I have two questions for you. First, do I have your permission to tell this story? And second, may I use your name?"

Ma LuBin's answer was immediate and unequivocal: "Yes, tell my story. It's not just that you have my permission, I ask you to tell this story. It is important for the world to know what happened."

Then he paused for a while, pondering: "My story is history. It is fact. This is not my opinion. Today, people in China can be jailed for their opinions. This story that I have told you is just what happened. No one can put me in jail for telling the simple truth."

Ma LuBin's father, Ma Qiyi, was born in 1930, in Gansu Province, a desert and semi-desert region, situated along the Silk Road that was once the western border of the Chinese Empire. During the Tang dynasty (618-907) soldiers were stationed there, on the edge of the steppe, in isolation, along the Great Wall and its many watchtowers. The poetry of this period describes their feelings as they watched interminably for the dust clouds of advancing nomadic horse-warriors, far from "spring breezes," metaphorically their friends and loved ones in the eastern, urban-agricultural coastal provinces:

Leaving For the Border Garrison

The Yellow River cascades down from white clouds in the sky,
A lone castle among mountains ten-thousand-*ren* high.
The Qiang flute need not blame the willow trees,
For the spring breeze never crosses Jade Gate Pass.[26]

Ma Qiyi, like many other Gansu residents, belonged to the Hui ethnic minority in a predominantly Han Chinese nation. Ma LuBin once told me that his father was "short, like me. He was practical and talked less than I talk, because he believed that talking was useless." The Hui are an Islamic people, descended from Arabic and Persian merchants who traded silk and spices in long camel caravans along the Silk Road. Because they were an adaptable, merchant class, they abandoned their aboriginal languages and spoke Mandarin as the voice of commerce.

In a time when few peasant children learned to read and write, Ma Qiyi attended the Kunlun Middle School, founded by governor and warlord, Ma BuFang. In 1948, just after World War II, when China was embroiled in a bloody Civil War, Ma Qiyi joined Ma BuFang's army, which was loosely allied with the Nationalist leader, Chiang Kai-shek in his fight against Mao Zedong and the People's Liberation Army (PLA). Because he was educated, he became a company secretary and worked in the political department at Division Headquarters. After the communists defeated his unit in 1949, the communists captured Ma Qiyi. They "re-educated" him and he joined the PLA to fight against the Kazakhs in the East Turkistan Republic. Following their military victory, the soldiers were ordered to colonize the conquered land, which was incorporated into China and renamed Xinjiang Province. There were no Chinese women, so family members back in Gonsu loaded young, eligible women into a truck and ferried them out to the new border regions. Ma Qiyi married one of these women, Saifeiying, who was "short and a bit fat, with white skin. Although she was timid, she was good at talking if she spoke, although she never had any schooling at all. She stopped working a few years after their marriage because of many children and remained a housewife for the rest of her life."

The Chinese built farms and cities because the Kazakh people were nomads and the Han rulers wanted them to engage in more conventional commerce and agriculture.

In 1955, Ma Qiyi went to agricultural college to study forestry. When he returned home in 1959, he became the commander of a small village farm. He specialized in growing apple trees, and Ma LuBin describes him, in great loving detail, working in his orchid with a sharp knife and saw, grafting branches of his beloved fruit.

"My father loved his work. He and my mother were happy and we always had enough to eat."

In 1960, Ma Qiyi joined the Communist Party. In one of our discussions, Ma LuBin explained, in cropped sentences, without description or elaboration: "My father was very dedicated. His whole life. In those days, there was no corruption. If you were a leader and became corrupt, they would kill you. People worked hard. Nothing else but work. Nothing. We were building a new China."

On another occasion, when Ma LuBin was visiting us in North America and we were sipping lattes on a summer morning in Moose, Wyoming, just south of Teton Park, we strolled past an old Conestoga wagon. Ma LuBin ran his hand along the curve of a cracked, bleached wooden wheel and told me, "These wagons. My father had a wagon like this. I remember riding in the wagon on his lap when I was a small boy. He would hold me and cluck to the horses. I remember the sound of their feet on the dirt road; I remember listening to their breathing. It was a happy time. When I was a young boy, there were only one or two trucks in our village and no cars."

Ma Qiyi and Saifeiying had six children: five boys and a girl. Ma Lu Bin was born in 1952, in Altai City, where we met him so many decades later.

In my experience, Ma LuBin never complains and seldom talks much about hardship. So when I have asked him, repeatedly, about his personal experiences during the Chinese Great Famine, for a long time he refused to answer. But I knew that it must have affected him in a deep visceral way. According to the official Chinese government histories, 15 million people died of famine during the "Difficult Three Year Period" between 1958 and 1961, although independent historians place the death toll at 20 to 45 million.

Then one day, sitting together around a campfire, near a gurgling stream in the great forests of British Columbia, Ma Lubin began, "I tell you that all the time you ask too many questions. You ask too many times about the Great Famine. I will tell you, now. Go. Get your pencil and your notebook."

I raced to my pack and returned.

"The famine happened between 1960 and 1962 when I was 8 to 10 years old.[3] At that time, everyone was hungry. We were hungry every day. We ate corn cobs. Sometimes we had noodles. Soupy noodles. Less noodles and more soupy. Sometimes, like a dog, I walked into the fields at night, after harvest, to dig some small carrots.

"In other provinces, not Xinjiang, provinces where there were more people and more cities, sometimes people ate other people.

"This is true."

After a pause, he continued, "No problem."

Then he stirred his dinner and looked into the distance, indicating that he was done talking. I slipped my note pad back into my pack and never asked about the Great Famine again.

In contrast, Mr. Ma talked frequently about the Cultural Revolution that occurred a few years later. Like most of the other

3 Note, that this is the only time, in all of his personal chronicles that the facts in Ma LuBin's story differ even slightly from the dates and names in conventional histories of China. I repeat Mr. Ma's dates, as he told them to me, even though they are slightly different from the dates given in conventional histories, and assume that the timing of the Great Famine was slightly different in remote and predominantly rural Xinjiang than in the more populated parts of China.

children of his generation, Ma LuBin went to school. Then one day, in May or June of 1966, when the students were practicing their lessons, army officers burst into the room to announce the start of the Cultural Revolution. From that instant onward, school was over. Done. Finished. The soldiers piled the tables and chairs in storage. Chairman Mao warned that bourgeois elements had infiltrated the government, the schools, and society at large, aiming to restore capitalism. It was everyone's duty to destroy these "revisionists" through class struggle, violent if need be, and maintain the spirit of the Revolution.

From here, our story splits into two parallel threads.

Ma LuBin's grandfather had been a wealthy trader (aka a capitalist). His great grandfather before him had been a wealthy trader. The family was Hui, not Han. Although he was now a member of the communist party, Ma Qiyi had once been in Ma BuFang's rebel army. As a result of all these "suspicious black marks" against him, the zealots of the Revolution declared that Ma Qiyi was an enemy of the state. One night a small group of soldiers came to the house and took him away.

Like most educated local leaders in China at that terrible time, Ma Qiyi was accused of speaking against the government and was therefore branded a criminal. The authorities interred him in a small adobe hut in solitary confinement, with shackles on his wrists and ankles. They interrogated him day and night, for days on end, with the accusers taking shifts, yelling, prodding, torturing.

One night, almost driven into insanity by the incessant pain and sleeplessness, he decided that he could take no more. He said that he needed to go to the outhouse, which was located a short distance from his cell. His interrogator gave him a lantern and he hobbled out, moving slowly because he was encumbered by the leg irons.

At this point in the narrative, Ma LuBin stood up, assumed a bowed, submissive stance, with his hands held together as if hand-cuffed, and hopped on two feet as one would walk if shackled.

Thus moving about the room, he continued slowly, looking at me intently, to be sure I was listening.

"My father hung the lantern in the outhouse. And then he ran away." At this point, Ma LuBin hopped as aggressively as he could, still fixing me in a direct stare. "He knew that they would come after him soon, so he buried himself deep inside a haystack, where he could sleep because he hadn't slept in a long time. Meanwhile, in our house, we heard the soldiers and villagers running about, screaming, 'Capture him! Capture Him!' And we knew that they were searching for my father."

Ma LuBin paused and reflected, "My mother was very worried."

Then Ma LuBin turned abruptly and asked me, "Do you understand?"

I wanted to say, "Yes, I understand," but actually I couldn't comprehend. I didn't want to interrupt the story with my thoughts and feelings, so I simply replied, "Yes."

"Sometime, in the middle of the night, maybe 2 or 3 in the morning, I don't know exactly, we didn't have a clock, my mother heard a quiet scratching on the window. It was my father. Still in chains, he returned home to see my mother. Just to look at her face. Of course, he was captured, imprisoned, and tortured again. Worse this time."

The first time Ma LuBin told me this story, he broke down at this point and sobbed uncontrollably. His face, which had been pale at the beginning of our bicycle journey, was now tanned, offset by a purple bruise above his left eye which he got when he had crashed on a rocky downhill. "I have never told this to anyone before. I tell it to you because we are bicycling together. We are friends."

He continued, more composed now, wiping the tears from his face. "My father was never a bad man. People who once were his friends, people who flattered him when he was a commander, suddenly distanced themselves. No one defended him. Many criticized him publically and claimed that 'he never was my friend.' The men who accused him just wanted to make him look dirty so they would look clean."

At this point, Ma LuBin, who is always fond of American idioms, smiled and told me, "A friend in need is a friend indeed."

Then he continued. "My father was taken back to the room, the prison, and tortured again. My mother would bring food and hand it to the guard and the guard would give it to my father. My mother was never allowed to see my father. Eventually he was released from solitary and sentenced to hard labor with other criminals. They did dirty work like cleaning cesspools, or heavy work like carrying stone for road-building or other construction projects. Things like that."

Then he continued, almost in a whisper. "Actually my father was lucky. He survived. In my village, they hanged a man because his father had been an official under the nationalists. They didn't hang my father."

Meanwhile, back in the village, 14-year-old Ma LuBin, along with all of the other children, was rallying under Mao's directive to abandon school and "Go up to the mountains and down to the countryside." The youth organized into Red Guard "fighting teams" with spiffy uniforms and bright armbands. Ma LuBin's job was to print propaganda posters using a rudimentary process that started with pieces of waxed paper. Ma LuBin would carefully write slogans and draw pictures by scratching the wax off with a needle. Then he duplicated the original with an inked roller to produce copies. Captions read, "Chinese People's Liberation Army is the great school of Mao Zedong's Thought" or called for the destruction of the "Four Olds: Old customs, Old culture, Old habits, and Old ideas." Then the "fighting unit" of 14 to 15-year-olds would parade through the village with raised fists, shouting slogans and hanging the finished posters on walls and doorways throughout the village.

"You have to understand," Ma LuBin told me, holding my arm and leaning close to my face. "We were happy to do this. We were proud. We were excited. We were doing this, not so much for China, as for Chairman Mao." Then he stood up, clenched his fist, jabbed at the air above his head, and marched around the room with a sweet, determined smile, shouting "Hooray for Chairman Mao. Long live the Revolution."

The "fighting units" were also responsible for interrogating and humiliating their former teachers. In a reversal of roles, the teenage Red Guard leaders stood in front of the class, while the former teachers would cower, heads bowed submissively, before them.

"Why are you against Chairman Mao?" a young teenager would bark.

"I am not," the educated elder would reply, head still bowed.

"But you said such-and-such against our Great Chairman."

"I did not."

The students would start yelling. Fiery, excited. They would punch the teacher. "This was no problem. As a member of the Red Guard, you could punch a teacher. Any time. No problem."

Ma LuBin became agitated as he told me this portion of the story, swinging his fists and kicking his feet at the air.

"You could kick the teachers as well. Punch and kick. No problem. Do you understand me?"

I nodded silently.

Invariably, this unruly, uncontrolled, undisciplined mob of children would condemn the teacher as a criminal. The teacher would then be given a gong and sentenced to parade through the streets, wearing a high dunce-cap with a billboard hung around his neck, with words like "reactionary," "bourgeois element," "landlord," or simply "bad element." Women would be further humiliated by being forced to hang a string of worn shoes around their necks, indicating that they were prostitutes. The victims, men or women, would march with bowed head, shuffling slowly, beating the gong for all to hear, while publically and loudly confessing: "I am a bad man (or woman)." Gong. "I am a reactionary." Gong. "I am a running dog." "I should be killed a thousand times." Gong.

Children would race by, punching, kicking, beating with sticks, pulling hair, throwing stones.

One day, while Ma LuBin was walking through the streets of the village, with his Red Guard comrades, he saw the silhouette of a bent-over, broken man, working by the side of the roadway. Although the stick-figure was far away and backlit by the sun, he recognized that this was his father, one of the condemned.

I looked up from my notes, silently, remembering what he had said to me just a few minutes before, "We were happy during the Cultural Revolution. We were proud. We were excited. We were doing this, not so much for China, as for Chairman Mao."

Quietly, almost in a whisper, Ma LuBin continued, "I did not walk over to say hello. I did not tell my comrades that the man over there was my father. I was ashamed of my father so I looked away."

Shortly after the schools closed in 1966, many workers quit their posts to join the Cultural Revolution, followed by administrators and officials. Ma LuBin tells me that in his household, with his father absent, there was little food or fuel. In winter, the inside walls of their house were coated with ice.

Official estimates vary, but published reports document that in rural China, alone, some 36 million people were persecuted, and throughout the country 750,000 to 3 million were murdered.[27] Soon, even Chairman Mao realized that the Cultural Revolution had escalated out of control and he tried to put the brakes on, but it's hard to stop a moving freight train.

Some time in there, maybe around 1970, maybe a few years later, Ma LuBin's father was released from hard labor and allowed to return to his apple trees. "But he was never the same man again. He died of lung cancer, from smoking too many cigarettes, in 2000."

In 1972, when he was 20 years old, Ma LuBin got a job working with a 30-person propaganda troupe, acting out short skits, singing, and dancing as part of Chairman Mao's vast "Thought Propaganda Team." Altogether, he spent seven years with the troupe, mostly on tour, traveling from one collective farm to the next. One day, when they were at their home base, the leader of the troupe gave Ma LuBin a key and asked him to go into a locked storage room and retrieve some props and costumes for an upcoming event. When Ma LuBin opened the door, he found not only the props and costumes, but a wall of banned books.

He stopped and looked, in surprise, fear, and mystery. Then he gingerly lifted a Chinese translation of Anton Chekhov's short stories, and slipped it under his jacket. Back home, in secret, he read. When he finished, he returned to the storage room and stole a copy of Gorky, followed by Dostoyevsky, and Tolstoy. And his life changed.

As Ma LuBin told me, "Gradually, as the decade wore on, many people realized that the Cultural Revolution was wrong. Terribly wrong. But change was slow. For me, once I started reading books about the outside world, I could no longer believe what I had believed so fervently for so long. The world was bigger than we thought it was."

In 1981, Ma LuBin married and together the couple had two daughters, one of whom was mentally disabled. Throughout all the time that I have known him, he has said very little about his first wife, other than, "She was very kind." In 1983, he enrolled in a self-taught, remote, TV University, and graduated two years later. He then got a job in a bank. With his experience in Communist propaganda, he worked in the advertising department. He divorced in 1991 and quit the bank the following year to start his own interior decorating company, which was successful enough to have 30 employees. He married a second time, to "a woman who was not kind" and they had a daughter. Mr. Ma then sold the company because he was "tired of the work and the rich lifestyle," divorced a second time, and returned to the bank. On his mother's and sister's advice, he tried to get back together with his first wife and she seemed willing, but then she died, tragically, of a stroke. In 1997, at age 45, he took early retirement from the bank due to an unspecified long-term ailment and became "a free bird." He met Noey and me in 2006 and became a bicycle nomad.

FOILED

Six years after we met the first time, Ma LuBin and I were together again, in a bustling airport, this time with Nina, but without Noey, preparing to ride across the Himalayan Plateau. In the intervening years he had traveled frequently alone, by bike, back and forth across China. Now he was tanned, self-assured, and fit looking, smiling from beneath his jaunty baseball cap.

Ma LuBin had stored our mountain bikes from the 2006 expedition, waiting patiently and expectantly for our return. They were low-end, hard-tail Specialized, with marginal front forks, but good enough. We did some basic maintenance, picked up spare parts, and then waited all afternoon in a noisy, crowded train station in Urumqi for our passage to Xining, our starting point. I was practicing how to vegetate, a handy skill while traveling in China. Ma LuBin initiated the conversation,

"Mr. Turk, you are worrying too much."

"Actually, Mr. Ma LuBin, just at this moment, I wasn't worrying about anything. I was just sitting here."

"Ah, Mr. Turk, but sometimes you are worrying too much and I do not know that you are worrying so I cannot warn you to stop worrying."

"Ah, Mr. Ma LuBin. Thank you. You are absolutely right. When I was in America, before I came to China, I worried too much that you would have a very bad map for us when we got here. So I brought my own map. A secret US spy map."

Ma LuBin smiled, "You are a spy?"

"Yes."

"And you have this map, really?"

I tapped the top flap pocket in my day pack.

"Ah, Mr. Turk. Remember I told you about the American, Mr. Poulson, whom I traveled with last year? You are just like Mr. Poulson."

With over two million people, Xining is the largest city on the Qinghai-Tibet Plateau. Long ago, it was a hub of dusty Silk-Road bazaars where sword-wielding caravan drivers rested their bleating, recalcitrant camels before the long climb into the mountains and the treacherous passage across the Takla-Makan Desert. After countless battles, revolutions, famines, and conflicting religious and political philosophies, the fundamental capitalism of the Silk Road traders has emerged supreme, now manifest in gleaming glass storefronts that sell Versace handbags, Tommy Hilfiger overcoats, and Clinique perfumes along with tubs of Kentucky Fried Chicken, served on orange, plastic tables.

Nina and I brought Ma LuBin a new sleeping bag, tent, a down jacket, and a waterproof wind-shell for our journey into the highest mountain range in the world. In the interest of traveling light, we carried little else besides extra underwear, a minimal tool kit, cameras, and money. No stove or pots and pans; we planned to buy food in towns and villages or rely on the kindness of strangers in more remote places.

We survived Chinese Traffic Roulette and started the long uphill pedal out of Xining onto the Tibetan Plateau. By the afternoon of the first day, we crested a hill to come upon a huge complex of red brick buildings where a sign, in Chinese, Tibetan, and English proudly announced, "The Qinghai Museum of Tibetan Culture: The first and only Tibetan cultural center using modern virtual technology and multimedia to fully display Tibetan history, religion, art, and customs." The entrance fee was 80 yuan each, or 240 yuan total, almost $40, compared to 60 yuan for a seven course dinner for the three of us at an unassuming local restaurant with a chef to die for. Meanwhile, in Tibet proper, civilians and monks had been setting themselves on fire to protest the physical and cultural conquest of their traditional homeland.

Before Nina and I joined our lives together, she had worked for fifteen years as a fire lookout, perched on a lonely mountaintop in the Bitterroot Forest in Montana. Even now, when she is "back in town" she is infused with the silence of the mountains, so I've learned to listen to small sentences or even sentence fragments.

"The money is going into the wrong hands, let's get outta here."

I nodded and we continued onward toward a huge, walled monastery. According to Tibetan tradition, pilgrims say their prayers while circling holy places—monasteries or mountains—in a clockwise direction. When we arrived, a middle-aged Tibetan woman, wearing knee pads, a dust mask, and peasant trousers covered by a pink smock, was performing this ritual. She would take three steps, hold her hands together over her head in supplication, drop onto her knees, touch her forehead to the ground, lie prone, stretch her hands out on the ground, stand up, and take three more steps. She might have been repeating these gestures and the slow forward progress for hundreds of kilometers.

Two Han workers, one with a pick and the other with a shovel, were laying stone to modernize the old dirt pathway. As she approached, they stood aside, perhaps out of respect, or maybe just, incidentally, to take a rest. A small tractor, pulling a wagon full of sand, showed no indication of stopping, so the pilgrim stepped out of the way, careful not to cheat by moving forward.

A Tibetan man, in his 20s, stepped out of the shadows, grasped me by the elbow, and asked in India-accented English, "Are you American?"

"Yes."

He looked nervously about, "I must talk to you."

Just then Ma LuBin burst into the scene, "Jon, Jon. You must take pictures of this woman."

The man slipped away, into the shadows, his message dissipating into the dust left hanging in the air by the tractor. I guess it didn't matter. No secret between us would deflect the Chinese juggernaut. I took some still photos and video, uncomfortably aware that, just like the Chinese conquerors, I was in a position to commercialize this woman's devotions.

We continued on to the monastery entrance where we were met by a uniformed Han Chinese soldier and another entrance fee of 80 yuan—each. For the second time that day, we refused to pay and instead pedaled onward to eat lunch in the closest village. Women in traditional clothing were selling imitation Tibetan cultural artifacts to wealthy Han Chinese tourists who were wielding Canons with long, in-your-face, 300 mm lenses.

When the soup arrived, Ma LuBin began reminiscing about the early years of the Cultural Revolution. He pushed his chair back and high-stepped around the outdoor patio where we were eating, an old man imitating the boy he was so long ago, raising his fist defiantly into the air and shouting, "Long live Chairman Mao! Death to Americans!" followed by a charming, sweet smile.

I looked around nervously, worried that the police might race in to cart us off to the gulag. Or an insane asylum. But the bustling, capitalistic street-scene continued unabated and uninterrupted. We were paying customers. Don't interrupt the flow of money. Once he was already revved up and dancing, Ma LuBin performed a credible imitation of Michael Jackson's Moon Walk, followed by a graceful, almost erotic Uyghur love dance. He then lowered his voice, with the one special secret that he wanted no one to hear, "Mr. Poulson is not a good dancer. He is too serious."

"I understand," I commiserated, "but let's talk about what is happening today. You told me, a long time ago, that the Dalai Lama's birthplace was near Xining, and that he was born in a simple mud hut, not an elaborate monastery. This can't be the Dalai Lama's birthplace? Or is it?"

He shook his head sadly.

"So, where is it?" I asked.

Ma LuBin went on to explain that it was close by, but sort of a secret, but maybe not really a secret, but, anyway, no one would tell him. "I don't know where it is," he finally concluded, a bit downhearted.

Perfect. We had come halfway around the world to find this place. But it was a state secret, guarded by a repressive faux communist regime that ruled over a free-wheeling capitalist society, that wasn't really capitalism, but really was. So we couldn't find it.

Perfect.

If I had been a real journalist, with an assignment from a prestigious magazine, an expense account, a tight time schedule, and a specific agenda, then I would have had good reason to be upset with my friend. More likely, I never would have trusted this joker in the first place. I would have done my research, had a GPS coordinate, perhaps, or at least made contact with a real guide, an inside "fixer" who knew the ropes, hired taxis, had a reputation for getting things done, in a hurry. "Time is money," after all, when you are on an expense account, working for a big corporation.

But somehow I had dodged that bullet—all my life. This pilgrimage that we were on, and the destination it implied, had always been kind of vague and I had felt that we had been kind of faking it either in the religious—or journalistic—or pilgrimage departments, anyway. Like an inexperienced house-cat, I realized that I would really not know what to do with the mouse if I ever actually caught it. And perhaps I was treading on dangerous grounds to "want" to arrive at the Dalai Lama's birthplace, anyway. His Holiness is a Buddhist, after all, and doesn't Buddhism have a lot to say about expectation and the disappointment when our expectations do not reach fruition?

In his very first teaching, the Buddha explained,

> Birth is suffering, aging is suffering, illness is
> suffering, death is suffering..... not to get what one
> wants is suffering;
> Now this, bhikkhus, is the noble truth of the
> cessation of suffering: it is the giving up and relinquishing
> of it, freedom from it, non-reliance on it.

So, I wasn't getting what I wanted. Or I wasn't getting what I said
I wanted, but really didn't want. Because it didn't matter. So, I
could choose to suffer. Or choose not to suffer. Perfect. Right now
I was sitting in this restaurant with two dear friends. My tummy
was full. We were laughing together at my friend's goofy dances.
Everything we needed in this world was tied onto our bikes. Nina
was smiling from across the table and that always warms my heart.
The trip had just begun and it was promising to be a true
adventure, because we had no idea where we were going, what we
wanted "to see," or what we would find along the way.

ONTO THE HIMALAYAN PLATEAU

We got back on our bikes, and for lack of any better direction, we
headed south, toward the heart of the mountains. It was our first
day and my butt was sore. Twenty years before, I ascended onto
the Tibetan Plateau in Sichuan Province on a climbing expedition.
We traveled with a string of pack horses on a dirt track, so narrow
that we feared that a horse would bump its load against a rock
outcrop and tumble down the mountainside. Now we pedaled
toward the mountains on a paved roadway. Big trucks honked
loudly, in warning, from behind and then honked again as
they thundered past. I got a flat tire. The next town was a few
hundred meters away. We were hungry and tired so we didn't
bother to fix the flat but walked the bikes the rest of the way,

hopeful we might find a restaurant. But instead, the first store-front was a tire shop, which seemed encouraging at first, but it really didn't matter because we had patching material and they had no interest in fixing a puny bike tire. Explaining that she'd never seen a foreigner before, except on TV, the woman of the house invited us for dinner. She was tiny and young, looking more like a high school cheerleader than a mother and manager of a tire shop for rough-looking long-haul truckers. Ma LuBin took a photo of our hostess, me, and Nina posing on the couch in their cramped living room/kitchen. Then she grabbed the chip out of his camera and ran off, half skipping with the lightness of the teenager that she was, but wasn't. Fifteen minutes later she returned with several prints. On one, she carefully wrote in English, "My name is Yang Ying Hua Hua, (Flower). Thank you. 2012.9.16."

Somehow, lovely, hospitable Hua Hua is part of the conquering Han presence here in the foothills of the Himalaya. She is, in a convoluted, obtuse, unclear manner, part of the reason that young men and women in Tibet are pouring gasoline over their heads and lighting themselves on fire.

The next morning, we had a high pass to cross before the next village and we had no stove to cook with if we fell short of our goal. I thought we should get an early start, but, under Ma LuBin's guidance, we started pedaling around 11:00 AM, rode for half an hour, and then stopped to talk philosophy for 45 minutes. Then we had lunch. By 1:00 PM we started to climb into a cold, steady rain.

In Canada and the United States, 16-wheel tractor trailer trucks rule the broad four-lane freeways. Here, on a two-lane paved road, with no shoulders, no guard rails, and a steep drop off on the downward side, heavy 22-wheelers were churning up the pass. You'd hear them behind you, then feel the windblast of the cab and the groan and clatter of a downshift, and then the truck would be beside you, barely an arm's length away, taking forever to pass, spewing water from the tires and diesel fumes from the exhaust, crowding you so tightly it felt as if 10,000 years of rising civilization were bellowing like a dragon, threatening your puny human-powered bicycle off the road, not out of any innate personal animosity, but out of something even more terrifying: unadulterated, uncaring, inhuman, petroleum-burning power that was gobbling up any wildness left on the steppe to fuel the inevitable, unstoppable, march of civilization. No one slowed down to give us space. "Time is money."

Nina was riding strongly and pulled ahead on the steep switchbacks. When I finally caught up to her, we stopped at a small space where we could pull off the road to wait for Ma LuBin. But when we looked back, we couldn't see him. Then, there he was, way below us, a tiny figure following a dirt track that must have appeared to be a shortcut, but was, in reality, a dead-end canyon. There are no short cuts to crossing a mountain pass in the Himalaya. I half walked and half slid down the steep hillside, covered with wet grass and slimy mud and then helped Ma LuBin push and carry his bike back up to the roadway. He was exhausted and it was getting dark. I was beginning to be resigned to a cold wet camp, by the side of the busy road, with no dinner. But a kindly, slightly portly man, in his mid-30s, driving a shiny black car, stopped, and offered to shuttle us and our bikes to the top of the pass, one at a time. We thanked him, exchanged pleasantries, and accepted. When the three of us finally congregated on the top of the pass, with rain morphing into cold, wet, snow, the man wrote his address in Xining on a small, crumpled, scrap of wet paper, and handed it to Ma LuBin with an invite to dinner at the end of our journey.

In the waning light of the late afternoon, soaked to the skin, we sped down the south side of the pass. Below us, fitting incongruously into the concrete landscape of the highway we were on, we saw numerous tents and yurts of a few local herders who held on to the old ways on overgrazed hillsides. I thought fondly of my visits to herder encampments on recent journeys in central

Asia. When you enter the dim, smoky, interior of a circular nomadic herder's home, you always move left, clockwise, a quarter of a revolution, around the central fireplace, and then sit on the rugs, carpets, or animal skins spread out on the trampled soil. If he is home, the male, head of the house, will be seated 180°, or opposite the door, in the commanding, "head of household" position. The women will be busy in the "kitchen" which always occupies the remaining space. Children scatter about, aimlessly. The tent smells warmly of humans, animal skins, yak dung fuel, grass, fermenting milk, and if everyone is lucky, boiled meat.

I looked at a nearby cluster of yurts, and suggested that we stop here, but Ma LuBin strongly vetoed my plan and insisted that we would find better fare further down. So, as dusk threatened to slide into darkness, we rolled down the cold, wet pavement, spray spinning out of my front tire, covering me with a wet, oily sheen. Finally, as the valley floor came into view, I saw something I had never seen in central Asia before, so gleaming new that it felt like an apparition: A tidy village of cream-walled, red-roofed, brand-spanking new row houses, all identical and symmetrical. Two young Tibetan men were herding yaks from motorcycles. We stopped and Ma LuBin asked if there was someone who would put us up for the night. One of the men whipped out a cell phone.

In the Rocky Mountains of North America, a ghost town forms when people have moved into an area, lived there for some useful lifespan, and then have travelled on, when the economy has collapsed. This place that we arrived at, at the bottom of the pass, was the reverse of a ghost town. It had been built by a central government agency and was so new that few people had moved in yet. We followed our directions down a wide, empty boulevard, with streetlights, past identical green gates closing around identical walled courtyards. Even in the blandest subdivision in North America, houses have at least some tiny semblance of personality, maybe only a national flag, a plastic pink flamingo, an absolutely perfect lawn, or a child's bike left carelessly at the front stoop. But if no one lives in any of the houses, or has never lived there, there is no personality, just construction scraps and concrete dust left by crews that finished their work and disappeared. The place felt like a movie set, and I half expected that we were passing a row of false fronts instead of real houses. We knocked on a door and to my surprise, it opened, revealing a beautiful young mother with bright red lipstick, rosy cheeks, a pink Muslim head scarf, and a baby on her hip. Ma LuBin greeted her, queried, and she cheerily agreed to feed the three of us and let us sleep on her floor, for about $10.

We entered the room to a welcome blast of heat and electric light that was blinding after riding in the near-dark. We stripped off the outer layers of our wet clothes, careful not to hang them where they would drip on something that looked clean, polished, delicate, valuable, or precious, and settled onto a white blanket spread out on the gleaming new tile floor. To me, the most dominant and remarkable fixture in that room was the fat-cheeked baby, unlike any creature I had ever before beheld anywhere in central Asia. She was plump, not obese, but plump, with the fattest cheeks possible, as if harboring two tennis balls inside her mouth, so that the cheeks almost met in the middle, obliterating the baby's nose. I snapped a photo of the little girl. She was wearing a spotlessly white dress and pink bonnet and was seated in a pink and purple plastic tricycle-like device, complete with two LED headlights and a Winnie-the-Pooh character on the front dashboard. This was accompanied by a drawing of a bird-like creature with floppy elephant ears, surrounded by images of brightly colored floating soap bubbles. In my photo, the infant has an almost perplexed look on her face, as if her DNA told her that she should be thin, with a snotty nose from a chronic cold, dressed in worn, patched cotton hand-me-down clothes.

With a cup of hot tea cradled in his palms, Ma LuBin reminded me of our conversation, back up there on the mountain, and challenged me by asking: "Isn't this better than a drafty, smoky, leaky herder's tent?"

And then, as if he felt threatened that I might offer up some hippie-romantic image of noble poverty, Ma LuBin repeated what he had told me earlier, on our first visit, "You have not suffered as much as I have. You know nothing about China."

The truth is, Ma LuBin's mind-reading was spot on; I was silently reminiscing fondly of the old herder camps, with their hippie-romantic noble poverty. Touché.

In fact, my whole life had been a journey into faux noble poverty, supported and encapsulated by the spinoff of the astronomically unimaginable opulence of 21st century North America. I had walked out of my career, with its promise of a nice house in a cul-de-sac subdivision coupled with membership in a green-lawned country club, and lived in what is considered to be poverty in the United States—a tipi, a renovated chicken coop, a log cabin in the deep forest of Alaska, and now a small run-down house-cabin in the Montana forest without a flush toilet.

Yet it's a funny kind of poverty. We always have abundance of high quality food to eat and a roof over our heads. I own four pairs of skis. And two cars. And two chain saws to cut firewood. And…on and on…. Certainly I know nothing about China, but in North America, I know for certain that if you dance around the system adroitly, you can live very opulently on little money. And furthermore, such a lifestyle is rich and satisfying because it opens lots of free time to relax and to follow personal passions not related to the hustle of earning more money. So, indeed, Ma LuBin is correct: I am guilty of reminiscing fondly of a simple lifestyle, both in my homeland and in China.

That evening, while eating twisted fry-bread and noodle soup in that warm, dry house, with that happy, healthy baby, I was in no mood for a moral, economic, or philosophical discussion or argument with Ma LuBin, so I smiled and stuffed my mouth with food to replenish calories expended during our hard, wet day.

But the dilemma comes back to me as I write this: Does my message of return to Deep Wild and perhaps even Noble Poverty stand up to honest questioning throughout the world? And now, specifically, in China, does it pass the acid test in a nation that endured perhaps as many as 45 million deaths due to famine within Ma LuBin's lifetime and memory?

I turn to the Dalai Lama for an answer. This is his land after all, and his people have suffered. In *Ethics of the New Millennium*, he writes: "The achievements of science and technology clearly reflect our desire to attain a better, more comfortable existence. This is very good." (I love that sentence. So clean. Complete. Final. Accentuated by a cliché that wouldn't pass the muster on a high school term paper.) "Who could fail to applaud many of the advances of modern medicine?"

But now comes the greatest contradiction of our age. The Dalai Lama continues: "At the same time, I think it is genuinely true that members of certain traditional, rural communities do enjoy greater harmony and tranquility than those settled in our modern cities." Liberalism, democracy, socialism, and consumerism "have all failed to deliver the universal benefits they were supposed to provide, despite many wonderful ideas. A revolution is called for, certainly. But not a political, an economic, or even a technical revolution. We have had enough experience of these during the past century to know that a purely external approach will not suffice. What I propose is a Spiritual Revolution."

The Dalai Lama then goes on to explain that this Spiritual Revolution must be based primarily on compassion—which arises *only* out of the "ethical value of our actions." He explains: Each action is driven by a person's *kun long*, which is the "overall state of heart and mind" at the time of that action. If the person's *kun long* is wholesome and compassionate, then the action will ultimately be positive, even if temporary, unintended negative side effects arise—with the reverse being true as well.

I leaned back against a comfortable red cushion. Nina was fussing over the baby. Our hostess was bustling about the kitchen, chatting with Ma LuBin in Mandarin. I thought back to those days, trapped in the ice in the Nares Strait, and then to a rapid flush of imagery of so many mountaintops and oceans, storms and sunshine, ice fields and jungles. From all those images and experiences, of deep contentment even in the face of physical hardship and great vulnerability, I believe that a reciprocal relationship with Deep Wild, or even an afternoon walk in a city park, is one way to achieve a positive *kun long*, and therefore one way to approach the Spiritual Revolution or, as I prefer to call it, the Consciousness Revolution that the Dalai Lama and so many other learned people speak about. Which leads us back full circle to my hippie-romantic imagery, which can be so much bullshit out here, and to the Dalai Lama's parallel dilemma that "The achievements of science and technology…are very good." Which gets too confusing to think about, if you choose to think about it and get confused.

THE END OF THE ROAD

For the next nine days, the three of us bee-lined southward, over numerous 4,000-meter passes. Nina, who is a small woman, intensely athletic, and over 60, found her stride and pedaled up each pass with a steady, relentless power. Ma LuBin walked the steep sections, but no matter, he smiled and danced at each summit before we shared some water and a snack, and rolled down into the next valley. Along the way, we saw herders who lived in adobe walled compounds with their goats and yaks. Women wore colorful dresses with bright sashes, headscarves, and abundant jewelry. Men appeared in cowboy hats, or baseball caps, Tibetan necklaces, and layers of worn suit jackets as if each person had repeatedly raided the local Salvation Army Thrift Store.

I reminisced, ever more vividly, about the horse-pack trip two decades before, the animal smell, the silence, and the views of the mountains getting closer at walking speed. Today, the ultra-modern paved roads were often cantilevered ingeniously over cliff faces, on rebar and concrete. Overpasses intertwined improbably over and under each other, anticipating bigger cities and a future full of traffic. The construction was ongoing, everywhere. Heavy equipment rumbled across the landscape, gouging rock, and rerouting rivers while small armies of sturdy men and women were digging and paving the Himalaya stone by stone, shovel-full by shovel-full—opening trade routes and transportation arteries to import Han Chinese culture into Tibetan landscapes, and thus complete the conquest that started first with swords and later with tanks and guns.

The Yellow River snakes through southern Qinghai Province, incising a deep, sinuous, often impenetrable gorge through the mountains. In contrast, the road cuts as straight southward as possible, repeatedly dropping into the valley and then rising over the next mountain. Flat roadway does not exist in this part of the world. On the morning of September 25th, we climbed out of the river valley, crossed a moderate pass, dropped down again, and then, almost immediately, started a second arduous climb. A black Mercedes stopped and a Tibetan man with a warm smile and a gold tooth stepped out and offered each of us a frosty-cold can of Red Bull, fresh out of his ice chest. After a brief chat, followed by an invite to visit when we reached the next town, he sped southward with the reassuring purr of expensive German machinery.

At first I was confused. Where did this man get the money to buy a high-end automobile? And then, I realized, that in the effort to pedal my bike, I had been unobservant. All day, men and women, some with families, and some without, had been passing us in expensive vehicles. Where was all this wealth coming from? Not yak cheese, certainly. Not sweaters made of handspun wool, knit by nimble fingers stitch by loving stitch, and sold at "fair trade" bazaars. No. The source behind this wealth is a fungus called caterpillar mushroom, also known as "summer grass, winter worm," or *Yartsa Gunbu*.

In our oil-soaked, internet crazed world, wealth is often not so much a function of how hard you work, or how smart you are—although these factors certainly play a role—but of how lucky you are. And if you happen to be born in a skin tent on a high, barren, overgrazed grassland—in the middle of a lucrative, almost violence-free drug culture—then you can buy a new house with a gleaming tile floor, a flat screen TV, and a luxury car. *Yartsa* grows on the high steppe as a five-centimeter long, matchstick-thick capless mushroom, with a deep, skinny root, that looks like a caterpillar. Ancient texts claim that it is a powerful aphrodisiac. Modern folklore lists the drug as a cure for jaundice, back pain, tuberculosis, bronchitis, hepatitis, anemia, emphysema, AIDS, and even hair loss. The only thing I know for sure is that the tiny little fungus grows abundantly on this high steppe and sells for $10,000 per pound, enough—well—to purchase a Mercedes if your ancestral land is rich in this crop and if you pick long and hard, or hire pickers, during the harvest season.

Propelled by a hefty shot of Red Bull, we climbed the pass by the end of a long afternoon, stopped beneath the ubiquitous strings of prayer flags that garnish every pass, drank some water, rested, and shared a snack. Then, late into the day, we rolled into the small city of Da Wu, where we found a restaurant and a hotel, after Ma LuBin dealt with the confusion and acrimony of the tourist, rip-off hustle.

My bike frame was inexplicably bent, which created a torque on the rear wheel, and for the past few days I had been breaking spokes with uncomfortable regularity. So, the next morning, we found a bicycle wheel repair guy, operating in the outdoor market from a crude wooden cart mounted on old bicycle wheels. He aligned my wheel and replaced broken and bent spokes for 7 yuan, about $1.00. While I was waiting, I looked about, counting a forest of construction cranes that dominated the skyline, busy erecting 23 new high rise apartments and office buildings that loomed over the older structures of an ancient village.

In Montana, I live in Darby, a small, quiet mountain town

with a characteristically precarious economy, which has advantages and disadvantages. Projecting from my own experience, I wonder what it would be like for the government to waltz in and build a bunch of office towers, eight to ten stories high. And then what? Both Darby and Da Wu are deep in the mountains, with no university, no rail link, a long and difficult drive to the eastern industrial centers and seaports. So what economic trickery could support such a building boom? I wanted to ask the bicycle-wheel repair man with the wooden cart what sort of commerce would congregate here, but I had the sense that he was just as confused as I was. It was the inexorable invasion of progress, for the sake of progress, with no one to question it.

The guy running the local internet café took us aside, and in furtive whispers explained briefly that he had been incarcerated in a Chinese prison for two months for failure to carry his identification card. After his release, he escaped to the Tibetan refuge settlements in India for a few years (where he learned English), but returned home because he missed his landscape and family. He concluded with, "So you are a writer, you tell me. Well, tell the world that Tibetans might appear to be free, but we are not, as long as the Han Chinese rule over our grass and our water."

Thank you for that, but I don't know what to tell the world. Somewhere along the line, in the 1950s, when Nina, Ma LuBin, and I were children, and before many of the readers of this book were born, the Tibetans had an ideal—to build a sovereign nation based on Buddhist principles. They had so little technology that their border army didn't even have a radio. And the Chinese tanks rolled in and squashed that ideal. And, in my own country, Richard Nixon squashed Tim Leary. And today, the horny, old, rich, capitalistic, communist-party geezers in Shanghai buying caterpillar mushrooms, and the capitalist Tibetans who sell to them, are continuing to squash that ideal. And so on. And we are all zooming full bore into the Anthropocene, with an ice-cold Red Bull in one hand, while texting a neighboring yak herder or Zulu warrior with the other. And it would be somehow "nice" if we could nurture something different—some lesson from the Arctic icepack in the Nares Strait, which no one has heard of anyway. Is that what I am supposed to tell the world?

At Da Wu, the paved road we had been following came to a screeching halt. Even the Chinese engineers, with their seemingly infinite cash and modern machinery, coupled with a timeless philosophy of steady persistence, had been unable to penetrate the formidable snowy mountains to the south. There were, however, several roads running in a general easterly or westerly direction. After a rest day, we pedaled out of town, still with no real idea where we were planning to go. Actually, we hadn't discussed our route very much. With everything else going on, it just didn't seem that important. But, when we came to the first junction, we clearly had to make a decision. I took out my map, but Ma LuBin refused to look at it. Instead, he mused, "Confucius said, 'A young man's duty is to behave well toward his parents at home and his elders abroad.'"

"Great, my friend, thank you for that," I replied. "But I don't understand; should we go left or right?"

Ma LuBin shook his head sadly, as he always did when I showed my ignorance.

"Oh yes, once again, you are just like Mr. Poulson."

I waited because I knew that the explanation would come.

"You see, my mother does not think it is wise for me to be traveling by bicycle with you two Americans. So, we are already disobeying Confucius, who believed that there is a right way to do things, and that 'right way' is guided by the wisdom and knowledge of our elders. Instead, we are creating a new life for ourselves, in a new world, wandering on our bicycles, and we can no longer rely on my mother's wisdom. We are free birds. As Lao Tzu would say, 'There is no right path.'"

With that preamble…we decided to travel westward, toward Snow Mountain, because it seemed like as good a place as any to visit. After a few kilometers, the broad, new, smooth paved 4-lane highway ended abruptly as if sliced by a taut string.

No, we weren't lost; we had already decided that "lost" was impossible because it assumed a correct definition of "found." We had just reached the thin but absolute line where the giant wave of progress had momentarily crested. It was if we were standing on the beach, staring across the ocean, wondering why the continent had suddenly been severed by tectonic forces. Or, perhaps, as a temporal analogy, it was as if we had reached to the edge of time, where, if we crossed this line, we would be stepping back into the past, last week or last century, before steam engines had been invented. Just wait, my friend, relax, have a cup of tea, allow yourself to grow a little older, and soon enough, a bulldozer and a paving machine will rumble into view, churning, clanking, and raising a cloud of dust, and, presto, a new road will roll out before you so you can proceed across the mountains in relaxed, air-conditioned opulence.

But in the reality of the present journey, silent, glaciated peaks rose ahead of us, while the noisy construction cranes of Da Wu toiled away behind us. The road ahead was rutted and rocky.

You don't often think of pavement as a mind-altering drug, but it is, because pavement is progress, and progress, itself, is a mind-altering drug. You might suppose that when a broad concrete roadway degenerates into a rutted track, and all those shiny, new, high-horsepower vehicles purchased with caterpillar fungus money are forced to slow down from 125 km/hr to 25 km/hr, people might become impatient and grouchy because their journey has slowed to a crawl. But actually the opposite is true. Remove speed and efficiency irrevocably from people's lives and their temperaments take a huge sigh of relief. People slow down, physically and emotionally.

That day, every single vehicle that motored into view—with no exceptions—stopped and the drivers took the time to visit with us. Tibetans in traditional clothing, with mountain winds etched into their faces, leaned over their motorcycles or peered out of their shiny late-model Lexus, BMW or Mercedes SUVs to chat and to offer us each a Coke or another Red Bull. The reasoning seemed to be, "As long as it is going to take me all day to get to my destination, I may as well take all day plus fifteen minutes. So I'll stop and talk to these crazy people on bicycles." Paradoxically, at least on this roadway, when you put a brake on progress and mandate a radical reduction in what we like to call "efficiency," then people relax and, as the Dalai Lama advised, "enjoy greater harmony and tranquility."

The next day, we pedaled over yet another high pass and stopped to rest above another narrow valley. The hillsides were totally brown and barren, overgrazed to the root-tops, with not a single stick of woody plant anywhere. The Tibetan Plateau covers 5 million square kilometers (2 million square miles) and is a critical global environment because it is the headwaters of many of central Asia's largest rivers, the reservoir of the largest stock of ice outside the Antarctic and Arctic, and a key climate modulator of Asian monsoons. Yet the integrity of its grasslands, glaciers, and rivers is seriously threatened by a host of factors, including global climate change, overgrazing, soaring overpopulation from both the Tibetan and immigrant Han Chinese communities, and rapid industrialization.

This ecological devastation has occurred in the space of a single lifetime. The Dalai Lama reports: "It is no exaggeration to say that the Tibet I grew up in was a wildlife paradise. My chief memory of my three-month journey across Tibet from my birthplace at Takster in the east to Lhasa where I was formally proclaimed Dalai Lama...is of wildlife along the way. Immense herds of *kiang* (wild asses) and *drong* (wild yak) freely roam the great plains. Occasionally we would catch sight of shimmering herds of *gowa*, the shy Tibetan gazelle, or *wa*, the white-lipped deer, or of *tso*, our majestic antelope..."[28]

We saw zero wild animals on our journey. You can feel

their absence in your bones when you gaze across the denuded landscape where every twig of woody plant matter has long since been tossed into someone's fireplace, followed by the animal dung that would otherwise provide fertilizer for the malnourished soil. And then, if you look closely enough, you might see a herd of hungry domestic sheep or yaks scampering high into the rocks to find tiny nubbins of greenery to sustain themselves.

We were tired and hungry and had very little food in our panniers, so we rode down toward a small cluster of buildings at a road junction, hoping that we could buy or scrounge some dinner. It turned out that one of the buildings was a tiny convenience store—which wasn't like any convenience store you'd see in North America, with its brightly lighted signs, glass doors, a pink Easter-Bunny display, and a bored, minimum-wage worker staring forlornly over the counter, thinking about anything other than making change for your gasoline and soda pop. Instead, this was a broken-down 5 meter by 7 meter concrete block structure, clearly built by a home-handy-man, not a professional mason, with a red tin roof that sheltered a tiny, ramshackle, poorly-stocked store on one side, and a living space on the other. A larger adjacent structure was still under construction, although I didn't see anyone bustling about with their tool belts on. A red motorcycle was parked out front, and its owner was inside the store, chatting, but not buying anything.

We entered and, speaking in Mandarin, which was a second language to everyone else in the store, Ma LuBin asked if we could buy some food for dinner and later camp in the back yard. The proprietor, a thin, quiet, middle-aged Tibetan man with a warm smile, ushered us into the cramped living space, which was lined with plywood benches and a large bed that was bolted to the walls and covered with worn, dusty, frayed pads and pillows. Our host stoked the cast iron stove with fresh yak dung to heat up a kettle of water for tea. After exchanging a few pleasantries, he returned his concentration to a tiny TV with so much snow and static that

I wondered why he bothered. Meanwhile, a very drunken couple frolicked on the bed in the corner, giggling, groping each other, and then sitting up long enough to drink more beer, while a fat, 6-year-old boy feasted randomly on junk food from the store. We bought some Ramen noodles, which Ma LuBin insisted only he knew how to cook properly. Nina and I relaxed quietly, drinking our tea, while our enigmatic friend fussed over his duties as chef, oblivious to the obvious fact that Ramen noodles are so bad that you can't make them good, but you can't ruin them either. When our meal was prepared to perfection, I added a few pieces of sausage of mysterious origin to my meal, while Nina and Ma LuBin demurred.

That night, the drunken woman tried to climb into the tent with Nina and me. For a threesome, I suppose? After Nina and I shooed her away, we slept soundly, until a hard, early-morning rain woke us. We packed up our wet gear, but it was too muddy to ride, so we all hung out in the shop, where confinement and boredom initiated conversation. The owner explained that his ancestral land was rich in *yartsa* so he owned a large house in a nearby city and two cars.

I asked the obvious, why, then, was he here, running this tiny shop, out in the sticks, scratching for spare change with almost no customers in sight. He explained that he was born here and he liked it here; it was quiet, away from the bustle of the city. Someday he would finish the larger house he was building, but with a shrug he indicated that work was low on his priority list. Someday he might dig a well or a trench to pipe some running water to this shack from the nearby river, but in the meantime, well, he didn't understand the urban need to take a shower every day anyway. Then he mentioned with a wry grin, that rural life had its advantages: For example there was abundant *yartsa* and tradition allows sexual liaisons outside marriage.

Hmmm. Now where have I heard that before? Voluntary poverty, a lack of bathing, and free love—enhanced by aphrodisiac drugs.

We sat, listening to the rain, and Nina leaned gently against me, in a silent affirmation of our adventure and our lives together. I thought about an evening in our past, before we had met, when we both attended the exact same Jefferson Airplane concert. There she was in the crowd of my imagination, so much younger, but with the same signature smile and hazel eyes, both of us in our own spheres, grooving to good drugs and music, neither of us knowing that the other existed, and that we would someday live together in the Montana forest.

Yes, there it was again,

Timothy Leary, 1969, walking across the stage in his white suit, urging us to affirm inner voices.

John Lennon leading us across Abbey Road to the Other Side.

The Octopus waving his tentacles from under that rock in his mysterious garden.

Jerry Garcia:

> It's just a box of rain
> I don't know who put it there
> Believe it if you need it
> or leave it if you dare
> But it's just a box of rain
> or a ribbon for your hair
> Such a long long time to be gone
> and a short time to be there—[29]

Hunter Thompson tells us that peace, love, community, and compassion will win out, simply because sanity will win out: "And that, I think, was the handle—that sense of inevitable victory over the forces of Old and Evil. Not in any mean or military sense; we didn't need that. Our energy would simply prevail. There was no point in fighting—on our side or theirs. We had all the momentum; we were riding the crest of a high and beautiful wave. . ."[30]

Or the Dalai Lama himself, "…my intention is to suggest that the individual, keeping his or her daily way of life, can change, can become a better, more compassionate, and happier human being. And through being more compassionate human beings, we can begin to implement our Spiritual Revolution."

But somehow, this journey, that so many poets and visionaries have imagined, has not "simply prevailed." Instead, inexplicably, all that momentum smashed against the bright lights of Las Vegas and ran aground against the oil-soaked Bligh Reef with the Exxon Valdez. How did we allow ourselves to trade the currency of peace, love, and material simplicity for the universal, global, modern Cultural Revolution called commercialism? How did our wily leaders and CEOs convince us to drop everything else in our lives, humiliate and kick our teachers, and march through the village square, with raised fists, and red armbands chanting in unison: "Hooray for Coca Cola."

Why did we listen to them?

The rain ended and I needed to climb out of my thoughts and back onto my bicycle, to pedal up the next mountain, and to feel poorly oxygenated blood pound against the inside of my skull.

FIRST SNOWFALL

We soon learned that Snow Mountain, which we had randomly chosen as a destination, was also a Holy Mountain, and, in this part of the world, people make pilgrimages to circumnavigate holy objects of human or natural origin, large and small. As the days passed, we encountered a steady stream of devotees, traveling alone, or in groups, on foot, with yaks, or in fancy cars, old folks, parents, men, women, and toddlers. Some were dressed in spiffy western-style clothing, as if they had just walked out of a board meeting, while others wore the colorful robes, coral and turquoise beads, and bright sashes of the nomads who have lived in felt tents and followed their herds across this steppe for millennia. Many spoke only Tibetan, which we did not speak, so our encounters involved smiles, handshakes, and sometimes hugs. Many pilgrims had cameras or smart phones and asked to photograph us, at which point we took out our cameras and photographed them.

This was not a special occasion, it was business as usual, and I have a strong sense that the procession is continuing right now, as I sit here writing this and as you are reading. There was only one problem. Worried, earnest, and concerned pilgrims repeatedly told us that to accumulate prayers you must circumnavigate a Holy Object in a clockwise direction—and according to our random trajectory, we were bicycling counterclockwise—as if to unravel our prayers. I meant no insult to the deities. So many times in my life, the wrong way just happened to be the way I was going.

The road was steep, climbing to over 4,500 meters, so our travel was slow. Towns and stores were spaced far apart. One morning, I pulled ahead of the group, concentrating on reading the ruts in the road and gasping for air. Then I stopped to look at the high mountains, as if I had forgotten that they were there. You can use any cliché you want—snow-white, glistening, soaring, jutting into the sky—but for me, mountains, beautiful as they are, are not predominantly a visual phenomenon. They are a presence, a feeling of expansiveness pervading space, thin air, and tired muscles. Photos of mountains are just blobs of ink on a piece of paper without the tired muscles and aching lungs to accompany the scenery. I took out my camera, and looking through a long lens, I saw Nina, pedaling up behind me, tired, breathing heavily, but determined to stay on her bike every meter of the way, even over rocks, loose dirt, and rain runnels. Ma LuBin came next, walking, also short of breath, looking wan, but forcing a smile into the camera. Above us, the road continued upward.

Clearly we weren't going to make it to the next town that night, as we had originally planned. I was carrying most of the food and was reluctant to tell my friends that we only had a few crackers and a handful of nuts for dinner. But the inevitably of our predicament was obvious. Oh well, I had gone to bed hungry before. Just when I was mentally preparing myself to accept our situation, and maybe even find a positive mindset within our enforced fast, we stumbled into a construction camp where Han Chinese workers were finishing a huge lunch and putting away the leftovers. I looked at the food hungrily, waiting for Ma LuBin to ask if we could buy some food, but we didn't need to beg or bargain. The cook came racing out of the green wall-tent that was her kitchen and fed us generously. Soon, all the workers were gathered around Ma LuBin, smiling and laughing, and then dropping the conversation long enough to remain vigilant that we always had meat on our plates. After my tummy was full, I asked my hosts what they were building here and they explained that they were running a drill rig to core rock samples for a proposed tunnel beneath the Holy Mountain.

"A tunnel to where?" I asked rhetorically. But of course I knew the answer—a tunnel to some mysterious as-yet-to-be-built city in the next valley or beyond. It wasn't a tunnel to go anywhere; it was a tunnel to deify progress, as an entity in itself. A tunnel to obliterate the slow, spiritual journey of pilgrimage, the crossing of a high pass, for whatever reason, clockwise or counterclockwise; to replace beauty with speed, to pretend that the Himalayas didn't exist, to conquer a landscape that had already been subdued and overgrazed. This is the Anthropocene, after all.

The noon sun was warm, while the glaciated mountains rose in the background. I was grateful for a second helping of rice, vegetables, and meat, courtesy of this tunnel under the Holy Mountain, the tunnel that I don't want anything to do with, but that I am linked to, regardless, like it or not.

By evening, we were still climbing and the road ahead stretched too far and high for our tired legs. So, without supper, but still fueled by our huge midday meal, we made camp beneath fast moving clouds, tying the tents to our bikes, so the tents wouldn't blow away, or at least so we would all blow away together. The next morning, we woke to a patina of fresh snow and an ethereal blue-red sunrise. We were shod in light-hikers, not mountain boots, but no matter, this would burn off with the heat of the day and, for me, the first snows of winter are always welcome because of, not despite, the wet feet, causing me to dream of floating down powder ski lines in the back country of British Columbia.

In an incredible show of hospitality and generosity, the construction workers drove up the road for the sole purpose of bringing us breakfast, because otherwise, they explained, we would start the day hungry. Nina told me quietly that she had been prepared to dislike the Chinese people, for the net effect of their actions on the Tibetan people and landscapes. But generalizations aren't that simple.

After eating, when the sun cast enough warmth to start melting the snow on the roadway, we rode past new groups of pilgrims, moving in the opposite direction, of course, one with yaks and another with a Mercedes Benz carrying their loads. Young children were dancing in the storm, as children do, playing with snow and splashing in puddles, before they learn that weather can be "good" or "bad."

At the top of the pass, we stopped to rest near a gold-gilded stupa, offset against the high glaciers. Prayer flags fluttered in the breeze as the midday sun melted most of the rest of last night's snow, leaving yellow grasses poking out of the fresh whiteness. The Holy Mountain, which we had been seeing for days, sometimes shrouded in clouds, at other times tucked in behind adjacent ridges, now dominated the landscape, a double-summited massif with a dominant east face that to my irreverent mind looked like it would be fun to ski. All my life, I have sought places like this Himalayan pass, isolated from sustenance and madness, from family and conquerors, even as some other elements of society have been drilling a tunnel beneath it, metaphorically or literally, to bypass it, so we don't incorporate the damp wetness of the season's first snowfall into our being.

In our deep history, humans have proven to be an adaptable species. We marched out of Africa to settle in desert and steppe, we crossed oceans, and learned to hunt seals and build igloos in the frozen Arctic. In the past, we have not only survived but thrived on climate change, when the jungles desiccated into savannah, when the great continental and alpine glaciers rumbled down from the poles and spilled over mountaintops during repeated ice ages, when temperatures fluctuated by as much as 15 degrees Celsius, compared to less than a degree of climate warming that we are experiencing today.

I have hope. But first we have to find some—for lack of better words—spirituality, or consciousness, that will rise above deification of stuff and a Walmart-focused consumerism.

Think of it this way:

In the best estimates of anthropologists, hominids began manufacturing and using stone tools approximately 3.4 million years ago, about 3.2 million years before *Homo sapiens* evolved. The earliest tools were hand-axes, little more than a river cobble with a sharpened edge, but no shaft or handle for leverage, or any means of converting it into a projectile. Then something strange happened. For the next 1.5 to 2 million years, more or less, tool innovation stopped dead in its tracks. Few new designs appear in the fossil record. Rick Potts, of the Smithsonian Institution, writes: "In our present world of rapid-fire technological advance, it is unthinkable that any single manufactured item could endure for so long…Today we tamper with just about everything we create or lay our hands on. The hand-axe people just kept on making hand-axes."[31] Yet during this extended time interval, our brains kept growing. Thus, we were getting smarter, but we weren't directing our intelligence toward major advancements in stone tool making. A dilemma arises because brain tissue is an expensive metabolic organ. A modern human brain consumes roughly 16 times as much energy per unit weight as muscle tissue.[32] As a result, early *Homo* had to go out and pick more berries, dig more roots, and walk long distances to hunt or scavenge more game; just to support this monster mass of gray matter perched precariously above their shoulders. Moreover, our ridiculously large heads caused problems in childbirth and increased both infant and maternal mortality.

According to evolutionary theory, natural selection prepares organisms "only for the necessities of the moment...not a squiggle more."[33] In other words, every adaptation must provide a selective advantage for the organism *at the time*. Countless generations of early *Homo* didn't spend their whole lives feeding and nurturing a metabolically expensive brain so that a few million years later, modern humans could design computers and send rocket ships to the Moon. At each step along the way, our hominid ancestors reaped a benefit from their huge metabolic investment in a bigger think-too-much-know-it-all brain.

What were we thinking about during this seminal few million years of our development? How did these thoughts provide selective evolutionary advantage for our *Homo* ancestors living on the African savannah? And finally: What does this legacy tell us about ourselves and our humanity in this modern world?

At the same time that we are a thumb-wielding, tool-manufacturing species, we are also an intensely social species. Chimpanzees move as a troop from tree to tree, foraging along the way, while early hominids built central campsites where they could protect the children while sending out foragers radially to collect food, return with it, and share. Crucial to sharing and dividing labor, we formed extended families and tribes. Using our marvelous big brains, we congregated in deep painted caves, singing, dancing, and chanting among flickering torches.

Thus, socialization, family, tribe, art, music, and dance formed us into what we are today. In our ancient prehistoric past, stuff and commercialism came secondary.

Let us not be seduced by advertising or by convenience to forget, or ignore, or lose this side of ourselves. Let us not be seduced into thinking that tools and technology come first. As my Koryak friend, Marina, from Kamchatka, said, "It is the magic in your life that gives you power."

AND WHAT WERE WE
LOOKING FOR, ANYWAY?

From the high pass, with its newly fallen snow, gleaming glaciers, and golden stupa, we rolled downward, back onto the high steppe, and then, eventually, out to the paved highway again. This road, the main commercial route to Lhasa, was smooth and fast, but just barely two full lanes, with no shoulder, and often treacherous drop-offs on either side. We rode for a few kilometers late in the evening, but the trucks were so big, moving so fast, and seemingly oblivious to our existence that we were terrified that we would get squashed and mangled.

We camped at a road construction site, where military officers first tried to bully us, but eventually relented and offered us tea and breakfast. Then we decided to hitchhike. After all the adventures of a lifetime, there was no way I was prepared to accept the risk of an inglorious end as a blemish of blood and protoplasm against the bumper of a red *Dong Feng* 22-wheeler, whose driver might be sleepy, inattentive, wired on Red Bull and who knows what else, carrying concrete to build a tunnel under the Holy Mountain. After a few hours, a flatbed truck pulled over, with a car chained on top, piggyback fashion. We negotiated a small fee, tied our bikes to the front of the flatbed, climbed into the car, fastened our seatbelts, and rode onward, as if we were being carried in an ancient, royal sedan chair, toward a maze of increasingly large highways, massive tunnels, and even more heroic construction projects. When we reached the next city, the drivers demanded a higher price than we agreed on and got into an angry argument with Ma LuBin. It was a rude re-entry into the real world.

The next day we rolled down the biggest hill I have ever experienced, on a six-lane highway that thankfully had a shoulder that was sufficient to give us a reasonable chance of survival. After all the work to gain all that elevation, I wanted to release my brakes and whoopie-ding myself down, but that pesky bent frame and unstable rear wheel, which we had sort-of-trued in Da Wu, and which I fretted about nearly every day, was so wobbly now that I didn't trust it. I got a flat, replaced the tube, and half-heartedly twisted a few spokes, but, fundamentally, the bicycle was on its last legs. After limping downward to a medium-sized city, Huangyuan, the tired, faithful, long-suffering wheel simply split apart and collapsed. The only bike shop in town did no repairs and had no spare parts, but recommended an itinerant repairman, who usually parked on such and such a street corner, with a wooden cart, like the man who repaired the wheel in Da Wu. The man carefully took the wheel apart, disappeared on his motorcycle to find a new rim, and returned to announce sadly that he couldn't find what he was looking for.

At a certain point, delicate machinery cannot be patched together with tape, wire, careful workmanship, and patience. So, while Nina and Ma LuBin pedaled, I rode on the back of the repair-man's motorcycle, carrying my bicycle-without-a wheel, for a terrifying ride through veering, churning, random left-turn-horn-blaring traffic to the bus station. And then, ingloriously in a way, but relaxing at the same time, and with personal relief that we didn't have to pedal along any more Chinese superhighways, we came full circle, away from the colorful pilgrims, the slow, frost-breathing yaks, and the rarefied air—back toward the noise, commotion, and pollution of Xining, where we had started our journey. Stepping out of the bus, we were greeted by a silent plastic Mickey Mouse, standing on a red carpet and beckoning us into a bridal shop.

We treated ourselves to a banquet, and Nina snapped a photo of Ma LuBin and me, freshly showered but still scruffy looking, tanned and lean, gazing in wonder at the clean, orange tablecloth and the opulent abundance of soup, meat, broccoli, and mushrooms, all piled high alongside a dozen other small plates of delicacies.

The next morning Ma LuBin pulled a crumpled, faded, wet,

barely readable scrap of paper out of his pocket and announced that he would now call our friend.

"Friend?" I queried. "I didn't know we had any friends in Xining?"

Ma LuBin shook his head wearily and sadly at my lack of memory, as if I were so hopeless that it wasn't worth his time and energy to point out, for the umpteenth time, that I was just as bad as the mysterious, and equally hopeless Mr. Poulson.

After some coaxing and prodding, with a little help from Nina, who is not as forgetful as I am: Yes, I remembered. On the second day of our journey, when we were cresting the first long pass in the rain, as the afternoon threatened to slither into evening, a kindly, pudgy-faced man in a black car had shuttled us, one by one, to the summit.

So Ma LuBin called this man, who, it turned out, was eagerly awaiting our return, and immediately announced that he would treat us to a banquet. I wasn't sure that my shrunken stomach could handle two banquets in as many days, but in the spirit of the moment, there was no choice. So we feasted and drank and told stories. The next morning, Ma LuBin informed me that, as is customary in Chinese hospitality and one-upmanship, it was my turn to host a lunch banquet. We weren't even remotely hungry— but oddly enough, eating isn't always about hunger. Anyway, it was raining, and we were hanging out, so…whatever. After seven courses, consumed with beer and abundant yoghurt, which for some reason seemed as crucial as beer, our friend announced simply, as if it were no big deal, "I will pick you up in my car at your hotel promptly at 4:00 this afternoon and take you to the birthplace of the Dalai Lama."

What? Had I heard correctly?

I had already accepted the fact that we had failed to find a specific place that we had come so far to find, which, I had decided long ago, wasn't important to find anyway. As Lao Tzu said, "Just as we take advantage of what is, we should recognize the usefulness of what is not." But suddenly I realized that I was on a pilgrimage, even though I wasn't, that it did matter even though it didn't, and I was again filled with the wonder of this journey, of all journeys of discovery that follow mysterious trails, sinuous paths, coincidence, or perhaps, even, dare I say it: Synchronicity.

I'm absolutely certain that Ma LuBin didn't plan our lengthy bike ride as a convoluted initiation rite for this eventual invitation. He is not nearly that devious. At the same time, I certainly don't believe in cosmic, karmic reward for good behavior and the hardships of a long journey. But I do believe that if you hang out patiently long enough, with low expectations and a smile on your face, more often than not journeys will take you to where you thought you might have wanted to go in the first place. Or maybe they will take you to a place, equally wondrous, that you never even dreamed you wanted to go to.

Our friend picked us up promptly at 4:00, in a light rain. He must have had his car washed and waxed festively for the occasion, because I could see my reflection in the newly hand-polished surfaces. Nina and I sat in the back seat and even though we were armored by so much metal, compared with our bicycles, it still felt scary to navigate the chaotic, honking, random-left-turn-making Chinese city traffic. A dashboard-mounted GPS unerringly led us through the labyrinth of roads and traffic circles. At the outskirts of Xining, a billboard under a shimmering grid of high tension transmission lines announced, in Mandarin and English, "The Center of the City—That's Where Money Grows."

Our friend had a small plastic solar-powered Tibetan prayer wheel mounted on the dashboard, and when the sun broke through the cloudy overcast sky, the prayer wheel began to spin rapidly—clockwise, of course. Ah, maybe this would neutralize all the prayers we had unraveled by bicycling around the Holy Mountain the wrong way. Weaving precariously through dense rush hour traffic at 90 km/hr, we passed a zone where someone in a big bulldozer had flattened several square kilometers of old adobe buildings, with their family histories buried beneath squashed, smashed, splintered doorways and lintels that had been meticulously hand-carved in some bygone era.

As we turned off the main road, the automatic transmission down-shifted and the engine revved to speed up steep switchbacks as if we were in a rocket ship, blasting away from the gravity of commerce. When the onboard GPS told me that we were 300 meters above the valley floor, the setting sun poked beneath the low hanging clouds to light up the city like a virgin wearing a dress made of hundred dollar bills, and perched under a halo. And then, suddenly, like the line from pavement to gravel road earlier in our travels, we drove into the cloud and the urban world disappeared. In the fields, patches of snow from the morning storm clung to stacks of barley, which had been cut with a sharp scythe and bundled by hand. An old Muslim man with a wispy beard and wearing a skull cap was herding sheep along the road with a long, weathered stick. A cold-weather drop of crystal-clear snot dangled from his nose. I recognized him immediately as the cosmic gatekeeper. He smiled when we mentioned the Dalai Lama and pointed toward a rutted track that disappeared into the fog.

As soon as we turned onto that track, the GPS freaked out. The map spun in circles, and the faithful red indicator arrow showed that we were now zooming off into the never-world of outer space. Blissfully, the audio was set on "mute" so the device didn't yell at us, "Recalculating," in Chinese, or any other language. We reached a small cluster of houses at another intersection. Another man, also wearing a Muslim skullcap, was peeing behind a tear-shaped block of granite with bright red Tibetan lettering carved into it.

Our friend asked directions without waiting for the man to stop peeing, and while he was shaking off and tucking back in with one hand, the man pointed with the other hand to an even smaller dirt road, with no recent tire tracks. A few hundred meters later, the road ended. And before us rose a brand new, only a few-weeks-old, walled complex, built of decorative block, with a brightly painted, curved orange and red lintel and an ornate door. There were two shiny-new green trash cans, lettered in Chinese and English. The English read "Organism" on one and "Recycled" on the other. The last visitors had tossed their litter on the ground nearby, not in the cans.

We got out of the car. Nina, Ma LuBin, and I stood in the fog, close-knit travel companions, weathered and tired, honed and lean, on this peaceful mountain top—surrounded, somewhere far below, out of sight, by the commotion called Western Civilization. Our friend and benefactor stood slightly apart. At first, I was prepared to be disappointed, again. Was this yet another chimera? Where was the sign demanding another 80 yuan entrance fee? But wait a minute. There, tucked away inside the courtyard stood a worn mud-walled hut, clinging to the old ways, like the man with the snotty nose and the sheep, like Moolynaut, silently asking not to be forgotten and bulldozed over.

Seventy-seven years ago, in that old weathered house, a peasant woman had screamed, or grimaced, or smiled blissfully in childbirth.

We knocked on the courtyard door and a woman opened the gate. She was about 50 years old, dressed in a plain brown wool shirt and a bright pink headscarf.

"Go away, please," she pleaded. "No foreigners are allowed here." But Ma LuBin charmed her and she relaxed into a smile. She was the Dalai Lama's niece, the caretaker, and she agreed to let us enter, as long as Nina and I covered our heads.

The four of us walked into a modest courtyard, with the remnants of the old farmhouse, ghost-like in the background, half hidden by the evening mist. A young tree was growing out of the center of the courtyard. Could it be exactly 77 years old, planted when Jetsun Jamphel Ngawang Lobsang Yeshe Tenzin Gyatso, soon to become the 14th Dalai Lama, was born? Suddenly

I wanted to believe that I was the pilgrim that I wasn't—and afraid that I was merely a gawking, camera-toting journalist intruding into a stranger's sacred home. But before I had the time to resolve my emotions, which were irrelevant anyway, an angry man poked his head out of a second floor window, and ordered us off the premises.

The world had not been kind to these people, so we smiled and retreated into the enveloping darkness.

I hate to say that a particular landscape or structure holds religious or spiritual significance, because then some true believer will start a war to attack or defend it. So I refused to think that I had visited a specific place; instead it was more about a feeling. In a sense, nothing significant had happened. We had reached our goal and received a frightened human reception, not a blessing or a mantra. Yet I still had a deep internal feeling that the house was a symbol of refuge in the madness: Humans herding sheep in the cold fog, snowy mountains, hand stacked sheaves of barley, and sun-baked bricks—sustenance, peace, and compassion, rising out of the land, sustainable and full of hope.

The Chinese government, autocratic and repressive as it is, could have flattened the old mud hut in an eye-blink. But instead they built a fancy façade around it, to commercialize it, I suppose, complete with an "Organism" trash can. I suspect that they will improve the road and then merchants will set up shops to sell curios. Restaurants will appear. I further suspect that the Dalai Lama's niece and the angry man in the second floor window understood what was about to transpire, and they expelled us, to hang onto just a tiny morsel of peace for a few more weeks or months, before the hordes appear. I'm glad we got there when we did and I have no desire to return and have a slim smiling tour guide with high-heeled shoes and bright red lipstick show me around the place, amid praise for the central Chinese government conquerors.

For us it was the end of a long, sinuous, pilgrimage, or non-pilgrimage. Maybe because I am a writer, or maybe simply because

I live in the 21st century and have learned to think in this manner, I felt that I needed some words to arise out of the place. But there were no words that day, so I let the Dalai Lama speak, from his homeland, his house, his parents' house, his fields, and neighbors, even though he has been exiled from this place, forever:

> When the driving force of our actions is wholesome, our actions will tend automatically to contribute to others' well-being. They will thus automatically be ethical. Further, the more this is our habitual state, the less likely we are to react badly when provoked. And even when we do lose our temper, any outburst will be free of any sense of malice or hatred. The aim of spirituality and, therefore, ethical practice is thus to transform and perfect the individual's *kun long*. That is how we become better human beings."
>
> "We find that the more we succeed in transforming our hearts and minds through cultivating spiritual qualities, the better able we will be to cope with adversity and the greater the likelihood that our actions will be ethically wholesome.[34]

We clambered back into the shiny black car, now spattered with mud, and headed down the mountain to where the GPS worked again, to the center of the city, "where the money grows." Because I have been economically successful in my life, I treated our friends to yet another banquet, our second huge and opulent meal of the day, which we ate to celebrate raw consumerism, not because we were hungry.

CHAPTER 4

LIFE IN THE CITY;
DEATH ON A GLACIER

GARDENER WITH A RAKE

When I was a boy, growing up on the shores of Tarrywile Lake, in Danbury, Connecticut, my mother carpooled with neighbors to drive us to school in winter, but during the fall and spring, we walked. It's about a mile from my house to that forbidding red-brick and grey-concrete block building that gives me cold chills even today, because it represents the time when they tried to crush the wild out of me. The walk to and from school was definitely the highlight of the day. The neighborhood kids would flock together, as if we were flowing out of our houses to join the Pied Piper, and proceed as a tribe, playing as we went. In the spring, we peeled maple seeds apart and stuck them on our noses, like so many green Pinocchios, a bit of innocent frivolity and silliness that was so much fun that I remember it to this day. But, despite the distractions, it was still a long walk on small legs, so we would shorten the distance appreciably by cutting across the too-green lawn of a three-story, southern-plantation type mansion. Then we would continue through a short patch of woodland and down the driveway of another, more modest, conventional, rectangular, New England home, which today I recognize as a Leave-It-To-Beaver House, after the iconic middle class houses popularized in the 1950s and 1960s TV sitcom about an inquisitive and often naïve boy named Theodore "The Beaver" Cleaver.

The only problem with this shortcut was that the owners of the mansion didn't want all of us six- to twelve-year olds walking across their perfect, neatly mowed, dandelion-free, pesticide and herbicide-saturated lawn. They were afraid that we'd scuff up the grass, bend over the tiny blades, and perhaps—God forbid—wear a brown path along our route that would be ever so unsightly. It would lower the property values. Bad for business. Or perhaps one of us would trip and break a leg and our parents would sue them. Who knows what they were afraid of? All of the above, perhaps. In any case, the owners of the mansion, who were generally invisible to us, as they almost never appeared outside, made it clear that we were not allowed to cross their property. And to emphasize their point, they instructed their gardener to be sentry and enforcer.

So, every morning, our urchin tribe would walk carefully up the road and hide, giggling and nervous, behind a large white pine. Then, when we felt the coast was clear, all of us, together, would make a mad dash across the lawn toward the security of the woodlot. But the gardener knew the routine. We showed up at the same time every day, after all. He, too, would hide, giving us the illusion that he had forgotten about us. And then, when we were in full flight, committed beyond reasonable opportunity for retreat, he would pop out into view and chase us menacingly with his iron rake.

He never caught us. We thought it was because we were fast and elusive, dodging like jack-rabbits. But, come on, he was a grown man and we were little kids. Of course, he could have caught us. And if he had bashed just one of us over the head with that rake, smashed just one tiny skull into bloody chunks of brain tissue and bone…Well, if he had done that, he would have been sentenced to the electric chair. Of course he didn't do that. His kids probably went to the same school as we did, sang Christmas carols with us—and this was just a job. My guess is that he was actually on our side, so he made a game of it. And what a fun game it was. We were terrified. It was the high point of our morning, and later, during those long afternoons in class, when Miss Maroney droned on and on about long division, we passed notes back and forth, planning the strategy for returning home after school, without getting whacked by the fearsome rake.

That was over sixty years ago. Twenty-five years ago, my brother, Dan, and his wife, Yuki, bought the Leave-It-To-Beaver House. The gardener at the mansion was long gone, so I thought that I would keep tradition alive and chase all the little school kids with a rake. Terrify them. Give them some excitement to live for, something fun to think about when they were supposed to be spending their time diligently memorizing the capital cities of all fifty states. But, in the past quarter of a century, I have never, not once, seen a kid try to shortcut through Dan and Yuki's property. Why? Because kids don't walk to school anymore. They ride the yellow bus. And after school, as far as I can tell, they don't walk anywhere. If there is unsupervised play happening in the neighborhood, I haven't witnessed it. Not even once. It has to be out there, somewhere. Children are children after all. But, when I hang out at my brother's house, I don't see them. Now, when I am visiting, as geezers, my brother and I take almost daily walks in a nearby woodland that we grew up in, which is now a huge and marvelous city park, left about as wild as it was when we were boys. I remember spending endless hours in those woodlots, catching frogs so that we could throw them at Mary Sue Fript and she would scream, or maintaining a Maginot Line of forts along the rock outcrops to protect our women and loved ones should the fearsome Wooster Heights Gang mount a nefarious back-door assault on the soft underbelly of the Tarrywile Lake community. Of course those were the days of innocence, when 8-year-old, red-blooded American males didn't pack 9mm Glock semiautomatic pistols with thirty round clips, and gangs weren't really gangs because we never actually fought. In fact, the Wooster Heights kids joined our backyard, unorganized, pond-hockey team to defeat the wimps and wannabes across town at Juniper Ridge.

Anyway, I don't see kids playing in the woodlots these days, away from their parents, unsupervised, pasting maple leaves on their noses, building forts, fishing, making mischief, getting dirty, tearing holes in their clothes, stealing apples, and coming home late for dinner.

Call this the anecdotal ranting of an old man. Haven't geezers, since time immemorial, carried on about those good-for-nothing young whippersnappers of the modern generation? "Honest Abe Lincoln walked three miles just to return six cents to an old widow. In my day, when boys were men..." And so on.

Only a few generations ago young, South Pacific shipbuilders walked into the forest with stone tools, cut down huge tropical hardwood trees, and fashioned ocean-going canoes. And then they sailed across open sea from Polynesia to Hawaii. And back. I argue, "I couldn't do that. No one alive in the world today could do that." Just as I now argue that kids don't walk to school.

Yeah, but honestly now, who cares?

For whatever reasons, I have followed my own internal voices, buoyed by Moolynaut's teachings, to come, as close as I am capable of, to emulating the connectivity that our aboriginal ancestors had with their natural environments. I have been inspired by their skill and endurance, their ability to withstand discomfort, pain, and suffering, because I have believed that by importing these character traits, I have lived a more meaningful life. But what do I know? Is there anything universal here, or is it just my own, personal, irrelevant madness? I'm a crackpot, after all, living in a glorified shack with a wife who is also a geezer and a crackpot, when we could be hanging out at the Club Med in Tahiti together, working on our tans. Meanwhile, it's an undeniable fact that out there in the Real World—in Canada, Rwanda, and places like that—more and more people are choosing to live increasingly indoors, in increasingly urbanized, hopefully more comfortable lifestyles. Why allow your children to be chased by a psychotic gardener wielding a deadly weapon when you can petition the school board to chauffeur them around much more sanely and safely in a yellow school bus?

In 1950, when I was five years old, only 30% of the world's population lived in cities; by 2015, when I was 70, that number has risen to above 50%, and by 2050 almost 70% of the world's people are expected to live packed tightly together: In apartments and shanty-towns, penthouses and slums, as oligarchs and beggars. And along with our urban living, we have become increasingly sedentary. This is the Anthropocene, after all. So I wait patiently in my brother's back yard, but there are no kids on the loose, hiding in the bushes, daring each other to race past that old and probably feeble, yet still fearsome-looking, mustached, white-haired man diligently guarding family territory with a mean-looking steel rake.

In September 2011, *Scientific American* ran a 50-page collection of articles titled: "Cities: Smarter, Greener, Better." In the opening essay, the magazine editors wrote, "For thousands of years, people lived in the countryside. They worked on farms or in villages, knew little of the world beyond their immediate families and neighbors, and generally got by on their own. Slowly they began to congregate. It happened in Mesopotamia and Egypt, later in Greece and Rome, and also in Europe and the Americas... And then, by 2008, the balance finally tipped: in the ebb and flow of daily births and deaths, the number of people who inhabit the world's cities ticked into the majority, for the first time ever..."

The editors continue: "This issue of *Scientific American* celebrates the city as a solution to the problems of our age. We have tried to present it in the true urban spirit: best ideas forward."

Cherry-picking two representative quotes from the anthology:

"Cities bring opportunities for wealth and for the creative inspiration that can result only from face-to-face contact with others. In fact, the crush of people living in close quarters fosters the kind of collaborative creativity that has produced some of humanity's best ideas, including the industrial revolution and the digital age.... By supercharging the flow of ideas, cities foster economic prosperity, innovation, better health—and even new ways to govern ourselves."

"Today's cities are by many measures greener than the suburbs—among other things, urbanites use less energy and emit less carbon dioxide per household than their suburban counterparts do because they live in closer quarters and use public transportation."

And so on.

But there's something missing in this tidy and rosy assessment all wrapped up in a red ribbon with soft music playing in the background. Because, I'm sorry, everything isn't quite that hunky dory.

First of all, in case you haven't noticed, by the way, people have to eat. And food is grown in the countryside, by people called farmers, who survive (and feed the rest of us) by paying careful attention to weather, rainfall, and the cycles of the seasons—to insects, molds, nematodes, bacteria and stuff like that. Okay, let's imagine that we can shrug off this inconvenient truth by arguing, "Yeah, well, with modern mechanization, farmers represent only a few percent of the population. Farmers aren't really in the center of the action." Or, "Yeah, well, we can grow food in urban vertical greenhouses, or produce food in algae farms and chemical factories. However you cut it, the real focus, our potential salvation, resides in the ideas and technology that arise from the cities." Don't let me get too riled up about this, and certainly don't try these arguments out on Noey, who is a farmer.

But, let's assume, just for laughs, that we can ignore the business of eating. Even then, I don't think that we should feel comfortable relying on cities and urban thinking as the solution to our problems. Try walking into the disease and crime-ridden slums and shantytowns of Rio, Mexico City, Karachi, Bujumbura, or Ouagadougou, and talk to those people about economic prosperity, innovation, better health.

And then, wait a minute, this rosy assessment doesn't even stand up that well in Toronto or New York. A report by Nobel

Prize-winning economist Angus Deaton and Anne Case showed that mortality among predominantly urban, white, middle class Americans has been rising since 1999, because basically, relatively wealthy urban dwellers are, as a group, fundamentally so unhappy with their lives that they are killing themselves through direct suicide or indirect suicide with overdoses of prescription and non-prescription drugs, alcohol, and French fries.

Another Nobel Prize-winning economist, Paul Krugman, asks: "So what's going on? In a recent interview, Mr. Deaton suggested that middle-aged white North Americans have 'lost the narrative of their lives...We're looking at people who were raised to believe in the American Dream, and are coping badly with its failure to come true.'" Krugman calls this, "existential angst," which means that an awful lot of people are doing what they are trained to do—*think*—when thinking is not only unnecessary, but a downright pain-in-the-neck. Certainly, a great many people in North America are having a rough go of it. Income inequality and concentration of wealth into the top 1% is a serious issue. But there are also lots of people who are opulent by any conventional standards, but who decide to conjure up this totally bogus invented story that their lives are deficient. So they dream up problems that don't exist, making their potentially wonderful and gratifying lives woefully out of whack. Then they jump out of windows, or drink themselves to death, or veg-out in front of the tube drinking Coke and eating potato chips until their heart says fuck-this-shit and stops beating. Or, if you agree with Krugman, they get so pissed off at the world that they support egomaniacal, psychopathic, war and hate-mongering politicians who tell everyone that anger is the solution. Whew. Humans are really too weird, including me, for sure, and probably you.

But we don't have to be so weird that we destroy ourselves and the planet. That's the point of this book. Talk with the Spirit Wolf or the Ice in the Nares Strait. Wash your face in a muddy river someday so the Grandfather Crocodile won't eat you.

Follow Ma LuBin's journey from an angry Red Guard warrior and a propagandist for Chairman Mao to a bicycle nomad, "free as a bird." Or listen to the Dalai Lama who learned compassion from oppression.

Yes, cities are wonderful and I was happy to fly into Ottawa so I didn't die an early and unnecessary death. But the constricted space, too-busy jobs, traffic, noise, and wacko politicians are not so wonderful. It's not so wonderful that corporations are constantly reminding us that we need more stuff. And it's not so wonderful that for some weird reason we are hardwired to listen. And then we go into debt and destroy the environment to buy stuff we never needed in the first place.

It doesn't have to be that way.

Because, just maybe, our brains are actually capable of saying: "Stop already. Enough. Fuck this shit." Then we can open our eyes and take a walk and watch the snow fall, or play with our children, or take the time to make slow luxurious love with our partner. Whew. It shouldn't be that simple—but actually it is. Or should I say: It shouldn't be that complicated, but actually it is.

There are a lot of people out there who are calling for a Consciousness Revolution. But there are also a lot of people who are ignoring this call. On November 11, 2015, Beijing had a cumulative air pollution rating of 191 (unhealthy), compared to 26 in New York (Good.)[35] So what are the Chinese doing? They're building a super-city around Beijing, the size of Kansas, to house 130 million people, six times more populated than the New York metropolitan area. If you took that many people, and laid them all down in a line, feet touching heads, they would encircle the globe five times. How do you get all the food in and all the poop out? How can clean, healthy air find its way through that labyrinth of buildings and factories into the lungs of little children? How can clean, healthy thoughts find their way through that labyrinth of buildings and factories into the minds of little children?

I can't prove my point, and I respect all those who disagree, but like the Dalai Lama, I just have this nagging suspicion that urbanization, for all its obvious advantages, also steals something vital from us and that a journey toward a *paleo attitude* has great value even in today's modern world.

I've said this before: It's not a matter of going back. There is no "back" to return to. The world has been changing ever since bits of dust particles began coalescing in the void of outer space; ever since the dinosaurs died off, leaving ecological niches for furry mammals; ever since the first hungry hunter planted a seed; ever since Alexander Graham Bell spoke into a device that we now call a telephone, "Mr. Watson—Come here—I want to see you." It's no great revelation to say that no matter what we do, there is no baseline, and the world of tomorrow will necessarily be different from the world of today. But it's also no great revelation to say that the world in my lifetime has changed more rapidly than it has in the generation or million years before that, so it doesn't hurt to ask, over and over again, in as many ways as possible, "Where are we going, anyway?" And if we have any choice about it, "Is this actually where we want to go?"

THE SHORT LIFE OF KWADAY DÄN TS'ÌNCHÍ, "LONG AGO PERSON FOUND"

About 300 to 500 years ago, a young—Warrior? Hunter? Trader? Messenger? Adventurer? Or Love-sick suitor?—18 or 19 years old, ate a hearty meal of crab, seal blubber, and beach asparagus. Then he wrapped himself in his ground-squirrel robe, tied on his medicine bundle, grabbed a few weapons and some dried salmon, and struck out from his homeland on the coast of what is now Southeast Alaska, to walk into the dark, damp, verdant rainforest.

If you have ever tried to hike cross-country through this forest, you will find it slow-going due to an abundance of fallen trees, some with trunks as big around as a person is tall, thick patches of devils club, bogs, and other natural obstacles. But the Native Americans who lived in these regions maintained closely guarded pathways to facilitate trade with their neighbors in the interior. Predominantly, the coastal people traded oolichan oil, (also called eulachon oil) which is a greasy, calorie and nutrition-rich extract of a local fish that were once abundant in the Inside Passage waterways of the region. I mention this tidbit of history because the publisher of this book is Oolichan Books, in memory of a bygone era and a bygone lifestyle.

Pollen residues discovered by modern archeologists indicate that this young man started his journey in late summer, probably August. Hiking about 30kms a day, he climbed above the rainforest and ascended into the mountains of the rugged Tatshenshini-Alsek range of Alaska, British Columbia, and the Yukon. His route here is less clear, but I believe that as soon as he reached the high country he hiked along a broad glacier to avoid the thick brush of the sub-alpine scrub. Three days after setting out, he reached a high mountain pass. Snow fell and perhaps the wind was blowing. He might have become disoriented or hypothermic in the storm. Maybe he fell in a crevasse. Whatever the cause, this apparently healthy young man, in the prime of his life, lay down and died. Fresh snow quickly encapsulated his body in an icy tomb—before scavengers or predators could reach him.

In August 1999, three hunters, Bill Hanlon, Warren Ward, and Mike Roche were in the vicinity, working their way slowly upwind, rifles over their shoulders, stopping frequently to scan distant alpine pastures for trophy sheep. Bill told me this story in the summer of 2012, over a flask of whisky by a back-country campfire, with the clang of horse-bells punctuating his tale. He explained that they might have taken a shortcut across the remnants of an old glacier, but Mike and Warren's wives had made them promise not to cross any snow or ice, so they skirted wide on the talus. There, on the ground, the men saw bits of wood, which was curious because they were well above tree line. Bill and Mike picked up a few of the sticks, and saw, to their surprise, that the pieces were notched and some had been carved. Alert now, the three men scanned the vicinity through binoculars. Then Warren almost whispered, "I think I found the poor fellow who lost all this stuff." There, not far away, framed in the narrow field of view afforded by the binos, he saw something unusual, not rock or snow— fragments of a body protruded out of the edge of the glacier.

Bill told me, "The air became electric and the hair stood up on the backs of our necks. It was one of those moments that don't dim with time; I can imagine every vivid detail to this day."

The three hunters had discovered the body of that ancient warrior, now known as Kwäday Dän Ts'ìnchí, "Long Ago Person Found."

The men left the remains untouched, returned to town, and contacted Greg Hare, lead archeologist for the Yukon Ice Patch Study at the Beringia Centre in Whitehorse. For the past few years, Greg and his co-workers had been exploring the Yukon high-country, looking for artifacts that were melting out of glaciers and snowfields under the influence of global warming. So far, they had found over 200 human tools and utensils ranging from a 9000-year-old projectile shaft to a 19th-century musket ball. But a complete ice-preserved mummy was the Holy Grail.

"You found what?" Greg asked, incredulously, his heart jumping. "A body? On the edge of an ice patch? Where? Hold on. Don't do anything." Greg obtained the coordinates of the discovery and raced off to the site in a helicopter.

The body had been broken in half by ice movement, leaving a torso and left arm displaced from a lower section consisting of pelvis and legs, missing the lower right leg and the feet. They found hair. But no head.

Four years later, Bill and Mike were back in the region, hunting again. In Bill's words, "Mike and I decided to return to the discovery site to look for more artifacts. We never discussed the possibility that we might find the head, but it was heavy on both of our minds. So much ice had melted that I was able to step up onto the ice from the gravel bar to view the surface. That's when I said, 'Hey Mike. Look, there it is. The head!'"

Mike replied, almost angrily, "Fuck off. You're freaking me out; the hair is sticking up on the back of my neck again!"

"No Mike, I'm serious, there's the head!"

And then, a few days later, Bill called the Beringia Centre again. "Hey Greg, Bill Hanlon here. How'z it going?"

Greg cut through the small talk, "Don't tell me you found the head?" he asked, in hushed expectation.

Bill Hanlon is lean, athletic, and wiry, a skier from Trail, BC, a seasoned horse-packer, and a master woodworker who lives in the mountains of southeastern British Columbia. He has an easy, jovial, happy-go-lucky, almost boyish enthusiasm about him, tied together with a photographic memory. If you've got nothing to do one day, with time to kill, just pick a date at random, and ask, "Hey Bill, tell me about that elk you shot in 2005." And then sit back to hear the story, in detail, about the horses, the partners, the weather, and the adventure in the mountains he knows so well.

After Bill told me about the discovery, I felt compelled to visit the glacier where Kwäday Dän Ts'ìnchí had laid down and died, simply because, once again, I wanted to feel the spirit of those forgotten times.

The best radiocarbon dates place Kwäday Dän Ts'ìnchí's demise about 300 to 500 years ago, or roughly between 1500 and 1700, with uncertainty due to technical difficulties in the dating techniques. It was a time when European monarchs were building castles and launching ships of discovery, or armies of conquest, depending on your world view.

Europeans had already landed in the Western Hemisphere and, depending on the exact dates of Kwäday Dän Ts'ìnchí's life, the Spanish, and possibly the French and English had established colonies and even significant cities on the continent, although

Vitus Bering didn't land on the south coast of Alaska, from the Russian side, until 1741. We have no idea whether, or not, Kwäday Dän Ts'ìnchí had heard about the Europeans, with their bulky wooden ships, guns, and smallpox. My guess, and it is just a guess, is that storytelling is such an innate part of human nature, and the European colonization was such a significant event, that the news would have traveled even into the most remote, pristine locations. But it was just news from faraway lands, almost mythic in content, and the Europeans made little impact on Kwäday Dän Ts'ìnchí's life.

At the time of his death, the young warrior carried a knife made of an iron blade hafted into a hemlock-wood handle. The iron could have moved across continents and seas as a trade item or perhaps it washed ashore in a shipwreck from a Chinese junk or a Spanish galleon. Less probably, it could have been chipped from an iron-bearing meteorite. Other than the knife, his clothing and tools were evidence of the highest level of Stone Age technology, with zero European influence. To the best of our knowledge, his only clothing consisted of a hat made out of split spruce root and a loose fitting, ankle-length robe made from 95 ground squirrel skins, sewn together with sinew from moose, blue whale, humpback whale, and mountain goat. Scientists did not recover shoes from the site. Possibly he was barefoot, which is hard for me to imagine, because he had been traveling across the ice. Therefore, it seems probable, to me anyway, that his moccasins were lost, somehow, after his death.

Let us imagine the process surrounding the manufacture of this robe. First, Kwäday Dän Ts'ìnchí, or a friend, trapped, snared, or cold-cocked 95 alert, sneaky little ground squirrels. Then he carefully skinned each one with his crude knife, and tanned the hides. Somewhere along the line, he and his buddies obtained some blue whale sinew, possibly by scavenging a carcass, or possibly by paddling out to sea in a cedar-log dugout and harpooning a 170-tonne blue whale, the largest animal that has ever existed on earth, using a stick, with a piece of rock tied to the end of it. Finally, someone—His mother? Girlfriend? Wife? Or did he do it himself?—sat down during the long, dark winter months to painstakingly and meticulously sew these tiny hides together, and waterproof the seams.

On his last journey, Kwäday Dän Ts'ìnchí carried a 4-meter walking stick, which probably doubled as a salmon gaff, and a curved wooden tool, which possibly was used to set snares for ground squirrels. Ceremonially, he wore a copper bead, fashioned from native metal deposits in the Alsek, and a small bag made of beaver skin. Representatives of the local First Nations tribes immediately recognized that this bag was a medicine pouch. They asked the scientists not to open the pouch and then reunited it with Kwäday Dän Ts'ìnchí's remains.

By studying his stomach contents and the isotopic content of his bones, scientists learned that Kwäday Dän Ts'ìnchí grew up on the coast, probably near Haines or Skagway, Alaska, eating a marine diet. Shortly before he died, he traveled inland for several months, consuming caribou, moose, and other inland food. He returned home for a brief sojourn, and then started back inland on his ill-fated final journey. Perhaps he had found a girlfriend among the interior tribes and returned home briefly to tell his parents and fetch a gift for his future in-laws, which he sequestered carefully in his medicine bag. Others suggest that he was a messenger, carrying important tribal news between settlements.

But why did he travel over this high, glaciated mountain pass when he could have followed the river valleys, which are so much lower and less prone to the full intensity of violent storms?

In the spring of 2014, Bill and I made plans to follow Kwäday Dän Ts'ìnchí's probable route over the glaciers to that fateful high pass. We were joined by John Bergenske, a geezer, like me, in his mid-60s, and the Conservation Director of Wildsight, a leading environmental group in southern British Columbia. John is an avowed vegetarian while Bill is a horse-packing, gun-toting, redneck environmentalist. John attacks Bill's hunting mania mercilessly, sometimes with good humor and sometimes with just a touch of a sharp edge. But it's all part of the game and Bill gives as good as he gets, often referring to vegetarian meals as "eating what food eats." But this banter is just chaff, overlying the tight bond between the two, based on their love of traveling in, and protecting, wild landscapes.

Under a dark sky and a weather forecast for a week of rain, we loaded our packs with ten days of food. For reasons of privacy, I won't give the exact location of the site, but suffice to say that it is located on the eastern edge of the Kluane / Wrangell-St. Elias / Glacier Bay / Tatshenshini-Alsek World Heritage site, a 10-million hectare expanse of mountains and glaciers, the largest protected wilderness in the world. I was hoping for sunny skies, of course, while at the same time aware that we were at the edge of the Southeast Alaska rainforest, where the clouds often hang heavily over the mountains for weeks at a time and I shouldn't be surprised, or bummed out, if we were encapsulated in the legendary, dripping, omnipresent sogginess that nurtures green-cloaked hemlocks, red-capped fungi, and broad-leafed devil's club down in the coastal valleys.

My first photo of the trip shows my two compatriots barely out of the parking lot, with smiles on their faces and still-dry clothes, slogging into dense wet undergrowth with the low gray clouds kissing the tops of the mountains. Although I missed it in the photo, a grizzly bear was feeding a hundred meters away. The following morning, we rose out of the brush and into the alpine, where the rock-strewn tongue of a glacier poked from between dark peaks, like a medieval gargoyle. On the third day, we descended a steep ravine to cross a river valley that had been recently glaciated. I've been in this situation frequently in recent years, where the maps are outdated because the ice is receding so quickly under the influence of global warming, and the rock and talus are dangerously unstable because they haven't had time to settle.

After several aborted attempts, we found a route through an improbable series of gullies, nearly devoid of soil or vegetation. After reaching the valley bottom, we donned our crampons to ascend the glacier on the other side. At a junction of two valleys, we veered into a refugium of high alpine meadows that was apparently ice-free 500 years ago; and was carpeted with mountain heather, glorious in abundance, the bell-shaped flowers hanging downward, so the delicate stamens face the ground, to survive the arctic wind by hoarding heat from the earth. Archeologists have found numerous wooden artifacts in this valley, indicating that in Kwäday Dän Ts'ìnchí's time, people routinely walked through this cathedral of ice, rock, and flower.

Why did they climb so high, into such harsh terrain? Was this the route of a spiritual walk-about? Perhaps, but after traveling in this country, Bill, John, and I think that there is a much simpler and more logical answer. From a hiker's point of view, it is so much easier to travel along snowfields, glaciers, and tundra than to bushwhack through the thick alders down below. Therefore, anyone walking into the interior to meet with the people in the southern Yukon might logically have followed this route. Or perhaps, our friend wasn't journeying into the interior at all. Bill suggests that he may have been here as his final destination, to hunt sheep. The question remains unanswerable.

Late in the afternoon, we reached the site where Bill and his partners had found the mummy, fifteen years before. In respect for spirits, past and present, we took no photos. Bill led us to a small cairn, built by members of the modern Champagne and Aishihik Nations to hold the cremated ashes of the young man whose spirit had been unsettled for so many years because he had never had a proper burial. I left a piece of string on the cairn, because string is so useful in the Real World, and presumably in the Other World as well, and so tedious to weave from the split roots of a spruce tree. Bill left a piece of elk jerky from his daughter's first elk the season before, a gift from one hunter to another. And then we sat there, silently, in the rarefied air of this remote place, amid a seemingly infinite expanse of mountains: rock and ice, high meadows and wildflowers. I felt that I had time out there. Time to stop thinking. Time to watch the mountains eroding into the sea. We glassed the hillsides for sheep, goats, and grizzly bears, and watched the long, Northern summer day settle, ever so slowly, into evening.

In 1999 and 2000, I kayaked from Japan to Alaska, following the ancient maritime passage of North Pacific Rim migrants who crossed over from Asia during the ice ages. Now, I was visiting the final resting place of one of the distant grandchildren of these ancient voyagers. These journeys have taken me through some of the most beautiful land- and sea-scapes in the world. But beauty is one of those words like "nice," that are, well, nice enough, but, in a way, missing the point. For me, mountains, oceans, prairies and icecaps are like living sponges. As I pass through the abundant, welcoming openings, millions of tiny tendrils reach out, capture the useless thoughts and petty worries I carry around with me every day, like filtering bacteria out of the ocean, and then sequester these worthless words in secret labyrinths, where they can do no more harm. And when I come out the other side, if I am lucky:

> It is on the space where there is nothing that
> The usefulness of the wheel depends.

Unfortunately, all too often, for some weird reason, my body builds defenses against the cleansing. Then, as I walk peacefully through the forest, I think about random bullshit. So I've devised little tricks to open some doors and close others. In a sense, I cheat. But in a larger sense, there are no rules, and hence it is impossible to subvert the rules by cheating. My major trick is to put myself intentionally in life-threatening situations. Then it becomes imperative to shut off the mind-chatter and open to what is real and in front of me. Or I die. Thus, for example, over countless winter days, I have dug deep into the mountain snowpack to examine the buried snow crystals, sometimes with a magnifying glass, to understand how well they had bonded together, to decide if the slope was safe to ski, or whether it will avalanche and kill me. On other occasions, I have studied rock faces with binoculars, to locate tiny cracks that would enable me to scale the high cliffs. So many times, when threatened by real, tactile danger, I have found that alertness to weather patterns, or the movement of bears, have helped me maintain that thin edge that makes life so possible, intense, and wondrous out here. But when I'm lucky, like on that day, on that high pass, with two dear friends, there was no danger, only nature being nature, and me opening to the memory of a young man who had perished here, in such an incomprehensibly different world, so distant and yet so close in time. And then those ruminations faded into the glory of a peaceful evening on a mountainside kaleidoscope of snow, talus, and wildflowers, with a vein of quartz cutting diagonally across a rock outcrop.

In his beautifully written and insightful book, *The Once and Future World: Nature As It Was, As It Is, As It Could Be*, J. B. MacKinnon argues that when the European conquerors arrived in the Western Hemisphere, they killed off 90% of many of the indigenous mega fauna, as well as 90% of the Native Americans who lived there. To add my own thoughts to this tragedy, I believe that these same European settlers, in creating an urban world, destroyed 90% of the Deep Wild possible within themselves. As my Koryak friend Lydia told me, "If you went to school in a square room and sat behind a desk, learning your letters and numbers, you can never, ever, in your life, no matter how hard you try, have the mind of Moolynaut, who grew up in a skin tent, herding reindeer." Thus, today, we all live in a 10% world.

The good news is that the 10% we have left, outside and inside of us, is pretty darn wonderful. Wonderful enough so that on that day, I sat on a high mountain pass, ate a small handful of nuts imported from California, the Amazonian Rainforest, and who knows where else, and then rallied my creaky old bones to drop into the valley below, to cook dinner, and make camp.

J. B. MacKinnon again, "Pay attention and we will value nature more. When we value nature more, we work harder to reverse its declines. Reverse the decline in variety and abundance, and nature becomes steadily more fascinating, more spectacular, and more meaningful. Awareness can be its own reward."[36]

Kwäday Dän Ts'ìnchí was born only about 6 lifetimes ago, a miniscule nano-spec of human history, just before James Watt invented the steam engine, freeing humanity from the yoke of human and animal labor, and, in the process, setting the foundation for catastrophic climate change. As I've said before, even if it were possible, which of course it isn't, no sane person would return to the Stone Age, where most people died in their thirties, warfare was common, and winters were long, cold, and dark as people huddled in smoky longhouses or around the blubber lamp in an igloo. Yes, this man died young, but humanity survived here for eons, with the barest of tools, on stormy oceans and frigid icecaps.

As I have mentioned previously, numerous anthropological studies have shown that Stone Age people, despite the harshness of their lives, despite the obvious time-consuming process of making ground-squirrel skin robes, "worked" 12 to 19 hours a week, and thus had loads more free time than most people have in our uber-efficient, consumer-oriented, internet-crazed, oil-soaked society. They revered and honored the earth, all its creatures, the water, and the rocks, as one would revere a loving grandparent. Our ancestors sat around campfires and chatted, played with their children, made music, danced, and painted on rock walls. The flute was invented by Stone Age hunters forty thousand years ago, approximately the same time that hunters and warriors were inventing the bow and arrow and other projectile weapons.

SYNCHRONICITY AND
THE SACRED SPACE

Travel books, like this one, romanticize exotic adventures in remote lands. But there are other books that romanticize staying at home and observing nature without wandering the globe. Noey and her partner Glenn make their living by operating a commercial organic farm that is not 100 acres, or five acres, or even one acre, but a 2,400 sq. ft. greenhouse, the size of an average suburban house. Noey suggests that if you want to create a meaningful life based on sound environmental ethic, "stay home and grow a garden."

To recognize and honor the many valid pathways toward this slippery and elusive journey that we paste names onto, like the Spiritual Revolution or the Consciousness Revolution, I end this book by leaving ice fields and jungles behind and telling a story about an urban adventure.

Between 2011 and 2015, I collaborated with choreographer Jody Weber and the dancers of Weber Dance to produce a performance called "Synchronicity and the Sacred Space." The show is an integration of my storytelling with the ecstatic artistry of dance to convey a message of the Sacred Space. In Jody's words, "Through storytelling and dance, this performance probes the strange landscape where scientific thought encounters the unknown, and where human perception and reality are fluid partners."

When we started creating the show, Jody had me stand on a blank stage and tell a story segment about my life-journey from the world of science to the healing powers of Moolynaut. Then I would walk off and the dancers would enter to interpret that word-image as motion. Repeat. But that format lacked vitality. So one day, in an abandoned warehouse in Boston, in the basement, in the city, Jody announced that I needed to integrate more intimately with the dancers.

"Great." I responded sarcastically, looking at the young,

intensely athletic, professional dancers around me. "Do whatever you want, but don't make me look clunky."

"I'm aware of the problem," she responded.

So we created a performance where I interact directly with the dancers (but hopefully not clunkily) where the words and the imagery intertwine. The high point of the dance, for me, occurs just after I talk about my healing with Moolynaut. As I am finishing my story, one of the dancers, either Jen or Kristy, walks up behind me. Even though I am facing the audience, and she approaches on bare feet, noiselessly, I can feel her presence behind me, her energy, just as I felt Moolynaut's healing energy on the day that I stood naked before her. When the dancer's presence is so palpable and tactile that I can no longer look away, I turn to face her. She reaches out her hand and I grasp it between two open palms. We stand there for a moment, looking into each other's eyes. And then I say, "I just told you what happened to me. But this is how it made me feel."

And then I quickly step back and out of the way, while Jen or Kristy explodes into a dance-interpretation of the ecstasy that I felt when my body was healed, or the ecstasy that I felt when Boomer and I paddled through the night, through the Nares Strait with the ducks skimming the water.

In the spring of 2014, we performed along the western slope of the Rockies in Central Colorado. One day, a man named Aaron Garland came up after a show and told me that he was the director of a "Youth Recovery Program" in nearby Glenwood Springs, and asked if we would talk to his students. He offered what was available to him, $200, for all six of us, $33.33 each, for a morning's work. We accepted. Performing in a modern dance troupe is not a get-rich quick scheme. It didn't matter. We were together in this beautiful place. Dancing. Like I told one audience during an informal discussion, "It was like running away as a youth to join the circus, only without the elephants."

Glenwood Springs lies at the down-valley end of the

Roaring Fork River, which flows past Aspen and drains some of the most beautiful mountain scenery in the world—as well as the playgrounds of some of the richest people in the world. But the building that housed this "Youth Recovery Program" was a somber brick structure, with tiny windows, and no proper entry-way, just a forbidding, locked, steel door, like the steel doors in my dormitory at Brown so many years ago; like a prison that closes you in, not a portal to something uplifting beyond. We knocked, and an aide, a teacher, a guard, or the janitor—I'm not sure which—opened the door, which creaked and groaned on its hinges, like in an old horror movie. We filed in tentatively but obediently and then the door clanked shut with a hollow metallic sound. Instinctively I looked over my shoulder, feeling that we had been tricked by the old witch and now were sucked into the bowels of some place that I had fought all my life not to be sucked into—captured—to be baked into ginger bread or forced to watch FOX News for the rest of eternity, or something like that. If it were possible I would have forfeited my $33.33 and asked the aide with the keys to let me out of here, *right now*, back into the March sunshine.

Aaron is a big man, well over two meters tall, with a large body to match, like a professional athlete, with a huge, warm, embracing smile. He ushered us into the faculty room and offered some foul-smelling institutional coffee that no one accepted, not even Jody, who usually embraces a hit of caffeine. He explained that these kids were, in fact, in prison, although he didn't use that term. Not a single one of them wanted to be here. They were between 14 and 18 years old; all had been at odds with the law for drug abuse problems, and some had been violent. He wanted us to inspire them. Turn their lives around. Make a difference.

"Right," I thought. "We're going to waltz in there, flipping our pink petticoats so to speak, and in one hour we're going to turn the clock back on a lifetime of neglect, abandonment, despair, alienation, abuse, drugs, violence. Dream on, Dude."

But we were here and we might as well get it over with.

We walked into the hallway and a dozen kids filed past us, moving in the classic poses of the defeated—heads down, avoiding eye contact, shuffling as if they were wearing leg chains, unsmiling, not talking, expressionless. Hardened children-people. One young woman, about 15 or 16 was chewing a water bottle, as if it were a baby bottle, as if she were about to retreat into a corner and suck her thumb.

Right. Let's get this over with and get outta here.

Jody, the dancers, and I had no idea what we were supposed to do or what we were expected to say. There had been no planning, no rehearsal. We followed Aaron and the kids into a large class-room, and they moved the chairs around the perimeter, backs to the windows, leaving us an impromptu performance space. Aaron brought in a small mobile sound system and Jody took a CD out of her briefcase.

Improv theatre. Wing it. I stood there with the four dancers and Jody. For this past week, this moment in time, we were a close-knit family, a tribe. Every performance depended on a reciprocal, emotional—joyous—connection among the six of us. On stage, our energies floated in the spaces between us, embraced, spiraled, and expanded.

I thought about last night's performance, before cultured, fortunate adults, from the Aspen Valley, who had navigated the 21st century, successfully enough, or luckily enough, to afford the price of admission. And then some. I thought about that moment when I had held hands with Kristy and said. "That is what hap-pened to me. And this is how it made me feel." And then, as she exploded into a solo that expressed my feelings through her artistry, I thought about ecstasy and connectivity. The power of synchronicity. About how fortunate I was to be born one of the lucky ones. Then I looked at the children-people, or convicts, whatever you want to call them. And I knew, instinctively and without doubt, that we had the power to make an impact.

Jody asked me to talk first.

I didn't know these kids, had never spoken even a single word to any of them. But I'd been there, where they were, not in as deep a hole, but been there. Because the world around me didn't make sense. Because my teachers around me were all upside down, trying to brow-beat me into believing that "learning" was the act of "conforming" to a set of rules and values that didn't make sense to me then—and still don't, not even now. All my life, disbelieving has been my yin and my yang, what has gotten me into trouble and then what has gotten me out of trouble. I had to tell these kids that there was actually a healthy path out of the madness, toward a journey that made some kind of universal sense, deep within our consciousness, a path now made ever so much more blurry by rejection, imprisonment, violence, and resentment.

With the first sentence spilling out before I knew what I was saying, I started, "We're here to talk about healing." Then I paused, because I didn't know what the second sentence would be. "We all become broken at times. We break bones. Sometimes we are hurt in other ways and we feel broken, even when our bodies are sound. Every one of us gets broken sometimes. This is normal. Sane even. This happens to everyone. So we all must learn how to heal."

Jody picked up the thread and talked about the dance we were doing. About the sacred synchronicity of healing. About Moolynaut and the Black Raven. About flowing water. She put on some music. The dancers exploded into motion that celebrated wellness on an emotional, visceral level. I talked; Jody talked; the dancers talked a little, but mostly they danced. The hardscrabble girl stopped chewing on her water bottle. One by one, smiles appeared on the faces of the condemned.

Near the end of the hour, Jody asked the kids to stand and dance the flow of water with us. "We will ride the wave of flowing water to healing." And every one of those "Youth Recovery" kids rose and danced with us. With smiles on their faces. Responding not to lessons or rules; demands or assignments; threats or promises; but to simple, unadulterated, artistry, motion, music, and joy.

At first I was surprised. But I shouldn't have been because deep inside every one of us, there is a primal yearning to shut off our think-too-much-know-it-all brains and open a space for music and dance to flow in, like a wave, like water. In my own youth, I, too, had stumbled and nearly fallen, because I didn't know that the search for ecstasy was the only sane, valid, career choice. My mother never told me. The rabbi never told me. The psychiatrist and the dean never told me. Ma Lu Bin had been a propagandist for Chairman Mao, even while the Cultural Revolution was torturing his father, because he, too, had been swept up to believe in hierarchies, political power, anger, progress, and nationalism. And then, on the cusp of old age, he waited outside our hotel room in the cool pre-dawn, with his cotton bedroll tied haphazardly on his piece-of-shit Chinese bike, because he could finally become a "free bird" after all those years, by simply dropping everything else in his life, *right now*, and ride a bicycle into the mountains with these two crazy Americans. This bike ride would become his own personal healing, ecstasy, just as he had understood the treasure of books when he entered that storeroom so many years ago.

And I think that it's safe to paraphrase what the Dalai Lama is so patiently and assiduously telling us: That if we free our minds of all the extraneous input and confusion, the random useless stories we invent for no good reason, we might be lucky enough so the empty space that remains will fill with ecstasy. And then ecstasy will morph seamlessly into compassion, for ourselves, our neighbors, and our planet. That one word—compassion—stands out loud and strong in all of the Dalai Lama's writings and teachings as the Consciousness Revolution that will be the beginning of healing. Is it really that simple? Or maybe we should ask: Why is it that complex and difficult?

In this dizzyingly insane world, with its tragic hostilities and abundant opportunity, dark prisons and sparking ice-fields, it seems that I've led my life as improv theatre, wandering around without a coherent plan, tripping over my own folly more often than I would like to admit, but, nevertheless assiduously avoiding people who tell me what to think or do, and listening carefully to those who have ideas that they are willing to share. And it's worked well enough, in a bumbling sort of way. I have no complaints.

I wrote this book about Deep Wild because that is where I have found my own personal teachers: Moolynaut the Shaman, Oleg the Hunter, Tundra, the crocodile and the wolf, the Arctic icepack, and the robin in your own backyard. And then, of course, there is Kwäday Dän Ts'ìnchí, our ancestor, who understood Deep Wild because this knowing of the unknowable gave him the power to survive, which in turn allowed us to be born into a mysterious and alien reality. Then I collaborated with the dancers who expressed my emotional communication with the natural world as joyous motion within an urban world. Because there are many paths. And that is all the simplicity and complexity, all the richness I could hope for. Every kid loves a circus, especially if there are no sad, captive elephants.

(ENDNOTES)

1   Taken from the lyrics of the Bob Seger song, "Against the Wind."

2   Joanna Harcourt-Smith. *Tripping the Bardo with Timothy Leary: My Psychedelic Love Story*, CreateSpace Independent Publishing Platform, 2013, 364 pages.

3   Steven Koonin, "The Tough Realities of the Paris Climate Talks," Opinion Pages, *The New York Times*, Nov 4, 2015.

4   www.urbandictionary.com

5   Bob Dylan. *Chronicles*, New York, Simon & Schuster (September 13, 2005)

6   William Faulkner, "The Bear." As part of an anthology: *Big Woods, The Hunting Stories*, New York, Vintage Books, 1995.

7   As quoted in: Calvin Luther Martin, *The Way of the Human Being*, Yale University Press, New Haven, 1999, 235 pp. Quote found on page 56.

8   *The New York Times* digital edition, July 25, 2013.

9   Jack Turner, "Gary Snyder and the Practice of the Wild," published in George Sessions, *Deep Ecology for the 21ˢᵗ Century*, Boston, Shambhala, 1995, 488 pp, page 45.

10   www.ditext.com/diamond/mistake.html

11   William Press, "What's So Special About Science" in *Science*, Vol 342, Pg 817, Nov 15, 2013

12   Ronald Bayer, Amy Fairchild, and Constance Nathanson, "Confronting the Sorry State of U.S. Health," *Science*, Vol 341, Pg 962, Aug 30, 2013.

13   Dirk Helbing, "Globally Networked Risks and How to Respond," *Nature*, Vol 497, pg 51, May 2, 2013

14   Paul Krugman, Talking Troubled Turkey, New York Times, Jan. 30, 2014

15   www.ted.com/talks/brene_brown_on_vulnerability/

16 As quoted in, Joan Halifax, *Shamanic Voices*. New York, Arkana Press, 1979, 266 pp. Quote found on page 6.

17 Timothy Wilson, et al. "Just Think: The challenges of the disengaged mind," *Science*, Vol 345, Issue 6192. July 4, 2014, pg 75.

18 *Tao Te Ching*, Chapter 20.

19 Proceedings of the Proteus Court of Inquiry on the Greely Relief Expedition ... By United States Congress, Published by Cambridge University Press, quoted from: http://books.google.ca/books?id=ZVemy nt78mUC&pg=PA252&lpg=PA252&dq=steamship+proteus&source= bl&ots=GBEoXE0m9J&sig=2Ugo_fxuUKSXK4L6A08gVrk9mWU& hl=en&sa=X&ei=vrXiUpG0Ks_joASR14GYDw&ved=0CE4Q6AEwB Q#v=onepage&q=steamship%20proteus&f=false.

20 Lennard Bickel, *Mawson's Will*, New York, Dorset Press, 1977, 237 pages. pg 152.

21 Kurt Vonnegut, *Cat's Cradle*.

22 Sam Van Schaik, *Tibet: A History*. New Haven, Yale University Press, 2011. 372 pg.

23 His Holiness the Dalai Lama, *Ethics for the New Millennium*, New York, Riverhead Books, 1999. Page 1.

24 Sam Van Schaik, *Tibet: A History*. New Haven, Yale University Press, 2011. Pg 238.

25 Ibid, pg 239.

26 Wang Zhihuan (688 - 742). Translated from the original Mandarin by my brother, Dan Turk.

27 Roderick MacFarquhar and Michael Schoenhals. *Mao's Last Revolution*. Belknap Press, 2008, 752 pp. And also, Jung Chang and Jon Halliday. *Mao: The Unknown Story*. Anchor, 2006. 801 pp.

28 His Holiness the Dalai Lama, *Ethics for the New Millennium*, New York, Riverhead Books, 1999. Page 129.

29 From Grateful Dead, "Box of Rain."

30 Hunter S. Thompson, *Fear and Loathing in Las Vegas*, New York, Random House, 1972.

31   Rick Potts, *Humanity's Descent*. New York, Avon Books, 1996, 325 pp. Quote found on page 139.

32   William Calvin, *A Brain for All Seasons*. Chicago, University of Chicago Press. 2002, 341 pp. Quote found on page 110.

33   Edward O Wilson, *Consilience: The Unity of Knowledge*, New York, Alfred A Knopf, 1999, 332 pp. Quote found on page 48.

34   His Holiness the Dalai Lama, *Ethics for the New Millennium*, New York, Riverhead Books, 1999. Quote found on page 29.

35   www.aqicn.org: Worldwide Air Quality

36   J. B. MacKinnon, *The Once and Future World: Nature As It Was, As It Is, As It Could Be*. New York, Houghton Mifflin Harcourt, 2013, 240 pp.

ACKNOWLEDGEMENTS

I meet many people when I travel, often in remote, chaotic, and potentially dangerous environments. Over a lifetime of passages, these interactions have, for the most part, been hugely positive. Oh, yeah, I've been held at gunpoint a few times, some jerk stole my GPS before a critical kayak passage, and the Politician begrudged us a few Band-Aids when we were hurting on Ellesmere. But those are the exceptions. So many individuals, over so many years, have offered me a bowl of rice or a cold Red Bull, a place to sleep during a rainstorm, or a friendly chat that enriched my understanding of a landscape, a people, and myself. My entire life would have been vastly different without all these warm, friendly, generous, smiling men, women, and children, many whose names I never knew. I take this opportunity to thank them all.

Within this matrix of humanity, there are numerous companions who deserve special thanks for their extraordinary contribution to my life and my journeys. I list them in order of appearance in this book.

First, I would like to thank Tyler Bradt for dreaming up the idea of linking an old man and a young gun to adventure together and combine their separate but interwoven perspectives and strengths. Unfortunately, Tyler broke his back and was unable to participate in the Ellesmere expedition, leaving Erik Boomer to pick up where he left off. How can I thank Boomer enough for his strength, fortitude, wisdom, and friendship? I hope the Ellesmere chapter adequately conveys the closeness and joy that lies in my heart.

Ah, yes, and then there is Ma LuBin, small, thin, wiry, a Falstaff-like observer of societies gone mad. Thank you Mr. Ma for your friendship, stories, and insights. I have done my best to convey your wisdoms, while recognizing what you have told me so many times; "You will write about China? But remember. You know nothing about China." My dear wife, Nina Maclean, joined us on the bicycle journey across the high passes. Nina, who has saved me from my own madness and has been my best friend and constant companion for the past decade; what can I say, but: Thank You.

Bill Hanlon and John Bergenske joined me, or should I say led me, over the high glaciers to Kwäday Dän Ts'ìnchí's final resting place. And then there is the wondrous, mysterious, ongoing synchronicity with Jody Weber, Artistic Director of Weber Dance, who incorporated a clunky old man—me—into a swirling, graceful dance, and gave me to opportunity to translate words into emotion. Finally, I would like to thank the dancers: Adriane Brayton, Shannon Humphreys, Kristy Kuhn, and Jennifer Sylvia. For wondrous, unforgettable moments out there, we shared ecstasy.

Thanks also to the sponsors of the Ellesmere Expedition. Travel in the North is expensive, and without the generous financial support of Eddie Bauer First Ascent and Polartec the Ellesmere expedition and this book would not have happened. I thank you both. I also thank Wilderness Systems for providing us with kayaks, AT (Adventure Technology) for paddles, and Kokotat for Fed Ex-ing dry tops at the last minute when we were in the midst of Great Confusion.

The chapter on the Ellesmere Expedition has been expanded from an article that originally appeared in Canoe and Kayak Magazine. I thank Jeff Moag, the editor, for his guidance and faith in me. Working together, the article won First Place in Print Journalism at the Northern Lights Award. In a parallel scenario, I published an early version of the Kwaday Dän Ts'ìnchí story in Explore. David Webb was my editor on that project, and we were awarded Honorable Mention in the Canadian National Magazine Awards. A part of the Ma LuBin story appeared first in Walrus, and I thank Marni Jackson for that opportunity.

Talking about Marni, again, she helped me through another period of Grand Confusion as my guide and mentor during two lengthy workshops at the Banff Centre.

A book breathes only after it is printed, bound, and sold; only after people read it. I would like to give special thanks to Richard Parks, my agent for twenty years, who tirelessly had faith in me, and then passed the torch when it was time for him to retire.

The torch was picked up by Randal Macair, publisher at Oolichan Books, who saw vision in this project. Randal is such a pleasure to work with, with his infectious smile. I always enjoy walking up the creaky wooden steps of the old-brick building, to visit with him and chat about this book, or literature in general. The office has the feel of the old guitar shop where I used to hang out—50 years ago—to escape the pressure of the Real World. Special thanks, also, to Carolyn Nikodym, Assistant to the Publisher, with her quiet demeanor and sharp ideas. Ron Smith, Editor, helped hone the manuscript with pointed suggestions. Thanks Ron, for being spot-on with your criticisms and suggestions. Michael Hepher, graphic artist and cover designer gave the book its finished look. Working together, as a family, the staff at Oolichan and I converted the initial rough manuscript into the book you now hold in your hands. Thanks also to Hannah Honey, in Hamilton, Montana, who designed my website.

Jon Turk received his Ph.D. in chemistry in 1971, wrote the first environmental science textbook in North America, and continued as an environmental science writer for 40 years. He has also engaged in numerous extreme outdoor expeditions. Jon's circumnavigation of Ellesmere Island was nominated by National Geographic as one of the top ten adventures of 2011. He has written three books chronicling his physical passages and the spiritual journey toward a Consciousness Revolution. When not out travelling, Turk divides his time between Fernie, BC and Darby, Montana.

You can visit Jon at www.jonturk.net.